Charitable Choices

Charitable Choices

Religion, Race, and Poverty in the Post-Welfare Era

John P. Bartkowski and
Helen A. Regis

NEW YORK UNIVERSITY PRESS
New York and London

NEW YORK UNIVERSITY PRESS
New York and London

Library of Congress Cataloging-in-Publication Data
Bartkowski, John P., 1966–
Charitable choices : religion, race, and poverty in the post-
welfare era / John P. Bartkowski and Helen A. Regis.
p. cm.
Includes bibliographical references and index.
ISBN 0-8147-9901-9 (alk. paper) —
ISBN 0-8147-9902-7 (pbk. : alk. paper)
1. Church charities—Mississippi. 2. Public welfare—
Mississippi. 3. Public welfare—Religious aspects—Christianity.
4. Church and social problems—Mississippi. 5. Church work
with the poor—Mississippi. I. Regis, Helen A. 1965–
II. Title.
HV530.B37 2003
361.7'5'09762—dc21   2002010095

Manufactured in the United States of America
10 9 8 7 6 5 4 3 2 1

Contents

Acknowledgments

The completion of any book is a collaborative endeavor, reflecting the efforts of many more people than those whose names appear on its cover. There are many individuals and organizations that we wish to thank for their contributions to this project, and sincerely hope that we have not overlooked anyone in doing so. Where we extend our gratitude to the multiple persons and organizations listed below, we do so alphabetically because it would be impossible to rank–order the contributions of so many.

We extend a special thanks to the religious leaders and benevolence workers in local congregations who gave generously of their time and insights to make this study possible. We are especially grateful to those who welcomed us into their congregations to observe and participate in their benevolence programs. Members of the religious communities whose stories are told here never failed to engage us on intellectual, material, and spiritual issues—and not necessarily in that order. Although we take full responsibility for the interpretations offered here, we have tried to be respectful in our dialogue with our subjects' experiences and viewpoints. We pay all these persons of faith the highest compliment in saying that we think about faith–based benevolence work quite differently now than we did going into this study.

Various organizations provided generous funding for the study, including the Joint Center for Poverty Research; the Louisville Institute; the MSU Criss Fund; the PricewaterhouseCooper Endowment; the Religious Research Association; the Rural Health, Safety, and Security Institute; and the Southern Rural Development Center. We also thank the reviewers of our research proposals, reports, and other writings submitted to these organizations. We are especially grateful to Mark Abramson, Paul Lawrence, James Lewis, and Scott Thumma in this capacity. Portions of this book were presented as conference papers at various annual meetings, including those sponsored by the Association for the Sociology of Religion; the Society for the Scientific Study of Religion; and the Southern Anthropological Society. Colloquia presentations that distill portions of material presented in this volume were given at Harvard University's Hauser Center, as well as the sociology departments at Baylor University and Brigham Young University. We have received incisive comments from countless people in such forums, and thank them collectively here for their remarks. We are particularly grateful for the comments provided by Nancy Ammerman, Mary Jo Bane, Kelly Besecke, Ralph Brown, Mark Chaves, Brent Coffin, Diana Garland, John Hoffmann, William Lockhart, Elizabeth Lower–Basch, Dale McConkey, Mark Moore, Carol Olander, Charles Tolbert, Heidi Unruh, and Christopher Winship. We hope that those familiar with our early writings and public presentations on this topic will recognize how our perspective has developed over the course of this project. The thoughtful feedback and encouragement of Ram Cnann and Bob Wineburg on this manuscript were most appreciated. Our work is very much informed by their careful scholarship. We have also benefited from friendly conversations—both brief and extensive—with Jerome Baggett, Melissa Barfield, Stephanie Boddie, Suzie Cashwell, Adele Crudden, Wanda Dodson, Patricia Duffy, Omri Elisha, Christopher Ellison, Gretchen Griener, Jeffrey Kosmacher, André Lewis, Stephen Lazarus, Matthew Lee, Mary Bogle Malzahn, Clyda Rent, Amy Sherman, Bonnie Teater, Stanley Carlson–Thies, Elfriede Wedam, Brad Wilcox, Pat Wittberg, and David Yamane.

We are thankful to the working group on faith–based benevolence at Mississippi State University that conducted portions of this research with us: Louis Bluhm, Melinda Chow, and Neil White—all of whom are coauthors of chapter 3. Our thanks to Carolyn Bryant as well for select data collection. In our home departments (Mississippi State University and Louisiana State University, respectively), our gratitude goes to all our colleagues for providing an atmosphere that was supportive of research and writing. We thank Thomas Kersen for his able research assistance during the early stages of the project, as well as Suzanne McClain and a large group of sociology graduate students for providing us with outstanding interview transcriptions. Heather Hanna helped with indexing.

Among colleagues who have helped to facilitate our work, we extend our special appreciation to Lionel Beaulieu, Arthur Cosby, Craig Colten, Martin Levin, and Miles Richardson. We will not be able to reciprocate the mentorship, feedback, support, and encouragement they extended to us during this project. But in lieu of specific reciprocity, we hope that we can do the same for junior colleagues sometime in the future. Others who have offered us insights about this work through constructive commentary or by carefully reading portions of the manuscript (albeit in different forms) include Nina Asher, Conner Bailey, Dydia DeLyser, Steve Janzen, Matthew Richards, Steven Rathgeb Smith, Gail Sutherland, Peter Sutherland, John Valery White, and Julie Zimmerman.

Jennifer Hammer and the staff at NYU Press offered the right combination of guidance, encouragement, and latitude with this project. We are grateful to them for their patience as well. Michelle Ashton provided crucial assistance in the production of the manuscript. Lastly, we are very grateful to our families, friends, and loved ones. They have encouraged us—and put up with us—during the long and sometimes arduous hours that it took to conduct this research and produce this volume. This book is a product of their sacrifice, forbearance, and emotional labor.

1

The Welfare Revolution and Charitable Choice

America has recently witnessed a revolution. No weapons were fired. No blood was shed. But this revolution has already influenced the lives of citizens by the millions. And it will undoubtedly shape every major social institution well into our nation's twenty–first century. The architects of America's welfare revolution promised, in prophetic words first uttered by then presidential candidate Bill Clinton, to "end welfare as we know it." And with the passage of welfare reform legislation in 1996, they delivered on this promise. It is not an overstatement to say that we have entered a new phase in our nation's history of social welfare. Given the benefits restrictions and work–first orientation ushered in through this new legislation, America has entered the post–welfare era (Handler and White 1999; Mink 1998; Schram 2000).

Apart from its profound political significance, there is every indication that the welfare revolution will alter the landscape of American religion. Under the legal provision, charitable choice, faith–based organizations of various stripes—religious congregations, interfaith ministries, and denominational relief agencies—have been thrust into the center of America's welfare–to–work transition and community revitalization efforts (Bartkowski and Regis 1999; Chaves 1999; Cnaan 1999; Bane, Coffin, and Thiemann 2000; DiIulio 1997; Glennon 2000; Lockhart 2001; Orr 2001; Sider and Unruh 1999, 2001; Walsh 2001; Wineburg 2001). Charitable choice makes it illegal for state governments to discriminate against social service providers whose organizations have a religious mandate. And on the heels of this policy change, several states have begun to underwrite faith–based social service programs with public funds (Griener 2000; Sherman 2000).

This volume takes charitable choice—and, more broadly, the changing relationship between religion and social welfare—as its primary point of departure for investigating faith–based poverty relief in the post–welfare era. Specifically, we hope to broaden current discussions of charitable choice to encompass issues—among them, racial inequality, denominational cleavages, and local cultural forces—that have not been given their due. With the hope of advancing a more grounded and inclusive dialogue about charitable choice, we explore how this policy initiative might affect religious organizations that vary by race, faith tradition, and local milieu.

Guided by the premise that social context matters, our work is intentionally idiographic. We produce detailed analyses of faith–based poverty relief as undertaken by religious congregations located in east central Mississippi. To accomplish this task, we analyze an array of qualitative data, including in–depth interviews with thirty local pastors in Mississippi's Golden Triangle Region, detailed field observations from five congregations with active service programs, and unstructured ethnographic interviews with religious relief workers in these programs. Given Mississippi's distinctively high rates of religious affiliation and impoverishment, there is not a more ideal state in which to explore the prospects and pitfalls of faith–based poverty relief. Our rendering of the complex organizational processes and cultural dynamics underlying religious benevolence poses a serious challenge to broad–brushed portraits that paint religious congregations with the positive gloss of virtue or the negative gloss of vice. We demonstrate that the work of congregational poverty relief is a more complicated undertaking than such one–dimensional caricatures would have us believe. Most public discussions of faith–based initiatives are overdetermined by the ideological agendas of political commentators. Too few of these social commentators are engaged with the empirical realities of faith–based service provision.

Finally, in our effort to push forward debates about the place of religious organizations in American civil society, our study draws together insights from several different theoretical traditions. We argue that religious groups define their collective identities with reference to a commemorated past, a palpable present, and aspirations for the future. Moreover, benevolence work and community outreach are key resources through which religious organizations define their moral character and draw social boundaries. As it turns out, religious definitions of morally appropriate responses to poverty vary considerably from one congregational context to the next. We explore the range of poverty relief strategies that congregations adopt to negotiate the countervailing ethical demands of compassion and moral rectitude. Lastly, we seek to extend the burgeoning literature on faith–based social capital. Where faith–based poverty relief is concerned, we demonstrate that social capital in religious communities can serve both integrative and exclusionary ends. We pay careful attention to the subtleties of religious networks, thereby revealing how different types of faith–based benevolence can either transform or reinforce existing social boundaries.

Religion Goes Public: The Emergence of Charitable Choice

How did charitable choice find its way onto the map of American politics? The most obvious answer resides in an examination of the debates over welfare during the 1990s. However, a more careful response to this question suggests that revolutionary changes in social policy are rooted in deeper philosophical transformations. If there is a guiding motif that captures the character of poverty relief during much of twentieth–century America, it is one of parallel tracks. Under welfare as we knew it, the fight against poverty was waged on many different fronts by largely independent parties. Public assistance and religious benevolence were distinct enterprises. When confronted with persons in need, of course, collaboration between religious leaders and social workers at local government offices was not forbidden and sometimes occurred. However, the ideal of church–state separation, along with the cultural chasm between religious organizations and government entities, meant that public-private collaboration was minimized.

The welfare revolution radically restructures the relationship between government agencies and faith–based service providers. The welfare–era motif of parallel tracks separating government support from religious benevolence has been supplanted by the post–welfare principle of partnership. In America's post–welfare era, religious communities and government agencies are now seen as allies whose mutual interests are served by the formation of public-private partnerships. The partnership ideal of welfare reform, part of a broader privatization of government (Savas 2000), is coupled with a new practical opportunity for faith–based providers. Under charitable choice, religious organizations can seek government funds to underwrite a whole range of social service activities including food assistance, job readiness training, and child care. It is, of course, too early to tell if this newly formed relationship will be a happy marriage or, for that matter, a collaborative partnership among equals. Religious suitors of government funds find themselves pitted against formidable competitors—secular nonprofits and private service providers—in the quest for what, in all likelihood, will be a limited pool of public resources. And, of course, the professional staff and social connections enjoyed by secular nonprofit organizations might give these agencies an inside track over their faith-based counterparts in the competitive bidding process. For its part, the Bush administration has argued for a level playing field in which all prospective providers will be judged on performance—that is, the degree to which funded programs can deliver in a clearly measurable way on their stated goals. The confidence of religious service providers is likely buoyed by a president who touts the distinctive merits of "rallying the armies of compassion"—virtuous, tenacious religious reformers—to combat America's most pressing social problems (Bush 2001).

How, then, did landmark legislation passed near the close of the twentieth century propel us into a post-welfare era of public-private partnerships? The short-term origins of welfare reform and charitable choice harken back to the early 1990s. With public opinion strongly favoring a major overhaul of America's welfare system, policy makers who supported the integration of local faith communities into welfare reform found a vocal advocate in Marvin Olasky. An academic and an outspoken evangelical, Olasky[1] initially catapulted the prospect for faith-based welfare reform into the public consciousness through his popular treatise, *The Tragedy of American Compassion* (1992). In this provocative volume, Olasky chided what he viewed as the bureaucratic detachment and lack of accountability of the modern welfare system. Olasky argued that prior to the rise of the twentieth-century welfare state, religious communities effectively redressed the needs of America's poor. By his account, religious communities provided the highly personalized care— and, as needed, the strict discipline—to lift the disadvantaged out of the mire of poverty. Based in part on this historical precedent, Olasky articulated a vision in which religious organizations of the late twentieth century could provide the needy with immediate material relief such as food, clothing, and temporary shelter while also promoting more permanent transformations in both the moral fiber and economic circumstances of the poor.

Although proponents of charitable choice sometimes disagree on the particulars of faith–based welfare reform and the best way to make it a reality (cf. Center for Public Justice 1994; Olasky 1992), they generally agree on its justification (Carlson–Thies and Skillen 1996). Charitable choice advocates call attention to the special repository of resources cultivated within faith communities—a robust sense of mission, high standards of moral integrity, close–knit relationships among coreligionists, holistic views of personhood, and a connectedness to the local communities in which religious adherents are situated. These resources are believed to give religious communities a unique role in assisting the poor and advancing the project of the welfare revolution. Consequently, champions of charitable choice agree that, when compared with government–based and secular solutions to social ills, religious organizations are superior providers of social services because of the moral values they embody and the holistic goals to which they aspire.

Throughout his term, President George W. Bush has consistently endorsed faith–based solutions to a wide range of social problems including unemployment, inadequate housing, persistent hunger, crime reduction, and substance abuse. Soon after being sworn in as America's forty–third president, Bush sought to expand the reach of charitable choice from state governments to federal agencies. At the same time, he called attention to collaborative partnerships that had already been forged between innovative state governments and the faith–based organizations to whom they had outsourced public services. To implement his vision of compassionate conservatism, Bush created the Office of Faith–Based and Community Initiatives. Soon thereafter he had every sector of the government's executive branch evaluated to determine their openness to partnering with faith–based organizations. These changes were predicated not on a policy of hands–off diagnostics, but aimed to create new avenues for the participation of faith–based organizations in federal programs.

Bush's ardent support for charitable choice reflects a broader social trend that began in the 1980s. It was then that evangelical religion dramatically broke out from the private realm of personal piety and family morality into the public realm of politics, social justice, and civil society. It is not at all difficult to discern the boldly public role that religion has played in the Bush campaign and the administration's legislative agenda. During his campaign for the White House, the born–again Bush called Jesus Christ his favorite political philosopher. And in the wake of the terrorist attacks of September 11, Bush invoked the Christian aphorism "love thy neighbor"—coupled, tellingly, with his advocacy of four thousand lifetime hours of civic volunteerism for every American citizen—as the best way to "stand up to evil" in the world. Many in the Bush administration would seem to share his view that faith is a bona fide public good, and a priceless civic resource at that. Bush selected Tommy Thompson, an outspoken conservative Catholic, to head the Department of Health and Human Services. During Thompson's tenure as Wisconsin's governor, his state's implementation of faith–based welfare reform initiatives was rivaled only by that of Texas under Bush's governorship. Moreover, Bush's Attorney General, John Ashcroft, was the principal architect of the charitable choice provision found in 1996 welfare reform law. Ashcroft, then a senator from Missouri and now the nation's chief legal figure, is a devout Pentecostal who seems strongly convinced that religion can restore virtue to American civic life.

The administration's Faith–Based and Community Initiatives Act (H.R.–7), more commonly dubbed the Charitable Choice Act of 2001, was passed by the House of Representatives on July 19, 2001. That bill proposed to create a "compassion capital fund" that would match private donations to small faith–based charities with federal funds. The bill, however, soon came under fire—particularly with regard to its protection of discriminatory hiring practices by religious groups who could exclusively employ members of their own faith if they so desired. Despite a watering down of the bill prior to its ultimate passage in the Senate and the resignation of John DiIulio as head of the Office of Faith–Based and Community Initiatives, Bush has shown no signs of backing away from his goal of creating collaborative partnerships between local faith communities and all branches of government. Indeed, Bush recently named Jim Towey—whose most touted credential is having conducted hands–on ministry to the poor alongside Mother Teresa—as DiIulio's successor at the Office of Faith–Based and Community Initiatives. Bush has promised to keep faith–based initiatives at the forefront of his domestic legislative agenda. What's more, in the wake of 1996 welfare reform law, several states have moved forward to implement extensive charitable choice programs (Griener 2000; Sherman 2000). While the majority of states (including Mississippi) continue to weigh the merits of forging service provision partnerships with religious providers, the exposure and momentum given to faith–based initiatives show no sign of reversing themselves anytime in the near future.

Debating Charitable Choice: Elite Disputes and Public Concerns

The charitable choice provision in welfare reform law and, more recently, the Charitable Choice Act of 2001, set off a firestorm of criticism (e.g., American Civil Liberties Union 2001; Americans United for the Separation of Church and State 2001; Boston 1998; Connolly 1999; Pinkerton 1999; Rogers 1999; see Fritz 1999; Raasch 1999; Sack 1999 for reviews). Some critics contend that these policy initiatives threaten religious liberty by allowing the government to favor particular religious groups over others as social service providers. And despite legislative clauses forbidding proselytization through service provision, others worry that charitable choice accords too much decision–making authority concerning staff hiring and client needs to religious organizations that might harbor coercive moral agendas. Americans United for the Separation of Church and State has begun to mount a legal challenge to charitable choice, making it likely that proponents and opponents of this initiative will exchange volleys in the courts to complement those that have already been traded in the media.

Still other critics assert that all the attention given to religious benevolence forestalls more meaningful discussions about the structural causes of poverty, thereby permitting the continued exploitation of the poor by elites. Hitchens's (1997) exposé of politicians and corporate elites who used their affiliations with Mother Teresa to advance their own political careers, ideological agendas, and economic interests provides many cautionary tales about the malevolent ends sometimes served by religious benevolence. Finally, some have warned that faith–based social service initiatives, at least as initially conceived by Olasky, are naive and impractical in the contemporary era (Wolfe 1993).

Lest it be thought that all opponents of charitable choice are motivated by an antireligious zeal, it is worth noting that many faith–based organizations have expressed reservations about forming partnerships with the government in this revolutionary era (Burger 1996; Jewish News 1999; Pinkerton 1999; Raasch 1999). Some religious leaders worry that vying for limited public funds to expand their relief efforts might lead to religious rivalries—particularly among groups that have only recently cultivated tolerance for those outside their faith tradition. Others are clearly anxious about the prospect of political regulation that might accompany public funding. And given the antiproselytization clause that accompanies charitable choice legislation, fears have arisen that public funding might undermine the effectiveness of religious organizations. From the standpoint of many Christian groups, religious believers' most valuable tool in fighting social ills is the life–transforming power of spreading the faith to nonbelievers. In those religious communities where spreading the faith is essential to their spiritual practice, concerns about any such gag rule run very deep indeed. In short, although the letter of charitable choice law is designed to placate the fears of religious organizations, many religious groups worry that the implementation of the initiative and actual formation of partnerships with the government may leave them vulnerable in ways not currently anticipated.

Debates about charitable choice have also been inflected by denominational tensions and racial dynamics, often overlaid upon one another. Only days after the Office of Faith–Based and Community Initiatives was established in February 2001, leaders from the Anti–Defamation League visited executive director John DiIulio to voice their concern about the prospect of the government providing public funds to the Nation of Islam. Similar concerns were soon raised about other "fringe" denominations, including the Church of Scientology, that were portrayed as not genuinely religious and too far outside the cultural mainstream. Just as the Charitable Choice Act was being debated by the House of Representatives in June 2001, Bush was heartened by the endorsement his plan picked up from none other than civil rights icon, Rosa Parks. Parks spoke glowingly of the Bush proposal at the 2001 U.S. Conference of Mayors. However, less than three weeks later and with congressional debates still in full swing, the NAACP passed a resolution opposing the Charitable Choice Act at its annual convention. Apart from voicing concerns about the quantity and manner through which funds would be made available to faith–based organizations, NAACP opposition to the Bush plan was chiefly concerned with the discriminatory hiring practices it would legally permit.

Elite debates and mobilization over charitable choice seem to have informed public opinion on this issue, though not in a deterministic fashion. The American public is overwhelmingly supportive of charitable choice in principle. A series of public opinion polls conducted by the Pew Research Center for the People and the Press (most recently, in March 2001) revealed that 75 percent of the national survey sample favored government funding of faith–based organizations, with only 21 percent opposed. Blacks and Hispanics (81 percent) were more favorably disposed toward charitable choice than their white counterparts (68 percent). The public's trust in the efficacy of religious benevolence is strongest for faith–based programs that feed the homeless, counsel prisoners, and mentor youth. Interestingly, support for government funding of faith–based initiatives is rooted firmly in the values of individual choice and religious compassion. A full 77 percent of Americans back charitable choice because they believe recipients of public services "should have a variety of options," while a nearly equal percentage (72 percent) believe that religious people "are more compassionate and caring" than nonreligious providers. Moreover, 62 percent cite the power of religion to "change people's lives" as a rationale for supporting public funding of faith–based organizations.

Despite such robust levels of general support for charitable choice, the American public remains wary of its specifics. High levels of support for the public funding of faith–based organizations dwindle significantly when the religious groups that would receive government monies are situated outside the cultural mainstream. Whereas between 60 and 70 percent of Americans back public funding for established religious charities, Catholic churches, and Protestant congregations, a scant 38 percent of Americans support government funding for service programs in Muslim mosques and Buddhist temples. Less than one in three (29 percent) supports the provision of government monies to Louis Farrakhan's Nation of Islam. The Church of Jesus Christ of Latter–Day Saints (Mormons) wins only weak public support for government funding (51 percent). And the Church of Scientology fails more than all others to gain the public trust, with only 26 percent of Americans favoring this scenario. Despite the preference for mainstream religion reflected in these figures, an overwhelming majority of Americans (78 percent) oppose discriminatory hiring practices that would allow publicly funded religious groups to hire only those of their own faith. In a nod toward religious pluralism, large percentages of Americans express fears about the infringement of religious expression among faith–based organizations (68 percent) and violations of religious liberty among service recipients (60 percent)

Deconstructing Charitable Choice: The Legacy of Calvin and Hobbes

In light of the widespread debates and deep public concerns this initiative has generated, it is important to recognize that its name, "charitable choice," is much more than a shorthand reference for government funding of religiously based service activities. In a political sense, the charitable choice moniker is designed to rally support for this initiative by underscoring the "new freedoms" ushered in by it. Charitable choice gives faith–based organizations the same freedom of resource procurement that secular nongovernmental providers have long enjoyed. With the passage of this initiative, faith–based organizations win the opportunity to receive state funding to underwrite a wide range of social service programs, including job readiness training, hunger relief, child care, and crime prevention. In addition, charitable choice protects the freedom of religious expression for faith–based organizations that receive public funds. Previously, religious organizations that received public funds (such as Catholic Charities and Lutheran Social Services) had to secularize themselves by stripping away all religious symbols, language, and practices from their service programs. Alongside these new freedoms, charitable choice aims to preserve the civil and religious liberties of those who utilize publicly funded social services. States that award funds to religious service providers must offer the same service through a comparable secular provider. Moreover, religious organizations that provide state–funded social services to the needy cannot legally force their clients to participate in religious practices.

In a sense, charitable choice seeks to meld two forms of social relationship—contract and covenant—that have long been at odds with one another (cf. Elizar 1994, 2000; Bromley and Busching 1988; Williams 1994, 1999). With the rise of Enlightenment philosophy, utilitarians like Thomas Hobbes and Adam Smith championed self–interest—the peculiar human ability to weigh costs against benefits and thereby maximize one's utility—as the defining characteristic of "economic man." Yet both these thinkers worried that economic man without an external check against self–interest could destroy himself. Hobbes ([1651] 1994:71) feared that, in a state of unbridled self–interest, society would devolve into a war of all against all in which life would be "solitary, poore, nasty, brutish, and short." For Hobbes, the external check against the excesses of self–interest was the Absolute Sovereign, a supreme ruler created through a social contract in which free citizens rationally "bargain away" some of their individual liberties for an orderly society governed by law.

Of course, other thinkers of the day disagreed with the Hobbesian diagnosis of a European society that was undergoing rapid social change.

John Calvin approached the problem of social order through religious—rather than a purely political—means. One of the most noteworthy aspects of Calvin's theology was his view of predestination (see Weber [1904–5] 1958). According to Calvin, God—in a sense, the original and omniscient Absolute Sovereign—knows all things, including who will be saved ("the elect") and who will not ("the damned"). As a principle for organizing Calvinist communities, the theology of predestination penetrated the religious believer with a burning anxiety about his or her fate—"Am I saved? Am I damned?" The Calvinist habitus of this–worldly asceticism produced subjects who lived a life of discipline, austerity, and impressive economic productivity. In his sociological examination of Calvinism, Max Weber (1958) charged that these religious ideas produced a sectarian subculture whose preoccupation with finding evidence of salvation through "signs of election" led to the unprecedented accumulation of wealth that is now the hallmark of capitalism.

American poverty policy, even with the most recent innovations in welfare reform law, represents a collective attempt to grapple with fundamental questions about freedom, citizenship, civic virtue, and the good society—the very questions that Calvin, Hobbes, and many social critics after them were seeking to answer. The passage of welfare reform suggests that we are heirs to an ambiguous heritage that is both Hobbesian and Calvinist in character. Welfare reform is Hobbesian, and more broadly utilitarian, inasmuch as it adopts the language of utility, economy, and individualism—evident in such terms as "choice," "competition," and "client"—to conceive of the relationship between the state and its citizens. Language that conceives of the poor as "clients" of the state or civic agencies, and that legitimates "competition" between social service providers (nonprofits, congregations, faith–based agencies) is consistent with the contractual logic of utilitarianism (see Schram 1995; Schram and Beer 1999; Schram 2000 on the contractual bases of welfare discourse). Indeed, the Republican "Contract with America" that promised, among other things, to promote "individual responsibility" by enacting a "tough two–years–and–out provision with work requirements" was an explicitly utilitarian means of kicking off welfare reform debates (see Schram 1997; Schram 2000: ch. 1). Here was the embodiment of a contractual order, with its view of individuals as atomistic entities that are tenuously connected through relations of expedience much like those between a buyer and seller.

Although those who advocate a consumer model of governance presume that it fosters freedom and equality, a contractual order—both as cultural metaphor and political practice—inscribes relations of power. Enlightenment–era utilitarians were notorious for overlooking structured social inequality, privileging instead a purely voluntaristic conception of individual choice. Consistent with the uncritical premises of utilitarianism, charitable choice assumes that religious organizations can compete on a level playing field with other nongovernmental providers when the latter have cultivated long–term working relationships with the government well before the passage of welfare reform. Moreover, this policy assumes that welfare clients move about freely in economic and religious marketplaces unhindered by the structural inequalities of race, class, and gender. Charitable choice also places great faith in the fairness of local political authorities to ensure the equitable distribution of block grant money. Among other things, it assumes a merit–based system, as well as the absence of cronyism and local political corruption.

Moreover, the block grant system instituted under welfare reform is consistent with utilitarian emphases on choice and freedom from the perceived constraints of social structure. In its effort to deinstitutionalize the provision of temporary public assistance, welfare reform law established a block grant system of financial disbursement to states.[2] A block grant is a fixed annual sum of federal monies which are dispersed to state governments and then matched by state funds. Whereas options for the administration of welfare payments prior to the passage of welfare reform law were limited by a highly bureaucratized disbursement system, welfare reform provides states and, ostensibly, local communities with greater freedom in the distribution of public assistance monies.

The block grant system itself is predicated on a philosophy of political devolution, which is guided by the assumption that state–level and community policy makers should "choose for themselves" the programs that will best redress the needs manifested in their local communities. According to this view, innovative relief efforts and effective welfare–to–work programs are best conceived and implemented by local officials who understand the unique dynamics of the communities in which they serve and reside. Consequently, block grants provide local officials with a broader range of choices in the implementation of poverty relief and community development programs.

At the same time, the legacy of Calvin—that is, the principle of covenant—is evident in welfare reform legislation and charitable choice.

Charitable choice accords a central place to religious institutions in public life and our nation's moral order. Consistent with the distinctive practices that led Calvinists to become the unwitting creators of capitalism, strict benefit limits under welfare reform aim to inculcate the values of austerity and self–discipline among the poor. Armed with the post–welfare mantra that "any job is a good job," welfare reform touts the merits of productive labor, defined as full–time employment in the paid workforce. The post–welfare-era assistance program, Temporary Assistance to Needy Families (TANF), is founded on the philosophy that virtually unlimited access to public assistance promotes welfare dependency among the poor and produces a class of citizens whose motivation to seek paid employment is undermined by unfettered access to government–sponsored assistance. By limiting the federal funds available for public assistance efforts, policy makers wished to redefine welfare from an entitlement–based system—that is, a system predicated on the government's obligation to provide benefits to anyone who qualifies—to a more restrictive temporary relief program. This antientitlement orientation among policy makers, captured in the law's reference to personal responsibility, was given force by the widespread unpopularity of welfare with the American public throughout the 1980s and into the early 1990s.[3] A 1990 national survey conducted by the National Opinion Research Center revealed that 70 percent of surveyed adults favored "reducing welfare benefits to make working for a living more attractive."

Such antientitlement views, however, were often replete with media representations that were themselves rooted in racist, classist, and gendered assumptions. The "welfare queen" was popularly depicted as a black single mother of multiple children whose childbearing practices were motivated solely by a desire to secure an increase in public assistance benefits (Cruikshank 1997). This same antientitlement orientation advances allegations about the dismal failure of antipoverty programs, and assumes that only wage labor qualifies as legitimate "work" in the current American economy (Gilens 1999). In a way that Max Weber could not have anticipated, idle hands have once again become defined as the devil's workshop.

Theoretical Perspective: Religious Ecologies, Congregational Stories, and Faith–Based Social Capital

Our study of faith–based poverty relief in the wake of the welfare revolution is informed by theoretical perspectives that, taken together, attune us to the relationship between congregational dynamics, religious narratives, and social capital.

Religious Ecologies: Contextualizing Congregational Life

Sociologists of religion have carefully investigated the interface between community dynamics, social change, and the culture of religious organizations (Ammerman 1990, 1997; Becker 1999; Becker and Eiesland 1997; Eiesland 2000; Kniss 1996, 1997). The concept of religious ecologies underscores the vast array of relationships that religious organizations negotiate, the cultural repertoires they develop, and the resources they marshal to thrive in their changing local environments (Ammerman 1997, 1998; Eiesland 2000; Eiesland and Warner 1998; McKinney 1998). Congregations—the backbone of American religion—are linked to other local voluntary associations and their communities at large through overlapping membership ties (Ammerman 1997:360–362; Chaves 2001). By establishing ministerial alliances and parachurch organizations, congregations commonly forge lateral partnerships with other faith–based groups on the local scene. And through cascading vertical relationships, religious congregations are linked to translocal organizations that are regional, national, or international in scope. So, "if there is a distinctively holistic or transformational approach to social service delivery that emerges from a religious base, it ought to be visible in the activities undertaken by the organizations—congregations—where religion is most central" (Chaves 2001:123).

Our study of Mississippi congregations reveals that they undertake benevolence work while balancing relationships with various social entities, including: other religious congregations, including neighboring churches whose denominational ties, theological orientations, and preferred relief–provision strategies may differ in noteworthy ways; supracongregational religious entities, such as ministerial councils and parachurch relief agencies, many of which are formed explicitly to address concerns about faith–based aid provision in the local community; local religious adherents and community members, given congregational efforts to balance member retention (inreach) with congregational growth (outreach); secular organizations of many persuasions, including political associations, government agencies, nonprofit organizations, and community merchants such as grocers, utility companies, and chambers of commerce; and the local poor—whose needs, desires, and demands are quite often met with a combination of compassion and judgment. We pay close attention to the ecological context within which religious communities operate to explore how the countervailing pressures confronted by local congregations produce synergistic collaboration in some instances and organizational conflict in others.

The religious ecologies perspective also highlights the influence of contextual particularities and community change on local religious congregations. The public prominence of religion in the South evinces an elective affinity with this region's distinctive demographic features. Population dispersion and a predominantly agrarian economy within many areas of the southern United States, in combination with these communities' geographical and cultural distance from large urban hubs, long ago thrust religious institutions into the center of civic life in the South.

Religion in Mississippi and the South bears the peculiar mark of a social institution whose member organizations were often polarized around the question of civil rights for African Americans (Marsh 1997). Many congregations and religious leaders fought for racial equality in the South, with black churches serving as a key site for the mobilization of activists in the Civil Rights Movement (Lincoln and Mamiya 1990). At the same time, church communities with long histories of racial separatism and class privilege provided an institutional base for those who defended segregation and sought to protect the tradition of Jim Crow politics. Consequently, the religious ecology of the South is marked by distinctive demographic features such as agrarianism and population dispersion that intersect with intense struggles over citizenship, equality, and civil rights. Our approach to faith–based poverty relief in Mississippi attunes us to the contextual particularities within which religious communities seek to solve the dilemmas associated with religious benevolence.

Imagined Faith Communities: Congregational Narratives of Poverty Relief

Our study is also informed by narrative analyses of religious experience. Recent scholarship has reasserted the importance of analyzing the narratives—literally, the stories—that religious communities tell about themselves (Ammerman 1994, 1997; Hopewell 1987; Roof 1993; Schreiter 1998; Wuthnow 1994a, 1997; Yamane 2000). These narratives are utilized to forge a collective identity among religious believers, to produce a shared history among the faithful, and to marshal support for future aspirations. Congregational narratives strive to answer a cluster of pressing questions faced by religious communities, typically centered around issues of identity (Who are we? What do we stand for?), memory (Where have we come from? What is our heritage?), and destiny (To what do we aspire? What type of community do we wish to become?). As imagined faith communities (cf. Anderson 1991; Spillman 1997), congregations collectively envision themselves in the present, past, and future through the use of narrative. Religious communities have long drawn on collectively imagined narratives—parables of virtuous action, metaphors of spiritual rebirth, myths of creation and redemption—in seeking to address these seminal questions.

It is important to recognize that congregational narratives do not offer definitive solutions to vexing questions of identity, memory, and destiny. Given community diversity, it is common for divergent factions within any religious group to coalesce and, at times, find themselves at odds with one another (Bartkowski 2001; Becker 1999). Like a building that contains many different levels, narratives are "storied"—that is, multilayered—accounts of identity, origin, and aspiration (Dunne 1995; Mishler 1986). Thus, current scholarship on narrative analysis recognizes that the conflicting messages and ambivalent sentiments contained within any story are as crucial as its central motifs.

Our study focuses on the ways in which religious communities imagine their identities—as well as their heritage and destiny—with specific reference to their ecological embeddedness and the antipoverty initiatives they undertake. These congregations' imagined identities, memories, and destinies are forged through collective ministerial practices that include relief provision for the poor. At the same time, local religious stories about poverty relief intersect with broader cultural narratives about American social welfare policy and civil society (cf. Schram and Neisser 1997). Religious narratives of congregational benevolence are replete with the motifs of judgment and compassion (Bartkowski 2001; Becker 1997; Wuthnow 1991) which, when woven together in distinctive ways, produce variegated religious conceptualizations of social and economic justice (Hart 1996; Wuthnow 1991, 1994b). Because religious organizations strive to define themselves as quintessentially moral communities, congregations are ineluctably faced with balancing these countervailing ethical imperatives.

The moral imperative of judgment rests on social distinctions that are constructed through boundary work (Lamont 1992, 2000). Although religious boundaries come in many forms, the most salient distinctions are drawn between pastors and congregants, longtime believers and newcomer adherents, and insider congregants and outsider nonmembers. These distinctions intersect with other forms of cultural difference, including racial, denominational, and regional cleavages. As a social practice, judgment entails the enlistment of accountability structures—formalized standards and thumbnail rules—that can be wielded to determine the righteousness of pastors, members, and, as needed, nonbelievers. By contrast, the moral imperative of compassion rests on the principles of equality and mutuality. Theological edicts that level cultural boundaries and invert social hierarchies bespeak an ethic of compassion. As a moral framework for social action, compassion mandates caring for the least of God's children, extending forgiveness to the contrite sinner, and eradicating social boundaries commonly separating in–groups from out–groups.

Interestingly, each of these moral imperatives finds support in religious theology, scripture, and tradition (Hart 1996; Smith 2000; Wuthnow 1991). Within the Judeo–Christian tradition, the metaphor of wheat being separated from chaff, the notion of lambs being privileged over goats, and the parable of the ten talents lend mythic substance to the moral imperative for judgment and legitimate strict standards of accountability. By contrast, Jesus Christ's mandate to minister to the least of God's children, his parables of the Good Samaritan and the laborers in the vineyard, and biblical injunctions against the harsh judgment of others convey themes of compassion and forgiveness. In her pathbreaking work, Becker (1997) astutely observes how these moral imperatives are collectively utilized by religious congregations to negotiate organizational conflicts. We augment these insights by applying them to a new domain of inquiry—namely, religious relief to the poor in an era of welfare reform. In doing so, we reveal how ethics inform congregationally grounded understandings of social justice.

Of course, while theological considerations and moral orientations are clearly part of these complicated narratives, the stories of relief provision, civic engagement, and community politics conveyed to us by local religious leaders are discourses that congeal around religious experiences and faith–generating practices. This experiential form of religious commitment—in a word, lived religion—has long been a central feature of evangelism and revivalism in the South. Therefore, we are not content simply to analyze the narratives conveyed in the spoken discourse of interviewed pastors. We explore the practical dynamics of religious benevolence by pairing an analysis of interview narratives with fieldwork observations drawn from several local congregations with highly active poverty relief ministries.

Throughout our investigation, we remain mindful that these narrative imaginings and practical undertakings are influenced by translocal social forces and political developments. The groundswell of support for faith–based antipoverty relief through Mississippi's pathbreaking Faith & Families program, and the apparent failure of this program in the Golden Triangle Region, has affected the way local pastors view their congregations and the practice of poverty relief. Moreover, the groundswell of nationwide political support for charitable choice has caused some communities to reconsider the conditions under which they would—or, conversely, would not—accept state funding for social services that they currently provide or hope to offer.

Janus–Faced Social Capital: Voluntarism and Gatekeeping in Religious Organizations

Finally, our exploration of faith–based benevolence is directly engaged with the growing literature on religion and social capital (Ammerman 1997; Baggett 2001; Cnaan and DiIulio 2002; Putnam 2000; Uslaner 1999). As we use the term in this study, faith–based social capital is composed of three key components: congregational networks, religious norms, and bonds of trust within faith communities (cf. Putnam 2000). Inasmuch as networks, norms, and trust promote reciprocal obligations and social embeddedness, religious congregations are powerful generators of social capital (Ammerman 1997). Religious organizations are characterized by enduring social networks and normative frameworks that facilitate collective action in the name of positive social change. Religious communities also provide their adherents with imperatives for morally grounded action. The voluntary sector to which religious communities belong eschews the values of self–interest, instrumentalism, and impersonality—the hallmarks of the state and market sectors of society—in favor of altruism and community service (Baggett 2001). Moreover, faithful congregants are often considered to be model citizens because religious involvement tends to promote civic engagement beyond the particularity of the congregation (Ammerman 1997; Greeley 1997; Patillo–McCoy 1998; Perkins, Brown, and Taylor 1996; Putnam 2000; Wilson and Janoski 1995; Wilson and Musick 1997; Wuthnow 1999).

Following recent innovations in social capital theory, we recognize that faith–based social capital can take two different forms. Bonding capital facilitates embeddedness within social groups that are already well established. Bonding capital, which is "inward looking" in nature and tends to bolster our "narrower selves," is "good for undergirding specific reciprocity and mobilizing solidarity" (Putnam 2000:22). Within the context of religious life, strategies of congregational inreach such as communal worship and mutual aid generate bonding capital. Bridging capital, by contrast, is "outward looking" and promotes new forms of connectedness between otherwise disparate social groups. Newfound linkages to "external assets" entail bridging because the social groups that forge such connections do not share a common history or identity. Within the context of faith–based relief, congregational outreach to disadvantaged nonmembers and the formation of interdenominational relief agencies are examples of bridging capital. Although organizations can generate bonding and bridging capital simultaneously, they are conceptually distinguishable: "Bonding capital constitutes a kind of sociological superglue" that fosters within–group ties, whereas "bridging capital provides a sociological WD–40" that smooths between–group alliances (Putnam 2000:23). However, an overabundance of bonding capital can create out–group antagonism right alongside in–group loyalty (Putnam 2000:21–24, 350–363)—a theoretical prospect which we take up momentarily, and an empirical pattern that we explore throughout the remainder of this volume.

Why is it that religious congregations have been able to produce such variegated and valuable forms of social capital in the United States? The sociological answer to this question resides in the voluntary nature of religious participation in the United States (Finke and Stark 1992; Stark and Finke 2000). Often couched in the language of microeconomics, this perspective asserts that the disestablishment of American religion has generated a pluralistic "marketplace" of faith–based "firms" that "supply" free social space to religious "consumers" with wide–ranging "tastes" or "preferences."

Because faith–based communities are literally voluntary associations, they are adept at producing collective bonds that are consensual and thereby facilitate highly coordinated collective action. Those members who choose to affiliate with a religious group do so by mutual consent. And, conversely, cultural consumers who opt not to purchase the capital produced by a particular religious community can invest their time and energy in another congregation within their local religious marketplace or a different type of voluntaristic firm altogether such as a secular civic association. The voluntary nature of religious affiliation, then, solves the problem of trust that bedevils any social group—"Who are my fellows, and upon what basis can I form relationships of reciprocal obligation with them?" (cf. Coleman 1990; Fukuyama 1995; Seligman 1997). By creatively addressing issues of identity, heritage, and destiny, religious communities create a high–trust ethos and, thereby, manage risk (cf. Fukuyama 1995; Lupton 1999; Taylor–Goody 2000). High–trust religious communities are characterized by normative frameworks that promote collective "investment" in networks of material and moral exchange.

Others have conceptualized social capital from a more critical perspective (Bourdieu 1984; Fellmeth 1996; Messer 1998; Popielarz 1999; Portes 1998; Portes and Landolt 1996; Schulman and Anderson 1999; Zand 1996). The generation, allocation, and acquisition of trust can reproduce asymmetrical power relations and can reify entrenched forms of social inequality. This critical view suggests that the same religious organizations which generate social capital in such abundance can, as the situation demands, effectively withhold the "investment" of social capital in persons perceived to be outside the network or undeserving of trust. This possibility is not unfathomable, given the homophilic (sameness–oriented) character of religious organizations, particularly those not self–consciously committed to cultural diversity (Popielarz 1999). Congregations are commonly segregated by race, ethnicity, and class—a situation that has led many sociologists of religion to conclude that Sunday morning is the most segregated time during any given week in America. Other forms of hierarchy and exclusion can also emerge among homophilic organizations. Such groups can reify social hierarchies based on age, gender, education, and cultural tastes—the last of which can subtly reinforce class–based distinctions (Bourdieu 1984; Lamont 1992).

Like any organization, congregations lend structure to social relationships. As such, they are capable of "weeding out" individuals who do not adhere to the beliefs and values collectively cherished in an established faith community. Such selection processes may be quite subtle. In this sense, it is appropriate to speak of coercion as the congregational flipside of consensus. In a structural sense, the coercive face of social capital is the "price of admission," including moral strictures and behavioral standards, that can be "charged" to outsiders seeking access to established, resource–rich organizations. In particular cases, admission may be denied altogether. Thus the coercive face of social capital essentially functions as closed doors to would–be clients.

Faith–based social capital, then, is Janus–faced inasmuch as the consensual and coercive elements of religious belonging often operate in tension with one another. Janus, the classical Roman god with two faces, is a guardian charged with monitoring the comings and goings of persons at sacred portals. Such gatekeeping is evidenced in the ability of faith communities to admit, exclude, or expel persons who fall outside the pale of religious networks, norms, and trust. Religious organizations, then, are best understood as semivoluntary in nature.

Primary Aims and Layout of the Volume

Whether it takes the form of community child care, hot meal programs, drug counseling, or the construction of affordable housing, religious communities throughout America offer a range of services designed to counter the effects of poverty and social disadvantage (see, for example, Ammerman 1997, 2001a, 2001b; Baggett 2001; Bartkowski and Regis 1999; Chaves 2001; Cnaan 1999; Dudley and Roozen 2001; Eng and Hatch 1991; F. Harris 2001; M. Harris 1995, 1996; Hogstel and Davis 1996; Humphrey 1980; Kniss and Campbell 1997; McRoberts 1999; Monsma 1996; Morrison 1991; Olson, Reis, Murphy, and Gehm 1988; Rawlings and Schrock 1996; Wood 1999; Wuthnow 1991, 1999). Recent survey research has underscored the importance of denominational, racial, and regional factors in faith–based outreach and community activism. Denominations differ in the level of faith–based community volunteering, philanthropy, and civic engagement they undertake (Dudley and Roozen 2001; Park and Smith 2000; Regnerus and Smith 1998; Regnerus, Smith, and Sikkink 1998; Tolbert, Lyson, and Irwin 1998; Wilson and Janoski 1995). Among white churches, those in liberal

Protestant denominations sponsor more outreach programs—though this difference is likely due, in part, to the more robust resource base such congregations enjoy (Ammerman 2001a, 2001b; Chaves 2001; Dudley and Roozen 2001).

Denominational differences in community outreach overlap with racial and regional factors. By most estimates, African American congregations are considerably more inclined to engage in community activism and social service provision, even when compared with white liberal churches (Cavendish 2000; Chaves and Higgins 1992; Dudley and Roozen 2001; Harris 2001). African American congregations were crucial in organizing the Civil Rights Movement (Lincoln and Mamiya 1990: ch. 8). Recent years have witnessed a continuation of this tradition in community outreach among black churches—manifested most pointedly among African American Pentecostal congregations (McRoberts 1999). Where community locale is concerned, rural congregations—particularly historically black churches—have many active relief ministries targeted at poor persons and disadvantaged families (Dudley and Roozen 2001; Williams and Ruesink 1998). Yet, perhaps because they are further removed from urban centers of political power, rural congregations lag behind others in offering ministries such as child care and health services that are required to meet government standards (Dudley and Roozen 2001). Taken together, this scholarship highlights the powerful influence of racial, denominational, and regional dynamics on faith–based community outreach and ministry to the poor.

To date, relatively few empirical studies have explored the extent to which religious communities might expand current relief offerings or launch new service programs with block grant monies in an age of temporary public assistance. Using survey data from the National Congregations Study, Mark Chaves (1999) found that approximately one-third of 1,236 surveyed faith communities would consider participating in a charitable choice program. Moreover, liberal and moderate congregations, as well as African American faith communities, were more likely to be favorably disposed toward charitable choice partnerships with the government. Only a scant 3 percent of the faith communities in Chaves's investigation were receiving government funds at the time of the study, a finding that underscores the dramatic transformation of faith–based service provision made possible by charitable choice. To their credit, Chaves and other scholars have fleshed out the character of faith–based service provision as currently undertaken in American congregations

(Chaves 2001; Ammerman 2001a, 2000b; Dudley and Roozen 2001). As it turns out, most congregational service programs are carried out by "small groups of volunteers . . . [who] conduct relatively well-defined tasks on a periodic basis" (Chaves 2001:125–126). Thus, concludes Chaves (2001:126), the actual "portrait of congregations' social service activities . . . is more modest—and realistic—than much of the public discourse on this topic."

In another treatment of this issue, Cnaan (1999) argues that local faith communities could effectively commit to a "limited partnership" with the state (see also Wineburg 2001). Cnaan's survey of faith–based service organizations in two local communities (Greensboro, North Carolina, and Philadelphia, Pennsylvania) reveals that religious providers offer a wide range of valuable services to various disadvantaged populations—the poor, persons of color, gays and lesbians, and women. These services could probably be expanded with an infusion of public funds, provided such partnerships are careful to honor the autonomy of religious organizations.

As a qualitative investigation focused in one local area, our study sheds new light on the context–specific dynamics of faith–based poverty relief. Specifically, our study highlights the wide range of motivations that undergird faith–based service provision, and identifies factors that complicate the practice of congregational poverty relief. We also explore the deeply ambivalent sentiments that local religious leaders articulate concerning charitable choice partnerships. Our general goal is to advance the emerging national dialogue about charitable choice by focusing attention squarely on the challenges that cultural difference—namely, racial asymmetries, denominational cleavages, and regional particularity—poses to faith–based initiatives (cf. Berrien, McRoberts, and Winship 2000; Coffin 2000; Gamm 2001; Harris 2001; Hehir 2000; Shipps 2001; White 2000; Winship and Berrien 1999). In many respects, Mississippi religious life provides the ideal empirical lens through which to scrutinize the relationship between cultural difference, charitable choice, and poverty relief. Although our primary commitment is to examine local cultural dynamics in all their richness and detail, we also take care to identify general social processes that are likely to affect faith–based initiatives undertaken in any locale. For example, our typology of congregational benevolence strategies can readily be applied to other social settings. Moreover, our analysis of the distinctive approaches to poverty relief exhibited by dominant and marginalized faith traditions yields generalizable insights about the influence of congregational positioning on faith–based outreach. While the specific religious groups that are marginalized will vary from one social setting to the next, hierarchies of dominance and exclusion among faith–based organizations are present everywhere. In the end, our study aims to shed new light on the quotidian practice of faith–based poverty relief while comparing pastors' standpoints on charitable choice across different racial and denominational contexts.

Our study unfolds as follows. Chapter 2 discusses the changing historical relationship between faith–based poverty relief and public assistance. Elizabethan Poor Law formed the basis of American social welfare policy from colonial times through most of the nineteenth century. For good and for ill, religious organizations were closely integrated into local community efforts to redress poverty during this time. Dramatic transformations witnessed around the turn of the twentieth century, including industrialization, urbanization, and successive waves of immigration, transformed cultural perceptions about the causes of poverty and religion's role in combating it. The rise of the welfare state during the twentieth century set public assistance and religious benevolence on parallel tracks. However, this pattern receded in the closing decades of the twentieth century and was dramatically reversed with the passage of the 1996 welfare reform law. A careful reading of American social welfare history reveals that the welfare revolution and its charitable choice provision are marked by historical residues from bygone eras.

Chapter 3 moves from the broad sweep of American history to the contemporary particulars of faith–based poverty relief in Mississippi. Using interview and field data collected from congregations in the state's Golden Triangle Region, we explore the strategies that faith communities utilize to engage in ministry to the poor. We describe the contours, motivations, and outcomes associated with four congregational strategies of relief provision: intensive benevolence, intermittent relief, parachurch initiatives, and distant missions of relief provision. We pay special attention to the way in which these strategies are influenced by distinctive assumptions about the causes of poverty, the character of the poor, and religious imperatives to address need.

Chapters 4 to 6 present a series of case studies generated from our research on poverty relief in select congregations. Each of these chapters contrasts the emergence and evolution of poverty relief efforts across two different congregational contexts. This comparative case study approach enables us to contrast how congregationally specific experiences in relief provision influence religious leaders' appraisals of welfare reform and the charitable choice alliances ushered in by this landmark legislation.

Chapter 4 compares two midsized United Methodist churches located in rural Mississippi. The first of these two churches is an African American congregation, River Road United Methodist. River Road has a legacy of civil rights activism, offers an expansive slate of social service programs, and evinces an overriding receptivity toward faith–based welfare reform. We compare this church with Green Prairie United Methodist, a white congregation that mirrors River Road in its size, rural locale, and denominational affiliation. Yet, there end the similarities between these two churches. Green Prairie is marked by racial insularity, a collective retreat from benevolence work, and pastoral pessimism toward charitable choice. This comparative case study clearly highlights how, despite many other points of commonality, racial differences can generate divergent standpoints concerning congregational benevolence and charitable choice.

Chapter 5 interrogates notions of welfare dependency and local empowerment through the eyes of two ministers and the congregations they serve—namely, a black pentecostal Church of God in Christ (COGIC) and a white Southern Baptist church. Each of these large churches is thriving, and both are located in the same town. The pastors at these congregations are highly critical of public assistance programs and are quick to valorize paid labor. Despite such similarities, racial and denominational cleavages between these two churches become readily apparent when their pastors articulate their views of dependency and community empowerment, as well as their memories of social life in the Old South. Their hopes and concerns for charitable choice are shaped significantly by these factors.

Chapter 6 turns away from the mainstream of Mississippi's religious landscape to explore instead its margins. In this chapter, we compare religious conviction and poverty relief in two transnational, minority communities. The first of these two communities is an itinerant Catholic ministry for Hispanic migrants who work on Mississippi farms. The second is a local Islamic Center composed of well–educated, upwardly mobile Muslims. Given their distinct faith traditions and their disparate positions in the class structure, each of these religious communities experiences a different form of marginalization from the Mississippi cultural mainstream. This comparative case study illuminates how minority faith traditions use their distinctive cultural repertoires to negotiate religious marginality. It also underscores how the practice of congregational benevolence and perceptions of charitable choice are shaped by the social location of minority faith communities. Consequently, this chapter raises important questions about the status of religious minorities in the post–welfare era.

Finally, chapter 7 steps outside the confines of congregational life to explore street–level benevolence and ecumenism in east central Mississippi. Here, we focus on the 1999 March for Jesus in the Golden Triangle Region. We analyze the march as a cultural performance that allows local religious communities to parade through streets traversing neighborhoods of privilege and impoverishment. With community traffic held at a standstill during the march, religious communities publicly display their commitment to benevolent ministry, racial reconciliation, and denominational collaboration. The 1999 March for Jesus marked a turning point in this annual event, as compassionate ministry to the hungry became the central focus of the march. We describe how this event was planned and executed by local religious leaders. We also discuss the impact of this daylong, liminal event on everyday religious benevolence and relations between local faith communities.

The conclusion of our volume begins by summarizing the core insights of our investigation and then moves on to delineate its implications. Our study reveals the diverse ways in which local religious communities understand themselves and their poverty relief initiatives differently in the wake of welfare reform and charitable choice. Religious benevolence in Mississippi congregations, like that in faith communities throughout the nation, is being transformed by the dramatic changes occurring in American civil society at the dawn of the post–welfare era.

2

Social Welfare and Faith–Based Benevolence in Historical Perspective

The revolutionary policy developments ushered in during the post–welfare era are best scrutinized in light of social welfare history. In this chapter, we examine the contours of American social welfare as it evolved during the past four centuries. In surveying this historical terrain,[1] we pay special attention to the place of religious benevolence in poverty relief. To be sure, our one–chapter treatment of such an expansive period does not enable us to render as detailed an account as that provided by excellent volumes and essays[2] devoted exclusively to the history of American social welfare and religious benevolence. Nevertheless, this chapter highlights how key social changes have affected public assistance and religious benevolence in America. Our overview is designed to highlight historical issues that are germane to our investigation—including the role of race, denominationalism, and shifting standards of deservingness in distinguishing the worthy poor from their unworthy counterparts. As our historical rendering makes clear, contemporary welfare debates are a reworking of issues with a long history in American social life. In the end, a keen understanding of complex historical processes enables us to scrutinize more adequately the prospects for faith–based initiatives in twenty–first-century America.

Poor Laws: Social Welfare in the Seventeenth and Eighteenth Centuries

Elizabethan Poor Law, first adopted and applied throughout England in 1601, grew out of a series of tensions rooted in remarkable social changes. In the early seventeenth century, a longstanding feudal order had begun to give way to new forms of social organization—most notably, a nascent mercantile economy and the emergence of civil government. Although some modifications to the Poor Law were made in the many years that followed, its core components formed the backbone of British and American poverty policy for over two hundred years.

Like many political initiatives that surfaced during the seventeenth century, Elizabethan Poor Law reflected the tensions of a social order in transition (Trattner 1999: ch. 1). Broadly, the Poor Law melded traditional feudal sensibilities in which individuals were conceived as the subjects of rulers (nobles, monarchs, God) with progressive notions of citizenship and civil society. The noble–subject relationship of the feudal period was defined by covenant—a series of mutual, though asymmetrical, obligations between persons occupying disparate ascribed statuses. Covenantal obligations inhered in the social status of persons and were seen as divinely ordained rather than as a product of social negotiation. By contrast, the relations of citizens within the nascent civil society were defined by social contract. Contractual relations, the defining element of contemporary American society, emphasized the rights and liberties of autonomous individuals whose status was negotiated through the shifting sands of social law.

Not surprisingly, Elizabethan Poor Law was characterized by an odd mix of policy provisions—some remarkably compassionate, others strikingly authoritarian. Through its more benevolent statutes, the Poor Law formally recognized the government's responsibility to relieve suffering among the helpless and to ensure a basic standard of living for all its citizens. The Poor Law was the first statute of its kind to establish the government's responsibility to support citizens who were incapacitated, helpless, or victims of misfortune—variously defined as the "impotent" and the "worthy poor." The worthy poor were guaranteed the right to relief of either the outdoor or indoor variety. Outdoor relief, also called home relief, provided support to the deserving poor outside a regulated institutional environment. Indoor relief amounted to support provided through institutional means—specifically, the local almshouse or poorhouse for the incapacitated and the workhouse for the jobless able-bodied. Apart from the worthy poor, Elizabethan Poor Law also identified other classes of dependents and prescribed specific courses of action designed to redress the unique needs of these populations. Apprenticeships were made available to needy children. And jobs were accorded to the able–bodied who lacked work opportunities.

Alongside these forward–thinking provisions, feudal sensibilities were also woven into this pathbreaking law. The Poor Law enjoined on individuals a series of obligations much like those imposed on the subjects of feudal nobility. Charity began at home, as primary economic responsibility for the disadvantaged was placed squarely at the feet of the poor person's family members. Parents and grandparents were legally charged with providing economic support to younger dependents (specifically, children or grandchildren). Likewise, younger generations were legally bound to provide care for their elders in old age. Those who failed to do so could be jailed. The Poor Law also enforced work requirements through what today would be considered draconian means. Able–bodied persons who refused work could be incarcerated, whipped, branded, and even put to death. "Vagrants," as they were called, initially had no legal recourse for challenging the verdicts and punishments meted out by overseers in the local community. In the early eighteenth century, the law was amended to provide the right to appeal.

Given the post–welfare era's clarion call for local empowerment, it is noteworthy that the Elizabethan Poor Law was rooted, first and foremost, in the principle of local responsibility for the disadvantaged. Each community was charged with caring for its own. Moreover, religious leaders and government officials were expected to collaborate in determining need and providing relief. As social welfare historian Walter Trattner describes it:

> the parish [local community] was to act through its church wardens and a small number of "substantial householders" who would be appointed annually by the justices of the peace to serve both as overseers of the poor and as collectors of the revenue—a wholly secular or civil position. Funds necessary for carrying the act into effect were to be raised by taxing every householder in the parish, with the threat of imprisonment for those who failed to pay such taxes. (Trattner 1999:11)

Poor laws in much of seventeenth–century colonial America were modeled after the Elizabethan Poor Law as first conceived in England (Bremner 1988: ch. 2; Trattner 1999: ch. 2). Yet when compared with their British counterparts, colonial Americans placed an even stronger emphasis on local responsibility for the disadvantaged. Frontier communities in the early American colonies faced many challenges. Most prominent among these were "anxieties about labor supplies and social order," concerns that "stimulated searching reexaminations of poor laws" as colonists sought to adapt them to their fledgling communities in the New World (Katz 1996:13–14). The great geographic distances that separated colonial townships, along with the rigors of everyday survival, gave each local community a vested interest in looking after its own poor while withholding aid to outsiders. Other localities were left to do the same.

Consistent with the basic premise of Elizabethan Poor Law, many communities distinguished between "pauperism"—an unwillingness to work among the able–bodied—and genuine poverty or misfortune. Initially, seasonal workers and the infirm were viewed as the worthy or deserving poor. They were given credit by local landlords and grocers until work returned or illness subsided (Katz 1996:9). Paupers—the undeserving poor—were scorned throughout colonial communities. Gripped by fears of transient men roving from one locale to the next to take advantage of each community's public assistance program, townships developed strategies and instituted systems designed to discourage pauperism. Many towns required proof of local residency before alms could be obtained. If the poor could not find work in town, they were given apprenticeships, sold off to a local bidder at poor auctions, or sent to the local workhouse in the larger townships where such facilities existed. Perceived as a potent deterrent to shiftlessness, poor auctions persisted in some small, tight–knit communities well into the nineteenth century.

Colonists' strong commitment to local responsibility for poor support stemmed largely from Puritan theology. From a Puritan standpoint, poverty provided an opportunity for the privileged to demonstrate material and spiritual benevolence toward the less fortunate. What's more, the exercise of such benevolence enabled each local community to reaffirm its commitment to order, discipline, and duty.

> The poor, mere pawns in a divinely destined universe and hence not responsible for their condition, were always present . . . not [as] a necessary evil, but rather a blessing, a God–given opportunity for men to do good—to serve society and their Creator. According to God's scheme, a well–ordered society was hierarchical; it had a series of ranks ranging from top to bottom. . . . Each had special privileges and obligations; the poor to work hard and to respect and show deference to those above

them, the well–to–do to be humble and to aid and care for those below them. (Trattner 1999:16–17)

Calvinist theology therefore gave relationships between the privileged and the poor a covenantal cast. Rather than focusing on individual rights and civil liberties, Calvinism placed a premium on social responsibility and the duty of all—privileged and poor alike—to uphold the general welfare of society at large. General welfare was understood to preserve order and divinely ordained social hierarchies.

Still, Calvinist theology itself was marked by contradictory imperatives concerning poverty and work. On the one hand, Calvinism was informed by Christian ideals that command benevolence toward the less fortunate. On the face of it, at least, the local community bore collective responsibility for its members and was obligated to demonstrate compassion toward those facing misfortune. Thus, compulsory taxation funded public assistance efforts within Puritan townships. Yet on the other hand, Calvinism lauded the intrinsic virtue of productive labor. The Christian's unswerving commitment to productive labor was a practical, this–worldly demonstration of religious devotion. The Calvinist valorization of labor and vilification of idleness emphasized the individual's responsibility for securing work. These theological imperatives dictated austerity in the treatment of the poor. "Sturdy beggars" would not find succor in Puritan colonies, leading Cotton Mather to proclaim: "For those who indulge themselves in idleness, the express command of God unto us is, that we should let them starve" (as quoted in Trattner 1999:22).

Social boundaries based on geography and race also influenced poverty relief undertaken in seventeenth–century colonies (Trattner 1999:19–27). Because resident townsmen were known quantities, they were treated more compassionately than strangers. But as colonial townships grew, knowing one's neighbors became increasingly difficult. In response, residency requirements—and, in some cases, immigration restrictions—were applied with more rigor to verify each solicitor's entitlement to public assistance from the local community. Free blacks were expected to solicit relief from "their own kind." And economic provision for black slaves fell on their masters rather than the community at large. Like blacks, Native Americans were widely considered to be members of a savage, inferior race. These "uncivilized elements" typically fell outside the safety nets provided by white townships. Though they might reside within these towns, they were not perceived as members of the community.

As colonies continued to grow during the eighteenth century, so did the ranks of the poor (Trattner 1999: chs. 2–3). Consequently, counties instead of townships became charged with overseeing poor populations and administering public assistance. Military conflicts and an abundance of dangerous occupations left widows and orphans in their wake, while a preponderance of seasonal jobs often left families in dire need for months at a time. Those emigrating to the New World typically arrived with very little in the way of material goods. Economic depressions and widespread health problems also created great need in many growing communities. It was at this time that wealthy philanthropists such as Benjamin Franklin began to supplement public relief efforts with donated funds.

Philanthropic efforts often had a religious cast to them. With the ranks of the poor multiplying, congregations regularly took up collections for those in need. Religious benevolence was further fostered by the First Great Awakening. Emerging in the late 1720s, the First Great Awakening was marked by a period of widespread religious revival centered on distinctly evangelical principles. Evangelical revivalism rejected Puritan notions of predestination and instead focused on the perfectibility of the world through religious conversion. A populist religious movement, evangelicalism emphasized the believer's spiritual rebirth, stressed the shared salvation enjoyed by believers of all social classes through Jesus Christ, and actively encouraged the dissemination of the Christian message among nonbelievers—regardless of social rank.

The revivalists' focus on perfectibility had important social welfare implications. Evangelical revivals commonly placed rich alongside poor, and blacks alongside whites. And in contrast to Calvinists, evangelicals redefined humanitarian benevolence as a generalized form of religious expression rather than a social obligation incumbent only on the most privileged. In this way, the religious fervor produced at mass revivals "fostered humane attitudes and popularized philanthropy at all levels of society" (Trattner 1999:36; see also Bremner 1988:20). Believers of every social standing were to do good for their neighbors. Religious benevolence had both a material and a spiritual aim—relieve suffering while growing the ranks of the faithful by spreading the Christian gospel. The Great Awakening "transformed do–goodism from a predominantly upper– and middle–class activity—half responsibility, half recreation—into a broadly shared, genuinely popular avocation" (Bremner 1988:20).

Yet with their individualistic theology, evangelical revivals promoted a form of humanitarianism that preserved systemic forms of social privilege. George Whitefield, a white evangelist and key leader in the Great Awakening, became popular for his frequent works of benevolence. Often his personal outreach to the poor crossed racial lines, as Whitefield himself provided economic assistance directly to many blacks. Whitefield also urged white masters in the South to educate their African slaves—in part to teach them the Christian message and save their souls. Yet, through it all, Whitefield was careful never to challenge the institution of slavery.

The eighteenth century also witnessed the establishment of private entities founded to perform benevolence work. Denominational relief groups, such as the Episcopal Charitable Society of Boston, were established in the middle of the eighteenth century. Moreover, with large waves of immigration into the colonies—and, following the Revolution, into the nation at large—private charitable organizations rose to prominence. These associations were commonly organized on the basis of a shared ethnic or national heritage. Such was the case with the Scots Charitable Society and the Charitable Irish Society. Germans and other immigrant groups soon followed suit by chartering their own private charitable associations. Private benevolence associations were also formed on the basis of gender, as manifested in an array of fraternal societies that sprung up prior to and soon after the Revolutionary War. These organizations, many of which persisted well into the nineteenth century (Beito 2000), offered mutual aid to their poor members and engaged in supportive outreach to the least fortunate within their local communities.

Whether secular or faith–based in nature, private relief organizations worked in concert with public entities in an effort to address the needs of the poor:

> Private philanthropy complemented public aid; both were part of the American response to poverty. While, from the outset, the public was responsible for providing aid to the needy who, in turn, had a right to such assistance, as soon as they could afford to do so, private citizens and a host of voluntary associations also gave generously to those in distress—orphans, widows, debtors, needy mariners, the religiously oppressed,

new residents of communities who were not covered by the poor laws, and others who could not care for themselves. In view of the antagonism later thought to exist between public assistance and private charity, this cooperative approach to the problem is one of the more noteworthy aspects of American colonial history. (Trattner 1999:35–36)

Other noteworthy historians agree on this point, with Robert Bremner describing colonial welfare as nothing less than a "joint public–private partnership. . . . The line between public and private responsibility was not sharply drawn. In seasons of distress, overseers of the poor frequently called on churches for special collections of alms" (Bremner 1988:23). Prior to the Revolution, welfare crises in Boston—which included a city fire of 1760 and, later, economic fallout from the Boston Tea Party—were relieved through the benevolent activities stemming from "individuals, churches, town meetings, and legislatures throughout the colonies" (Bremner 1988:25). This relief was undertaken by colonial churches across the denominational spectrum.

The Revolutionary War enhanced the cause of American benevolence (Bremner 1988: ch. 2; Trattner 1999: ch. 3). The war magnified poverty among various constituencies in the newly formed United States. Consequently, it expanded the opportunity for benevolence work through the massive social dislocation it produced. The Revolution left in its wake disabled veterans, the widows and orphans of soldiers killed in battle, and transient populations who had lost their homes. Victory in the Revolutionary War also increased Americans' collective commitment to democratic, populist, and humanitarian causes. Nevertheless, the decentralized political structure and church–state separation that distinguished the United States from many European countries reinforced local responsibility for the provision of social welfare. Municipal authorities worked in concert with local religious congregations, and enlisted the help of charitable organizations such as mutual aid societies and fraternal orders.

From Poor Law to Poorhouse:
Nineteenth–Century U.S. Poverty Policy

By the dawn of the nineteenth century, indictments of outdoor relief—and, more broadly, of poor laws—reached a crescendo (Bremner 1988: ch. 4; Katz 1996:47–54; Trattner 1999: ch. 4). Some critics charged that outdoor relief was inequitable. While local responsibility for the poor was an attractive ideal in principle, it created various practical dilemmas. Standards for public assistance varied greatly from one town to the next. And localities heavily populated by low–income citizens could not raise enough tax revenue to support the sizable number of residents needing assistance. Another group of critics charged that public assistance programs instituted under poor laws were inefficient. Local overseers of the poor were unpaid, untrained, and typically inept at discharging their responsibilities effectively. Furthermore, local oversight of public assistance programs with few accountability structures outside the community led to welfare corruption. Opportunistic overseers could provide relief in exchange for personal favors, while unscrupulous administrators could disburse aid on a preferential basis that was motivated more by cronyism than a genuine sense of need.

Such criticisms drew force from dramatic social and economic changes that took place during the nineteenth century. America's first full century as a nation was marked by massive immigration and geographical expansion, coupled with industrialization, urbanization, and the rise of wage–labor capitalism. Small, tight–knit agricultural and mercantile communities had begun to give way to sizable cities in which low–wage factory work was in abundant supply. The ranks of the poor grew significantly during this time. And despite considerable increases in local taxes, public assistance was the most expensive item in the budgets of most American towns and cities.

Critiques of poor laws were further amplified by dramatic changes in nineteenth–century economic theory and radical transformations in the social organization of work. Poor laws were predicated on mercantilist notions of mutual responsibility between the privileged and the poor. Under mercantilism, noblesse oblige demanded that the privileged confer benevolence on the poor—at least the worthy poor. In return for such relief, the poor were obligated to present themselves as deserving of such aid and to demonstrate a spirit of respect and deference toward their benefactors. Much like a religious covenant, this set of social arrangements was justified, by both theological edict and social convention, on the grounds of duty and obligation. Yet with the proliferation of nineteenth–century laissez–faire capitalism, covenantal relationships between the well–off and the poor began to assume the cast of stuffy sentimentalism (Elazar 1994). In both theory and practice, nineteenth–century capitalism facilitated the rise of contractual relationships. Contractual relations are predicated not on the principles of duty, responsibility, and obligation but rather on the precepts of individual rights, self–interest, and civil liberty.

As argued forcefully by laissez–faire economists of the day, capitalism demanded nothing less than an industrious and mobile labor force "freed" from the safety net of public assistance. From this vantage point, financial support to the poor inhibited economic productivity. Poor laws were charged with undermining the incentive to work, diminishing the labor supply, and artificially inflating the wages that could be commanded by workers. Nineteenth–century economists lamented that the poor, who would be forced to work for wages in a free market, could instead seek refuge from productive labor through public assistance. Finally, laissez–faire economists criticized poor–law residency requirements for discouraging mobility in the labor force. Initially established to protect local communities from vagrants, residency requirements coupled with public assistance hampered the free movement of labor from the countryside into urban factories.

On the heels of these massive demographic, economic, and ideological changes, nineteenth–century Americans began to see poverty and the poor through eyes quite different than their colonial forebears. No longer part of a Calvinist predestined order, poverty was now interpreted as clear evidence of deficient character and a lack of moral virtue. In the language of classical economics and contractual relations, poverty was the legitimate consequence—indeed, the "natural right"—of citizens who lacked the values to accumulate wealth in a free market. If the poor were devoid of the Lockean virtues of industriousness and rationality, they were entitled not to public assistance but to the natural consequences of their immoral character—meager compensation at the wages set by market forces. The rise of this individualistic ideology was fueled by the Second Great Awakening, a wave of nineteenth–century revivalism that assigned ultimate responsibility for spiritual and worldly affairs to the individual rather than to his or her milieu. "Poverty and damnation were personal matters; only the individual could overcome them" (Trattner 1999:55).

This confluence of forces gave rise to the poorhouse and scientific charity movements of the nineteenth century (Bremner 1988: chs. 4–6; Katz 1996: chs. 2–4; Trattner 1999: chs. 4 and 5). Advocates of the poorhouse movement wished to abolish outdoor relief and replace it with institutionalized assistance. Strangely, from today's vantage point, the earliest proponents of the poorhouse cast these institutions as a more caring response to poverty than other methods of relief. The poorhouse was envisioned as a compassionate replacement to the harshness of poor auctions. Poorhouses, their proponents contended, would teach the able-bodied poor how to engage in respectable forms of labor such as farmwork, weaving, and small–scale industry. Designed specifically for the able–bodied poor, the workhouse would be distinguished from the almshouse, with the latter set apart specifically for the deserving poor (that is, the sick, disabled, aged, and mentally ill). Whatever its form, institutionalized relief would promote closer and more sustained contact between the poor and these institutions' overseers, who were charged with the twin responsibility of monitoring and mentoring poorhouse residents. Apart from these anticipated virtues, poorhouses were also championed as a means for ensuring that children in impoverished families were properly schooled. Parents in the poorhouse could have their children cared for in separate institutions—orphanages. In this way, children could be prepared for a life of productive labor and would be less likely to internalize the idleness, lack of self–discipline, and bad habits that plagued their parents.

In addition to these apparent virtues, poorhouses were championed as a corrective to various forms of inequity that beset the old poor law system. Prior to the poorhouse movement, urban areas allocated as much as three times more money toward poverty relief than their rural counterparts. Under this new system, each county would have a poorhouse—two, if both a workhouse and almshouse were needed—and all townships in the county would be expected to support this institution. Moreover, settlement disputes, expensive inquiries through which counties sought to identify the particular local community responsible for providing relief to poor persons, would no longer be needed. A poorhouse that was supported by every township in the county shifted the responsibility of poverty relief from the local community to a common county–level institution. Thus, poorhouses reflected an effort to spread the burden of poverty relief more equitably between rural and urban areas, thereby addressing geographical disparities, while avoiding expensive settlement disputes.

Despite such high–minded ideals, poorhouse proponents were not wholly motivated by humanitarian concerns. Advocates of the poorhouse movement won public sentiment and political support based on the grossly utilitarian claim that they could provide care for the poor more cheaply and efficiently than the old poor law system. Given the sizable budgets for poor relief found in many municipalities, this claim of cost–effectiveness was compelling indeed. Poorhouse proponents also claimed that institutionalized relief would finally make it possible to distinguish between the able–bodied pauper and the deserving poor. If other work was not available, able–bodied men would at least be expected to cut wood and break stone in exchange for their supper and bed. Able–bodied women would be expected to sew or engage in other appropriately "feminine" work. Once determinations about able–bodiedness had been made, overseers could "inculcate virtue" by threatening to withhold food and shelter if paupers refused to work. To cure "intemperance"—a condition that today would be defined as a drug addiction—alcohol was prohibited in workhouses. And because intemperance was believed to have been caused in part by an "absence of religion" (Katz 1996:11), exposure to religious doctrine was deemed essential to the project of effecting moral reform among the poor.

Workhouses aimed, then, to reform the poor by requiring inmates to adopt respectable lifestyle habits and to engage in labor that would offset the cost associated with providing institutional support. Stringent work and lifestyle requirements, along with deplorable living conditions, in poorhouses were designed to have a deterrent effect. The able–bodied would not want to seek out support from the poorhouse if the conditions there were sufficiently reprehensible. Properly structured, it was thought, poorhouses would move the undeserving, able–bodied vagrant into the workforce while converting those with a defective moral character to a life of respectability.

Virtually all reputable historians today agree that poorhouses were a failure. Poorhouses were more expensive to establish and maintain than originally thought, and ultimately became notorious for financial mismanagement and graft. Many counties could not afford to support both an almshouse and a workhouse, exacerbating the already difficult task of distinguishing between the deserving and undeserving poor. Housing different classes of the poor together rather than separating them by condition made it virtually impossible to provide specialized services to poorhouse residents. In urban areas where poorhouse staff were significantly outnumbered by residents, official policies such as work requirements and abstinence from alcohol often went unenforced. And the original vision of poorhouse staff teaching productive skills and inculcating virtue among their residents rarely materialized. In rural areas, even the most successful poor farms—those that grew enough crops to feed their workers and the overseer's family—often struggled to make ends meet in the summertime when able–bodied men left to find seasonal employment elsewhere.

At its root, fundamental contradictions plagued poorhouses. Poorhouses were expected to be both humanitarian and punitive, caring and authoritarian, efficient and specialized. Moreover, poorhouses were expected to eradicate poverty even as overseers were afforded no professional training, given meager pay and resources, and supplied with minimal staff. In practice, poorhouses could not meet the demands of these conflicting imperatives. As Katz concludes, poorhouses were caught between

> the incompatibility of deterrence and compassion: the spread of fear and the kindly treatment of poverty could not coexist. One or the other always prevailed. This was the reason poorhouse critics increasingly argued for the separation of the able–bodied into special workhouses. By dividing the inmates into the able–bodied and deserving, two separate policies could exist: one harsh, punitive, and centered on work, the other more compassionate and generous. However, . . . in practice, the division of individual cases rarely was as easy as commentators implied. Some people were helpless because they were sick, insane, or old. But for others, the line was not nearly so clear. . . . Occasional bursts of sentiment aside, poorhouses were not supposed to do more than keep old and helpless inmates from starvation. They existed to deter the impotent as well as the able–bodied poor from seeking their shelter. . . . By the close of the [nineteenth] century, at the latest, dread of the poorhouse was nearly universal. In the end, deterrence won. (Katz 1996:34–35)

With the mid-nineteenth–century recognition that the poorhouse was not fulfilling its promise, advocates of scientific charity emerged on the scene (Bremner 1988: ch. 6; Katz 1995; Katz 1996: ch. 3; Trattner 1999: ch. 5). Reflecting the formal rational values predominant in America at this time, this movement professionalized poverty relief and gave it a new name—charity. The shift of language from relief to charity is telling. The notion of relief calls attention to the burdens besetting the poor and, implicitly at least, highlights the privileged class's obligation to give succor to the disadvantaged. Charity focused attention away from the recipients of relief by underscoring instead the goodwill and voluntary acts of kindness undertaken by generous, upstanding citizens.

Through the carefully planned and coordinated actions of professional charitable organization societies, scientific charity would do what poorhouses alone were unable to accomplish—repress pauperism, reform the character of the needy, and restore the poor to a life of self–sufficiency. Champions of the poorhouse and advocates of scientific charity could agree about many issues. Both condemned outdoor relief. Both argued that objective distinctions could be drawn between shiftless paupers and the worthy poor. However, scientific charity proposed to professionalize the poorhouse, and to institutionalize relief in general, by enlisting the careful calculation of science in the fight against poverty. Josephine Shaw Lowell, generally considered the founder of the movement, was the first to dub charity a "science." As Katz (1996:71–72) astutely observes, Lowell believed that "philanthropic experience around the world had developed a body of hard, definitive principles about poverty, charity, and relief"; moreover, leaders of the professional charity movement proposed a "method for gathering the data with which to further develop the laws of charity and reform. Charity organization societies . . . should study as well as help the poor."

The middle and latter parts of the nineteenth century witnessed the flourishing of charitable organization societies, the practical outgrowth of scientific charity theory. These societies, including the Association for Improving the Condition of the Poor, sought to reform the moral fiber of the poor while coordinating the activities of local relief agencies—all with the aim of eliminating "waste and duplication" among such agencies (see Katz 1996:71). Motivated by these goals, Lowell herself was instrumental in forming the New York Charity Organization Society. On the heels of the Second Great Awakening that swept America early in the nineteenth century, Lowell's vision was one of providing broad–based charity that fused the efficiency of science with the self–sufficiency embodied in middle–class Protestantism:

> the best help of all is to help people help themselves. . . . The poor man or woman should have the road cleared so that they may themselves march on to success—that their brains should be released from ignorance, their hands freed from the shackles of incompetence, their bodies saved from the pains of sickness, and their souls delivered from the bonds of sin. (Lowell, as quoted in Cammisa 1998:33)

The distinctly Protestant impetus that motivated this wing of the scientific charity movement put it squarely at odds with Catholic immigrants who had recently arrived from Ireland and Germany. Protestant reformers motivated by Lowell's vision "found the new Catholic immigrants to be lazy, indolent, prone to drink, and far too ready to accept public relief" (Cammisa 1998:34)—labels that would later be applied to African Americans and Hispanics. In the eyes of many Protestant charity workers, Catholics quickly became the undeserving poor. The solution to such moral depravity was obvious: convert the Catholic immigrants to Protestantism. Taking a page from tract societies that first emerged during the Second Great Awakening, Protestant charitable organization societies often delivered tracts (cliff–note summaries distilling key sections of the Bible) as they provided assistance such as food, clothing, rental payment, and employment contacts to the poor. The Catholic Church, whose own adherents were the target of tract society evangelism and relief throughout most of the nineteenth century, countered by forming its own benevolence organizations, including parish–level relief organizations and St. Vincent de Paul, a churchwide society. Not coincidentally, Catholic hospitals, orphanages, schools, and young women's homes also sprang up throughout the states at this time. At every turn, Protestant hegemony and proselytization efforts left Catholics to set up parallel institutions. New York Protestants had a Children's Aid Society for neglected youth and delinquents. Catholics who had recently settled in the city formed their own organization—the Catholic Protectory.

Another major reformer in the scientific charity movement was Stephen Humphreys Gurteen, an Anglican minister who envisioned a less sectarian yet highly centralized system that would promote the "co–operation of all charitable institutions in the city with one another, and with the distributors of official relief" (as quoted in Katz 1996:77). Gurteen set up a charitable organization society in Buffalo and assisted in establishing them in other American cities. Like Lowell, Gurteen charged that indiscriminate charity was itself a leading cause of poverty because it undermined the work incentive among the poor. Thus, charitable organization societies typically did not dispense material relief. Rather, they created review committees that fielded and scrutinized aid solicitations received by local relief organizations. If such requests were deemed worthy of support by the committee, the charitable organization society then served as a referral agency by sending the aid solicitor to the appropriate local charity. Given its commitment to the coordination and centralization of charity work in local communities, each society kept a central registry that recorded the receipt of aid by the poor. This registry was regularly updated and made accessible to all local relief agencies in the city.

Gurteen's vision of scientific charity also entailed regular follow–up visits to the homes of those receiving such charity. The New York Association for Improving the Condition of the Poor specifically designated males for the task of in–home visitation, and appropriately dubbed them "paternal guardians." The guardians' visitation of the poor in their homes served several purposes—friendship, guidance, and, as needed, admonishment. In Gurteen's own words (as quoted in Katz 1996:79), the poor needed "a real friend, whose education, experience, and influence, whose general knowledge of life, or special knowledge of domestic economy are placed at the service of those who have neither the intelligence, the tact nor the opportunity to extract the maximum of good from their slender resources." As such, visitors were instructed to "point out, in a firm but loving spirit, the degrading tendency of a life of dependence and the real dignity of honest work." And, if the home was found unkempt, the "visitor should . . . endeavor to induce the poor to keep their dwellings in a wholesome, healthy condition."

Historians now recognize that the motives underlying visitation—and, more generally, scientific charity—were at best marked by ambivalence and at worst reflected fear and hatred. In assessing the practice of in–home visitation, Katz (1996:79) argues: "In truth, the visitor was to be at once a sympathetic friend, an official, a teacher, and a spy." Concerning the broader accomplishments of scientific charity, Trattner (1999:72) surmises that "moralism superceded humanism; public aid and private charity were transformed from acts of justice and benevolence into mechanisms for bringing order and stability to a new and unsettling social environment." And Anne Marie Cammisa asserts that the white Protestant reformers during the era of scientific charity

> had a difficult time absorbing the [newly freed] black and immigrant populations into their midst. At their worst, social reformers . . . viewed the new population as subhuman and incapable of being reformed. Even at their best, social reformers often had paternalistic attitudes toward both blacks and immigrants, wanting to rehabilitate them by inculcating middle–class Protestant values to which the poor did not necessarily aspire. . . . Rather than accounting for cultural and religious differences,

they tried to create middle–class Protestants out of poor Catholic immigrants, many of whom resented their efforts. (Cammisa 1998:33–34)

Like poorhouses, then, charitable organization societies struggled to realize the promises trumpeted by their advocates. As the "first great secular organizations of urban philanthropy" (Katz 1996:78), charitable organization societies—particularly those beholden to Gurteen's vision—failed to win the trust of many local religious organizations. Fearing that religious zeal would inflame rivalries across faith traditions, many charitable organization societies eventually forced religious groups to set aside their creedal convictions and prohibited the proselytization of the poor. These became the first two cardinal principles of charitable organization societies, as described in Gurteen's *Handbook of Charity Organization* (see Katz 1996:78).

It should come as no surprise, then, that the relationship between such societies and local religious communities was often marked by tension and distrust. Religious organizations, particularly those of the evangelical variety, had long integrated proselytization into their relief efforts. And given the longstanding tensions between faith traditions, many charitable organization societies wished to sideline religious convictions as an organizing principle for charity work. In the place of creed–specific ministry to the poor, scientific charity demanded a businesslike model. If religious at all, the orientation and practices of charitable organization societies were covered by a thin veneer of generic Christianity. Rule 5 in Gurteen's handbook put the matter plainly: "There must be no sentiment in the matter. [Charity work] must be treated as a business scheme, if success is to attend its operations" (as quoted in Katz 1996:78).

Religious groups of many stripes found the cool detachment of this scientific business model unpalatable where benevolence work was concerned. The newly formed Salvation Army, with its "open–air outreach" conducted from urban street corners in major metropolitan areas, directly challenged the bureaucratic model of nineteenth–century scientific charity (Winston 1999). For Salvationists, real benevolence had to be thrust out of the philanthropic boardrooms—as well as out of the church—and into the "cathedral of the open air." Thus, Salvationists staged raucous street parades flanked by loud brass bands, held outdoor services several times a week (called simply "open–airs"), and undertook indiscriminate street–level benevolence—all of which stood in bold contrast to the stuffiness and stinginess of charitable organization societies.

The reactions of established religious groups were more subdued but nonetheless critical of charitable organization societies. Even the Indianapolis Charitable Organization Society, widely recognized as one of the more successful of its kind, was chided by Presbyterian leaders as a "system of espionage" for its condescension toward the poor and its intrusive monitoring of recipients' lifestyle habits; and area Baptist and Methodist ministers together voiced complaints about the unfair advantages enjoyed by some Indianapolis pastors who were perceived as cronies of the local charitable society (Katz 1996:86).

Regardless of the form such reactions took, the logic of formal rationality that undergirded scientific charity was starkly at odds with the benevolent impulse in many religious communities. Given the lip service that charitable organization societies paid to Christian mandates about ministering to the poor, critiques of these societies emanated from all quarters. John Reed, a critic of the societies who penned the introduction to a 1917 exposé called *Crimes of Charity*, wrote: "There is nothing of Christ the compassionate in the immense business of Organised Charity; its object is to get efficient results—and that means, in practise, to just keep alive vast numbers of servile, broken–spirited people" (as quoted in Katz 1996:87). Poet John Boyle O'Reilly was even more succinct and damning (in Katz 1996:86):

> That Organized Charity, scrimped and iced,
> In the name of a cautious, statistical Christ.

From Welfare State to Post–Welfare Era: The Twentieth Century

The twentieth century brought several remarkable developments in social welfare policy and faith–based poverty relief. With the decline of scientific charity, interdenominational relief agencies grew dramatically (Skocpol 2000; Thiemann, Herring, and Perabo 2000). Religious relief organizations thrived in urban areas which, by 1915, had become home to nearly half of the American population and were the destination of many new European immigrants. By this time, the Salvation Army boasted a following four times that of its 1890 membership rolls. The Young Men's Christian Association (YMCA), which had attracted a scant 10,000 volunteers in 1865, grew to 263,000 thirty years later. By 1915 the YMCA far eclipsed these numbers with 720,000 volunteers. Other religious associations, such as the Independent Order of Good Templars (IOGT) and the Catholic Knights of Columbus, also flourished at this time. The IOGT, a Bible–based organization of men and women, sought to overcome Protestant denominationalism through the collective pursuit of Christian temperance. The Knights of Columbus, the counterpart to Protestant fraternal societies, united Catholic men across ethnic lines (Skocpol 2000). Although this organization was founded by Irish Catholics, it later expanded to include Italians, French Canadians, and others. The proliferation of such groups signaled the rapid growth of America's voluntary sector in the early twentieth century. However, their growth also reflected broader changes in the landscape of American religion. Overall membership in American religious communities boomed, with national rates of religious affiliation doubling and the number of churches blossoming from 75,000 to 225,000.

Many reformers of the Progressive Era reacted strongly against the institutionalization of the poor that had taken place throughout much of the nineteenth century (Berkowitz and McQuaid 1992: ch. 2; Handler and Hasenfeld 1991:50–81; Trattner 1999: ch. 10). With the goals of preventing poverty and reforming the poor, settlement houses sprang up in many urban areas with large immigrant populations during the late nineteenth and early twentieth centuries (J. Schwartz 2000:109–121; Trattner 1999: ch. 8). Hull House, established amidst Chicago tenements in 1889 by Jane Addams, became a model for settlement houses in other urban areas. These large neighborhood homes served as centers for instruction, fellowship, and recreation. Settlement house workers took up residence among the urban poor, commonly situating themselves in immigrant communities. Many were beholden to Christian edicts about caring for the disadvantaged. They sought to teach new immigrants about American culture in the hope of facilitating their assimilation into U.S. society. Settlement workers also taught immigrants a range of practical skills, regularly providing them with child–rearing advice and preaching the good health that could be obtained by following hygienic practices. Unabashed advocates of assimilation, settlement house workers sought to change the lifestyle habits of immigrants to conform to early-twentieth-century U.S. culture—actually, that of white middle–class America. Consequently, settlement worker "do–gooderism" frequently raised suspicions among immigrants.

Social Gospel Christianity also enjoyed its heyday in many urban areas (J. Schwartz 2000:121–130). Reformers like Walter Rauschenbusch and

Washington Gladden chided the excessively individualistic qualities that had long distinguished American Christianity. They sought to promote social transformation through the application of biblical principles about social justice and progressive change. Social Gospel reformers critiqued the exploitative character of industrial capitalism while lobbying for better factory working conditions, the right to a living wage for American workers, and the abolition of child labor.

Although these reform movements had begun to decline by the late 1920s, both had an enduring impact on American understandings of poverty and U.S. social welfare policy. Both the settlement movement and Social Gospel Christianity understood poverty as the product of systemic inequality. Both sought structural solutions to poverty through the progressive reform of social welfare policy. And most importantly, the successes of these movements were rooted in religious arguments about social justice. To be sure, settlement house workers and Social Gospel reformers did not come anywhere near eradicating poverty during the first three decades of the twentieth century. But they transformed cultural understandings of poverty and, in so doing, sowed the seeds of social welfare reforms that were to flourish for much of the twentieth century.

Several social policy innovations coincided with the Progressive Era. One of the most striking developments was the establishment of mothers' pensions (Skocpol 1992). Repudiating the breakup of families common during the poorhouse era, progressive reformers urged states to develop public assistance programs for widows with dependent children. Mothers' pension programs were, in fact, seen to complement another social assistance program that had been introduced just years earlier—a veterans' benefits program for Union (though not Confederate) soldiers who had fought in the Civil War. Near the turn of the twentieth century, veterans' benefits were extended to the families and survivors of soldiers from the North. By 1910, one third of men in the North aged sixty-two and older were receiving payments from the federal government that were considered generous by international standards (Skocpol 2000:26).

Although women's suffrage was still years away, settlement house leaders like Addams and an array of women's federations were instrumental in fostering the passage of mothers' pensions. One of the most formidable advocates of mothers' pensions was the National Congress of Mothers, a Protestant organization not shy about publicizing its Christian convictions and its hope to "maternalize" government. In a 1911 speech to the National Congress of Mothers, a Tennessee woman addressed the group with strong words of encouragement:

> Do not rise up in indignation to call this Socialism—it is the sanest of statesmanship. If our public mind is maternal, loving, and generous, wanting to save and develop all, our Government will express this sentiment. . . . Every step we make toward establishing government along these lines means an advance toward the Kingdom of Peace. (as quoted in Skocpol 2000:36)

Many states—forty in all—followed suit in short order. This new program was born of the assumption that providing cash assistance to mothers would allow them to care for their children at home rather than having their youngsters sent to an orphanage. Based on the concept of republican motherhood, reformers portrayed the nurturing mother as essential to the project of American democracy. Properly reared children, it was thought, would grow up to be morally upright, economically productive citizens.

However, such programs were to be made available only to "fit"—that is to say, widowed—mothers (Gordon 1994). Given the dominance of the family wage ideal and widespread concerns about providing public support for "deviant" family types, these pension programs excluded deserted and never-married mothers. Where the concept of republican motherhood failed to quell criticism, the programs were commonly defended by enlisting a compensatory wage analogy: Widows should receive "wages" from the state in exchange for the successful discharge of their child-rearing responsibilities. This analogy had real-world implications, as aid was "highly conditional, dependent on the recipient's ability to demonstrate a class- and race-defined standard of maternal success measured on a scale difficult for many mothers to perceive, let alone achieve or accept" (Gordon 1994:52). The meager stipends commonly provided by mothers' pension programs gave "immorality" considerable appeal. Some mothers tried to find a man who would lend them financial support to supplement their aid—a practice that was expressly forbidden under the programs. Others would work for "real wages" clandestinely. This practice, when combined with an absence of day care, left them at risk of being branded "child neglecters." America's first generation of family policy makers, then, were doing what they could to maternalize public assistance, so long as they did not undermine the two–parent domestic model that was thought to be ordained by God and selected by human history. This program set the stage for debates about female–headed households that would persist for much of the twentieth century.

Broadly understood, then, the Progressive Era marked an important shift away from local control over social welfare policy. Poor laws from colonial times through the nineteenth century had placed responsibility for social welfare provision at the feet of local governments and private charities (religious and secular). Yet with the advent of the Progressive Era, states took more of a hand in providing for the social welfare of those in need and began to do so with cash assistance programs targeted at mothers deemed fit for such relief.

The stock market crash of 1929 ushered in one of the bleakest periods in American social welfare history—the Great Depression, from which emerged revolutionary New Deal programs (Berkowitz and McQuaid 1992: chs. 5 and 6; Handler and Hasenfeld 1991:85–106; Katz 1996: ch. 8; Trattner 1999: ch. 13). Following the crash, the unemployment rate increased until one out of every four Americans was out of work. With the advent of the Great Depression, the old poor law system came under increasingly critical scrutiny. Under the poor law system, disadvantaged persons were expected first to seek help from their own family members. However, given the profound economic problems wrought by the Great Depression, family members were in no position to lend assistance to one another. Religious and secular charities also figured prominently in the old poor law system. However, private charities of all kinds were being overrun with requests for assistance during this period. Given the flagging donations offered to religious and secular charities during the Great Depression, many organizations struggled to meet the pervasive demand for relief. Finally, sharp declines in the tax bases of local and state governments left these political entities at a loss to address the economic dislocation effected by the Depression.

Given these developments, Depression–era Americans began looking to the federal government for relief. And out of the ashes of the Great Depression rose of the phoenix of federal welfare policy. Soon after assuming the presidency in 1932, Franklin Delano Roosevelt proposed a broad slate of initiatives designed to combat the economic strife wrought by the Depression. In so doing, Roosevelt's New Deal programs dramatically revolutionized the American social welfare system and carried forward many reforms that had begun during the Progressive Era. New Deal initiatives, many of them passed within Roosevelt's first one hundred days in office, included the establishment of unemployment compensation, aid to farmers, a massive public works program, and federal regulation of the stock market. Not long after, in 1935, architects of the New Deal unveiled a revamped social welfare system that provided social insurance for the elderly (then called Old Age Insurance, now called Social Security), as well as categorical assistance for children in families that lacked a breadwinner (Aid to Dependent Children, or ADC). While pensions for mothers, and even the elderly, had cropped up in some states, ADC marked an important break with the past by establishing a welfare provision relationship between the federal government and the states. Both contributed funds to support the program.

This emerging relationship between the federal government and the states was marked by tension over the questions of single motherhood and the "Negro problem" in the South. Concerning the motherhood question, federal government officials favored a system in which aid would be provided to all families with children, including homes headed by never–married mothers and families left fatherless by husband desertion. State governments, however, preferred the mothers' pension model of withholding aid from never–married and deserted mothers. At this point, the debate was resolved in the states' favor. The "Negro question" was, in many respects, more vexing. New Deal architects had counted on opposition concerning "worthy widows," but failed to anticipate Southern resistance to the initiative based on race:

> Southerners were more unexpected opponents. During the hearings on the Economic Security Act, Senator Byrd spoke for Southern fears that Social Security might "serve as an entering wedge for federal interference with the handling of the Negro question in the South." Southern senators, he pointed out, wanted to prevent the federal government from withholding funds from states whose administration of old-age assistance discriminated against blacks. [Director of the federal government's Committee on Economic Security (CES), Edwin] Witte told Byrd that it "never occurred to any person" on the CES "that the Negro question would come up in this connection," and he agreed to modify the bill to permit Southern states a great deal more administrative autonomy. (Katz 1996:248)

Given potential opposition from white Southerners, then, the New Deal ensured that states' rights—at least where racial discrimination was concerned—would be protected. As another form of compromise with white power brokers in the South, FDR repeatedly refused to endorse antilynching laws (Katz 1996:252). FDR's unwillingness to challenge racial discrimination, however, was tempered by his wife. Eleanor Roosevelt manifested an "outspoken commitment to racial justice [through] support for the NAACP, speeches to interracial audiences, and meetings with black leaders. . . . The result [of Eleanor's unflinching support for more progressive race relations] was dramatic. In 1936, blacks exchanged their historic commitment to the party of Lincoln and voted for Roosevelt" (Katz 1996:253).

The New Deal, then, solidified many of the changes to social welfare policy that had first begun in the Progressive Era. The New Deal gave legal currency to progressive reformers' definition of poverty as a public issue rather than a private trouble. Given the economic fallout of the Great Depression, it was difficult for most Americans of this era to conceive of poverty as purely an individual matter. The New Deal also established the involvement of the federal government in a policy area—social welfare—that had for over two centuries fallen largely under the jurisdiction of local communities. Over the course of a scant forty years, responsibility for social welfare provision had moved on a steady course from being implemented predominantly by the local municipality, then by the state, and now by the federal government.

Apart from grappling with longstanding questions about gender and race, New Deal initiatives contained other moral residues from the past. Architects of the New Deal were careful to distinguish between social insurance programs (unemployment compensation, Social Security) that were paid for through user–taxes and categorical assistance programs (Aid to Dependent Children) in which recipients drew assistance from the program but did not contribute to it. This two–pronged approach to welfare provision enabled New Deal architects to reinforce the longstanding distinction between the deserving poor (beneficiaries of social insurance programs) and the undeserving poor (recipients of categorical assistance programs). Ever since they were first established, social insurance programs have been quite popular while categorical assistance programs have been subject to criticism and stigmatization. For these reasons, it is most accurate to conceive of New Deal programs as ushering in a "semiwelfare state" (Katz 1996) rather than a full–blown commitment to state–sponsored welfare.

Moreover, the New Deal involvement of the federal government in social welfare provision did not end the ties between local governments and religious activists in American communities. Government officials and religious organizations in many locales continued to collaborate as the country struggled to revive itself economically. Winston's (1999) historical treatment of the Salvation Army describes the extensive collaborations between Salvationists and the local government in New York during the latter years of the Depression and throughout the New Deal era. Salvationists worked closely with local elected officials, business leaders, and other religious organizations (including Catholic and Jewish relief agencies) to provide hot meal programs at soup kitchens and employment services through its job referral bureaus. The Salvation Army also supervised various temporary housing units for unemployed men. Given neighborhood settlement patterns within New York City, the Salvation Army was careful to oversee several units segregated by race and class. The Gold Dust Lodge catered to white professionals displaced by unemployment in lower Manhattan, whereas the Salvation Army Colored Men's Hotel and Food Depot offered lodging to black working–class men in Harlem. These efforts won public appreciation and accolades from prominent city officials. The city's Police and Public Welfare Commissioner warned that "any break in the program of the Salvation Army would throw the city's welfare machinery seriously out of gear, and would entail an immediate menace of social disturbances by the destitute unemployed" (as quoted in Winston 1999:237). And New York Mayor Fiorello La Guardia was not shy about calling attention to "the close relationship between the city and the [Salvationist] religious group" (Winston 1999:240). This partnership stretched on for years, as the New York City Salvation Army collaborated with local government officials to implement New Deal programs such as the Works Progress Administration.

Further south, Catholic leaders and laity emerged as key players in organizing the Pittsburgh steelworkers union during the New Deal era. As aptly charted by Kenneth Heineman (1999), Catholic priests and bishops stood on picket lines alongside local steelworkers, forged interracial and interfaith alliances among the workers, and participated in the formation of the Steel Workers Organizing Committee. During the great steel war of 1937, Catholic leaders and laity also called attention to the discriminatory tactics of steel companies that tried to replace striking white Catholic workers by importing Southern black and Appalachian white "scabs" into Pittsburgh. Local Catholic politicians served as valuable liaisons between the steelworkers and the city government. Thus, while many religious organizations struggled with resource shortfalls during the Great Depression, faith–based charities were instrumental in community development, the provision of social services, and progressive economic change during the New Deal era.

From the 1930s through the middle decades of the twentieth century, some social welfare programs initially ushered in under the New Deal were expanded and reformed. The original Social Security Act named particular professions to which retirement benefits would not be extended—among them, personal service and agriculture jobs. This provision discriminated against employed women and rural laborers—most notably, black men in the South.

> New Deal agricultural policies [including federal crop subsidies] hurt Southern blacks by forcing land out of production and shrinking the base of black employment. Although farmers were supposed to share their federal crop subsidies with their displaced workers, few did so. The consequence was widespread rural black poverty and the acceleration of black migration to cities where, of course, they found little work. . . . Of all groups during the Great Depression, black men had the highest unemployment rates, and black women, confined largely to agricultural and domestic service, did little better. (Katz 1996:252)

As it turned out, the overt gender inequities originally promoted by the New Deal were easier to fix than the racial stratification it reinforced. By 1939, policy makers amended the Social Security Act to make benefits available to a worker's family rather than just to the worker himself. Thus, widows previously covered under Aid to Dependent Children (ADC) were now provided for by Social Security—the more popular of the two programs. At the same time, ADC was expanded to cover divorced, deserted, and never–married mothers. ADC, already stigmatized for supporting mother–headed families, became a lightening rod for criticism. Defenders of traditional morality warned that the ADC expansion would promote immoral behavior, including out–of–wedlock births. By the 1950s, many states adopted "suitable home provisions" that allowed state workers to inspect the homes of ADC recipients to be sure single mothers, particularly African American women, were not living with a man. As Cammisa (1998:47) describes it: "State public officials actually raided recipients' homes in the wee hours of the morning to make sure that there was no 'man in the house' whose presence would make the mother ineligible for benefits. To make matters worse, suitable home provisions were often aimed at black women, who were more likely to have children out of wedlock." It was during this same time that African Americans began to mobilize against long standing forms of discrimination. They were soon to be followed by women and other oppressed groups. America's "rights revolution" (Schudson 1998), begun during the early twentieth century with the settlement house and Social Gospel movements, had reached its apex during the 1960s.

The 1960s brought the further expansion of welfare programs by the federal government (Handler and Hasenfeld 1991:106–127; Katz 1996: ch. 9; Trattner 1999: ch. 14). Upon taking office in 1963, Lyndon Johnson declared a War on Poverty. In the midst of economic expansion, Johnson's Great Society programs were intended to do no less than eradicate poverty. He proposed to do so by helping the poor—particularly urban blacks—left behind by the shortcomings of laissez faire capitalism and systematic discrimination. Welfare benefits were expanded through Aid to Families with Dependent Children (AFDC), whose new name reflected this revamped program's broader emphasis than that of its predecessor, Aid to Dependent Children (ADC). Other federal initiatives, including Head Start, Job Corps, public housing, and affirmative action were launched as well. Great Society initiatives such as the Work Incentive Program (WIN) made job preparation classes available to welfare recipients.

The Economic Opportunity Act of 1964 formed the centerpiece of Johnson's revolutionary legislation. This act created the Office of Economic Opportunity and chartered community action agencies to receive federal grants from the newly established office. "Community involvement was encouraged at all levels, and many programs required that boards be set up containing not only local officials but also members of the population that was to be served" (Cammisa 1998:49–50). The forging of direct ties between the federal government and local community groups was a new development in social welfare provision. Recall that the New Deal initiated programs cofunded by states and the federal government. Johnson's move to work with local community officials raised the ire of states, whose policy makers felt bypassed in the pursuit of the Great Society.

The community action agencies that were established under Great Society programs met with strong resistance in more conservative regions of the country, including much of the South. Given the history of racism in the South, many of the white community leaders in the region were deemed untrustworthy by progressive policy makers at the federal level. In the aftermath of *Brown v. Board of Education* (1954), Mississippi business leaders and professionals formed the White Citizens' Council "for pursuing the agenda of the Klan with the demeanor of the Rotary" (Payne 1995:34). With increased federal scrutiny over Southern lynchings, the Council aimed to preserve white supremacy through legal means—specifically, through economic reprisals against civil rights activists. Many Council leaders were also presidents of local banks and were thus able to control area residents by refusing to renew farm mortgages and leases, arbitrarily doubling rental prices, and refusing to do business in any form with black activists or those perceived to support them.

Therefore, when it came to forming community action agencies, parceling out grants, and implementing Great Society programs in much of the South, federal officials worked around local political leaders. Resentment grew among political representatives in Southern communities, who "felt that power was being wrongfully taken from them. . . . Great Society programs . . . specifically took control away from the local government, putting it instead into the hands of the local community action agencies, which were to be racially mixed and include members of the target population" (Cammisa 1998:51).

Melding the civic language of rights with religious visions of social justice, black churches found their political voice. Indeed, black churches in the South became a key institution in organizing the Civil Rights Movement (Lincoln and Mamiya 1990: ch. 8; Morris 1984). "The black church provided the civil rights movement with a collective enthusiasm generated through a rich culture consisting of songs, testimonies, oratory, and prayers that spoke directly to the needs of an oppressed group. Many black churches preached that oppression is sinful and that God sanctions protest aimed at eradicating social evils" (Morris 1984:4). Moreover, the South's long legacy of racism meant that Southern blacks—many of whom were inspired by biblical imagery of the "promised land"—were leading the charge for civil rights. While many protests were nonviolent, others were not. On the heels of church bombings and slain civil rights workers, "Birmingham blacks took to the streets . . . and pioneered a form of social protest new to the 1960s: the urban riot" (as quoted in Katz 1996:260; see also Lamonte 1995). Mississippi churches emerged as a key battleground in this larger struggle, with vocal advocates and opponents of the Civil Rights Movement surfacing from many of the state's religious communities (Marsh 1997). The Civil Rights Movement gave rise to a host of other social protest movements, including the National Welfare Rights Organization (NWRO). Many racially progressive churches supported the NWRO, whose backbone was formed by poor black women and others opposed to gender and racial discrimination effected by "suitable home" provisions.

The semiwelfare state that emerged subsequent to the New Deal had coincided with an emerging division of labor between public welfare and private charity. State assistance programs and religious benevolence initiatives had become situated on largely parallel tracks. Great Society programs, however, forged small but significant bridges across these parallel tracks. Public funding of local nonprofit organizations was initially ushered in on a small scale by Great Society programs, and was expanded soon thereafter (Smith and Lipsky 1993; Thiemann, Herring, and Perabo 2000). A 1965 survey conducted by the Family Service Association of America revealed that 8 percent of private nonprofit providers' funding came from public sources, while another study found that 80 percent of eight hundred nongovernmental service providers received no public funding whatsoever. Yet the passage of a 1967 amendment to the Social Security Act "specifically encouraged states to enter into purchase–of–service agreements with private agencies" (Smith and Lipsky 1993:55). With the passage of this new law, government outsourcing of service provision to private agencies began in earnest. Spurred on by a large increase in federal welfare spending (from $812 million in 1965 to $2.2 billion in 1970), contracts between the government and private nonprofit providers became commonplace (Salamon 1995; Thiemann, Herring, and Perabo 2000).

Religious organizations with established records of broad–based service provision, such as Catholic Charities and Lutheran Social Services, were able to capitalize on these developments. In some measure, then, the parallel tracks that for decades had divided public assistance from private charity began to be breeched. The case of Catholic Charities is particularly intriguing (Brown and McKeown 1997). The Catholic principle of "subsidiarity" recognizes the joint responsibility of various social actors—religious and government alike—for the poor and conceives of the person as both sacred and social (Hehir 2000). The principle of subsidiarity gave the Catholic Church a culture that was particularly predisposed to church–state partnerships. Moreover, by the 1960s, the children and grandchildren of Catholic immigrants had assimilated into the mainstream of U.S. society. This development, along with the inclusive Vatican II vision of serving the non–Catholic poor, made Catholic Charities a particularly attractive partner for government contracting (Thiemann, Herring, and Perabo 2000).

With the expansion of the federal government's authority over welfare, resentment against Johnson's Great Society programs and the War on Poverty eventually grew. By the end of Johnson's last term in office, Great Society programs had come to stand for all that was wrong with the federal government and the new social welfare "system"—centralization that seemed to promote top–down management of local affairs from distant bureaucrats. With the Great Depression and the New Deal serving as little more than distant memories for most Americans, discussions of states' rights and local empowerment came to dominate public debates over American welfare policy during the 1970s and 1980s. However, the Great Society push to enlist private service providers into public welfare programs would survive. In fact, even as Great Society programs came under greater fire in the 1970s and 1980s, policy makers acted to expand public–private partnerships (Bremner 1988: ch. 13; Savas 2000).

By the 1980s, America had retreated from its War on Poverty and began waging what some observers have called a "war on welfare" (Katz 1989, Katz 1996: ch. 10; Trattner 1999: ch. 16) and others have described quite plainly as the "war against the poor" (Gans 1995). This broader campaign contributed to the demise of the welfare state and the rise of the waiver state (Cammisa 1998:55; Katz 1996:309–312; O'Conner 2001:289–290). Under the waiver state model ushered in by Ronald Reagan's New Federalism and codified in the Family Support Act of 1988, states could appeal to the federal government for waivers that exempted them from the strictures of national welfare programs. Many states formulated innovative means of disbursing welfare. Such innovations included the adoption of mandates that required teen welfare mothers to live with their parents, the stipulation of school attendance and academic performance levels for the continued receipt of welfare, the withdrawing of benefits from women who had additional children while on welfare, and the expanded privatization of welfare service delivery through the disbursement of public monies to private nonprofit providers. During the 1990s, many states received waivers to pursue these program innovations (Cammisa 1998:70; O'Conner 2001:289–290).

In three senses of the term, then, the last several decades have witnessed the rise of a "contracting government" (Schram 1999, 2000). First, as noted, government entities now regularly enter into contracts through which they purchase the services offered by private providers. In point of fact, "government contracting with nonprofits grew throughout the 1970s, increasing from 25 percent of total public social service expenditures in 1971 to 49 percent in 1978" (Thiemann, Herring, and Perabo 2000:54). Second, this proliferation in the practice of government contracting has led to a shrinking of the government's responsibility for the welfare of its citizens (Katz 1996:312–314; Salamon 1995). Government outsourcing has been undergirded by the rhetoric of contraction, in which big government is the foil for political devolution. The architects of devolution promised a leaner, meaner form of governance—including a "get–tough" approach to welfare abuse and dependency. And finally, there is the danger that all this contracting could ultimately endanger democracy in America. The metaphor of contract governance—and its attendant practices of service outsourcing and competitive bidding—pits factions of self–interested citizens against one another. As Thiemann and colleagues (2000:54) soberly remark: "The dramatic increase of government spending on social services led not only to the creation of a great number of secular and religious nonprofit organizations to deliver contract services; it also led to the explosion of special interest groups founded to combat or promote certain government policies." Strangely, what is championed as a partnership model of governance can easily give way to "adversary democracy" (Mansbridge 1980).

In the post–welfare era, then, the old poor law system has made a comeback—though now as a more sophisticated contractual order. Political devolution has moved the lion's share of responsibility for welfare service provision from the federal government back to state and municipal authorities—local empowerment for the twenty–first century. Welfare reform legislation of 1996 pushed forward the "devolution revolution" (Nathan 1996). And the advancing of this revolution has, rather strangely, thrust us back into the Elizabethan past of poor laws and local oversight—if not local overseers.[3] What's more, the post–welfare era is once again a time for "experimenting" in the "laboratory" that is American democracy (on the limits of this metaphor, see Schram 1999). Welfare reform law permits state governments to "partner" in every sense of the word with religious organizations in order to deliver an array of social services to disadvantaged citizens. What are we to make of such experimentation? Proponents of faith–based welfare reform have been encouraged by the novel choices afforded to today's welfare clients (see Bartkowski and Regis 1999; Chaves 2001 for reviews). Many of them tout the merits of a new respect for the "preferences" of welfare "clients" who can now choose to "consume" services from a religious or secular provider. However, critics charge that welfare reform amounts to a new paternalism (L. Mead 1997; O'Conner 2001:289), composed of policies that introduce more insidious prospects for regulating the poor (cf. Piven and Cloward 1993) and punishing black single mothers long stigmatized as "welfare queens" and "dependent abusers" of public assistance (Cruikshank 1997; O'Conner 2001; Quadagno 1994; Seccombe 1999). Such debates notwithstanding, the historical trend is clear: The compassion of the maternalistic state manifested in the early decades of the 1900s had, by century's end, given way to the discipline and austerity of paternalistic governance.

Conclusion

We began this chapter by discussing the formative influence of Elizabethan Poor Law on two centuries of American social welfare policy. Outdoor relief was the primary mode of social welfare through the eighteenth century. Poverty relief under poor laws was widely viewed as the responsibility of local communities. In many locales, public assistance and religious benevolence were viewed as complementary rather than contradictory means of poor support. However, local communities regularly discriminated against those they deemed to be "outsiders"—often doing so on the basis of race. With the advent of the nineteenth century, advocates of institutionalized social welfare (indoor relief) mounted an offensive against outdoor relief, thereby giving rise to the poorhouse movement and scientific charity. These movements focused on the institutionalization of the needy. They were motivated by the twin hopes of monitoring and mentoring the poor—that is, policing the needy while inculcating "respectable" middle–class values among the lower classes. Given immigration trends during the nineteenth century, Catholic émigrés were disproportionately represented among the urban poor of industrializing America. With Protestant efforts to convert immigrant Catholics to "real religion" (read, American Protestantism), the Catholic Church organized parallel charitable and social service organizations at this time.

The twentieth century witnessed the growth of interdenominational relief organizations such as the Young Men's Christian Association, and the rise of religious reform movements such as Social Gospel Christianity during the Progressive Era. Progressive reformers focused attention on the structural causes of poverty, marking an important shift in American conceptions of poverty and social welfare. Such ideas were further reinforced by the Great Depression. Like secular organizations, many religious charities struggled to find adequate resources to meet the extraordinary demand for relief during the Depression. Still, religious groups quickly emerged as valuable allies of government entities in the provision of social services and the implementation of some New Deal programs.

As the welfare state grew from the 1930s to the early 1960s, religious groups were active participants in America's voluntary sector. However, formal collaboration between religious communities and the state was meager until the late 1960s. Near the end of the War on Poverty, the federal government began outsourcing social service provision to private nonprofit providers, a move that expanded significantly during the 1970s. Some religious providers, including Catholic Charities and Lutheran Social Services, were poised to take advantage of this development. In the post–welfare era, charitable choice significantly expands opportunities for the forging of public–private partnerships between the state and religious organizations.

3

Faith–Based Poverty Relief
Congregational Strategies

Coauthored with Louis Bluhm,
Neil White, and Melinda Chow

Having provided a broad historical overview of American social welfare and religious benevolence, we now turn our attention to
local narratives and practices of faith–based poverty relief in Mississippi
congregations. In many respects, Mississippi is the ideal state in which to
study faith–based poverty relief. Despite recent reductions in welfare
caseloads, Mississippi has long been marked by high rates of poverty
and public assistance use. The state also has a distinctive history of racial
struggle. And like many of its neighboring states in the South, Mississippi features a highly churched population that is dominated by Southern Baptists, Black Baptists, and United Methodists. (The social and religious ecology of Mississippi is discussed more extensively in the appendix to this volume.) In this chapter, we explore the origins of faith–based
welfare reform in Mississippi and the organizational strategies that local
religious congregations have developed to minister to the poor in their
communities. We outline four key strategies that local congregations utilize to provide poverty relief—intensive benevolence, intermittent relief,
parachurch collaboration, and distant missions. We also carefully assess
the motivations and implications associated with each of these aid–provision strategies.

"God Doing What Government Can't":
Faith & Families of Mississippi

Mississippi was the first state to propose and implement a collaborative church–state approach to combat poverty. Even prior to the passage of federal welfare reform, the office of Mississippi Governor Kirk Fordice formulated and implemented, with the assistance of the Mississippi Department of Human Services, a statewide program called Faith & Families of Mississippi. This innovative program—established November 1, 1994—attracted nationwide attention and led to the implementation of similar initiatives in other states such as Indiana and Texas (Harrison 1995a, 1995b; Indianapolis Star 1996; Loconte 1995; Sherman 1995; Yardley 1996). Mississippi's trail–blazing status in faith–based welfare reform is consistent with its leading role in other facets of welfare reform policy. Given its privileging of states rights and self-sufficiency, federal welfare reform was modeled largely on the traditionalistic political culture that has long held sway in Mississippi and the Deep South (see Breaux, Duncan, Keller, and Morris 1998).

As originally conceived, Faith & Families of Mississippi aimed to connect needy families on welfare with religious congregations in the local community (Faith & Families of Mississippi nd–a, nd–b; hereafter, FFM–a, FFM–b). Ideally, a welfare family would be sponsored by its adoptive local church. Adoptive churches were charged with providing the resources—from material assistance and job training to an inculcation of moral values—needed to move welfare families from public assistance into stable, long–term employment. To enlist local faith communities in this state–facilitated effort, Faith & Families of Mississippi distributed brochures to religious congregations statewide. One brochure introduced the initiative: "FAITH & FAMILIES OF MISSISSIPPI . . . 'GOD doing what Government can't' . . . LIFE CAN BE BETTER THAN LIFE ON PUBLIC ASSISTANCE."

Faith & Families flyers soundly criticized the "life of dependency" bred by welfare programs. Faith & Families cast its primary goal as the cultivation of self-sufficiency among the poor. Faith & Families flyers not only provided religious communities with the racial, family, age–related, and educational characteristics of the "average" welfare recipient.[1] These brochures defined the very subjectivity of this "average" recipient—that is, her motivations, moral sensibilities, and "skill deficiencies," the last of which were said to include: "Accepting personal responsibility," "Examining personal values," "Living a disciplined life," "Delaying gratification," "Becoming more assertive," "Developing critical thinking skills," and "Learning effective parenting skills" (FFM–b:7).

Faith & Families utilized several rhetorical strategies to solicit the participation of congregations. First, it asserted that faith communities have a moral responsibility to assist the needy, citing biblical imperatives such as "'If we see a brother in need and will not help him, how can God's love be within him?' 1 John 3:17." Faith & Families flyers also reminded local congregations of the apostle Paul's exhortations that Christians must mentor, affirm, and encourage one another, as well as "correct and direct" their fellows (FFM–b:4). The equation of social morality with biblical edicts is, of course, a longstanding feature of Southern culture.

Second, beyond articulating a discourse of moral responsibility, Faith & Families pragmatically charged that congregations have the actual ability to assist the needy. One of the Faith & Families flyers quoted directly from Marvin Olasky's *Tragedy of American Compassion*, and concluded: "*FAITH COMMUNITIES CAN MAKE THE DIFFER-ENCE* . . . by providing hope; helping remove barriers to acquiring jobs; providing a support system for families confronted with problems and questions during their transition to greater self–sufficiency, and by providing a vision for life" (FFM–b:3–4, emphasis in the original). The discourse of ability, now intermeshed with the language of moral responsibility, charged: "The church is the only institution that deals with the ultimate issues and provides the perspectives that give dignity to mankind. It is also the only place where people can find true commitment, compassion, healing, and love." Yet, in addition to providing "love, wise counsel, [and] encouragement" to recipients of public assistance, faith communities could offer "admonishment" as needed to encourage "gainful employment" for welfare families (FFM–b:4).

Finally, Faith & Families invoked a discourse of social utility to enlist churches' participation in the program. The Faith & Families program, according to its own account, produced positive results for all parties involved—former recipients of welfare, local churches, and communities at large. Faith & Families touted itself as "an example of how faith communities are making a difference in the lives of welfare recipients and reducing welfare rolls" (FFM–b:5), and boasted about having registered 325 churches, referred 380 families, placed 120 families in churches, and acquired jobs for 64 single-family mothers. Critics of welfare have alleged that public assistance programs promote out–of–wedlock births and undermine marriage by supporting female–headed families. Consistent with such arguments, the brochure stated flatly that under Faith & Families: "Only 13 illegitimate births [were] recorded . . . [and] 18 single parent mothers have been married." Utility here was inflected with moral presuppositions about the propriety of marriage and the inappropriateness of premarital sexuality. In light of this evidence, the brochure ended by boasting that outreach ministries such as Faith & Families "can make the difference by providing bread for the bodies and souls of welfare recipients" (FFM–b:8).

Despite the auspicious beginning and self–proclaimed accomplishments of Mississippi Faith & Families, the program eventually faltered and was scaled back to a few churches in the Jackson (state capitol) area under the Fordice administration. Under the subsequent administration of Governor Ronnie Musgrove, Faith & Families no longer functioned as a church–state collaborative relief effort. Accounts of Faith & Families' demise, which preceded the changeover in the governor's office, vary.[2] Some political insiders have offered religious rationales for its failure. According to these accounts, the theological conservatism of "fundamentalist" churches in Mississippi made it difficult for local congregations to cultivate and maintain a relationship of trust with the state government. From this viewpoint, fundamentalist churches' preference for cultural separatism, political disengagement, and religious autonomy kept these congregations from forging antipoverty partnerships with the government. Pointing to the fact that then–Governor Kirk Fordice was the first Republican governor in Mississippi since Reconstruction, other accounts suggested that political factors—namely, Democratic party entrenchment—caused the program to perish. One key informant suggested that party politics and "racial antagonism"—putatively, vigorous opposition from a small but powerful group of black Democratic religious leaders—combined to undermine the program. Finally, some have traced Mississippi Faith & Families' demise to the fact that it was immediately implemented as a statewide program without a pilot venture. Consequently, political expediency and lack of solid bipartisan support may have caused Faith & Families to falter.

During the peak implementation period of Mississippi's Faith & Families program and on the heels of federal welfare reform legislation, we collected in–depth interview data concerning faith–based poverty relief and charitable choice partnerships from a diverse group of thirty religious communities in east central Mississippi. (Our research design is discussed more fully in the appendix.) Our purposive sample of local religious bodies included congregations that varied by denomination, membership size, and community locale. We also conducted fieldwork[3] in a subsample of five congregations—a white Southern Baptist and black Missionary Baptist congregation, a white United Methodist church, an African American Church of God in Christ [COGIC], and a white Church of God congregation. All these congregations were engaged in extensive benevolence work and offered a wide variety of services through their church programs. Field data were also gathered from local interfaith relief agencies, community development organizations, and Department of Human Services officials. While this latter body of field data is not central to our congregationally focused investigation, it permits us to explore the relationship between local faith communities and other poverty relief organizations. The remainder of this chapter outlines the strategies that congregations utilize to provide aid to the poor, and explores the meaning of relief work for local pastors and the congregations they serve. Pastors often justify their preference for particular aid–provision strategies through vocabularies of motive that weave together themes about the poor, the nature of poverty, and the responsibility of religious communities to those in need (cf. Mills 1940; Wuthnow 1991).

Holistic Poverty Relief

The religious leaders we interviewed are virtually unanimous in defining faith–based aid broadly enough to include both a material component and a nonmaterial dimension. Local religious leaders commonly argue that faith–based aid provision is a holistic endeavor that—unlike public assistance programs—aims to address the material needs of the disadvantaged while simultaneously providing the means for moral development and spiritual sustenance. Pastor Nancy Evans[4] from River Road United Methodist suggested that her African American church's work with the local elderly was quite successful precisely because this program assists older individuals "financially and then spiritually also." This particular church has a jail ministry program founded on the same principle. The jail ministry entails not only visitation with the imprisoned, but a personal grooming service for them. References to holistic aid provision abound in pastoral testimonies of poverty relief.

Many congregations meld material and nonmaterial forms of relief quite creatively. Virtually all local religious communities in our study offer special programs during the winter holiday season from Thanksgiving to Christmas. While the specifics of these programs vary, they all generally complement the provision of material aid with worship services for those who wish to attend them. Thus, several congregations pair special praise and worship activities with free dinners at the church. Even forms of aid that at first blush would seem to be one–dimensional often subtly combine various types of relief work. Revivals, for example, are designed to inspire religious conviction among the unchurched and newcomer while rekindling the faith of the regular churchgoer. In this sense, revival–based ministries would seem to center primarily around the satiation of spiritual needs. However, the spiritual fervor produced in congregational revivals is often pointed toward a material outlet. At many revivals, special collections are taken up for local charitable organizations. Sometimes canned goods and clothing are collected from revival attendees to support the church's own social ministry efforts or those of a parachurch relief agency. In addition, these special services often provide pastors with a forum for recruiting congregants into volunteer aid programs. In such venues, the boundaries between tangible and intangible forms of aid are blurred while both monetary and human resources are deftly drawn together in the service of social ministry.

Despite this pervasive commitment to holistic relief, many congregations develop a preference for particular poverty relief strategies. In what follows, we describe four key strategies through which local congregations typically offer relief to the poor. To be sure, these aid–provision strategies are not mutually exclusive. Many congregations use several of these strategies simultaneously. Nevertheless, pastors often justify their preference for a particular style of relief provision by invoking two key vocabularies of motive—heartfelt compassion and discerning judgment toward the poor. All religious leaders in this study wrestle with these moral imperatives.

Intensive Benevolence

One aid–provision strategy utilized by several local congregations is intensive benevolence. Intensive benevolence entails sustained, face–to–face engagement with the poor. Many of the congregations that practice this aid–provision strategy do not need to look far to find the poor. These congregations are typically located within or near low–income neighborhoods and housing developments. In many cases, the congregations include working poor and disadvantaged persons among their members. Various types of disadvantage are fought with intensive relief efforts—hunger and malnutrition, substance abuse, inadequate housing, educational deficiencies, as well as job insecurity and unemployment. Thus, long-term food assistance, child care, and tutoring programs, as well as marriage and substance abuse counseling, fall under the rubric of intensive benevolence.

Because many of the congregations that practice intensive relief identify with the poor, these forms of disadvantage are viewed not as private troubles but, instead, as public issues. According to this logic, the poor struggle with the fallout from broad social forces that include racism, classism, family dysfunction, underfunded county schools, and lack of economic opportunity in the local area. Among congregations that utilize this aid–provision strategy, ministers defend the merits of sustained interpersonal contact with the disadvantaged. These pastors commonly argue that it is only through such intensive, enduring contact that they can cultivate solidarity and friendship with the poor, can become a trusted and reliable source of basic necessities to the needy, and can offer lasting emotional support to those who face persistent poverty. Terms such as "personal," "human," and "direct" are used to describe the seemingly redemptive power of the enduring relationships claimed to emerge from this strategy of relief provision.

Feed the Body and Nourish the Soul: Intensive Food Assistance

In many cases, faith communities that favor this approach to poverty relief have structured their congregation so that close contact with poor persons can be maintained on prolonged and predictable bases. Congregations with on–site food pantries and hot meal programs regularly welcome the poor onto their physical premises and into their congregational community as they make sacks of food available to the hungry. Consistent with the holistic approach to aid–provision discussed earlier, food pantries in congregations highly committed to intensive benevolence foster enduring social bonds between aid providers and relief recipients. In many cases, the relationships cultivated in many on–site food pantries are marked by familiarity with the aid recipient's name, life circumstances, and immediate social circles. Such venues transform the nameless, faceless "poor" into actual living persons whose struggles can be heard, understood, and redressed—at least in part—through the intensive benevolence of the religious community. At the same time, a congregation's choice to house a food pantry on its grounds serves as a publicly visible emblem of that church's commitment to the needy within the local community.

More than virtually any other form of relief, intensive food assistance aims to weave together material provision and spiritual sustenance. Providing food to the hungry on a regular basis is, of course, materially significant given the pressing nature of hunger. Recurring hunger and chronic malnutrition can pose a threat to one's physical health and psychological well–being. Moreover, episodic starvation can severely diminish the quality—and even longevity—of one's life. While these concerns are not to be minimized or dismissed, many faith communities that provide intensive food relief via on–site pantries are not content only to feed the body. They intend to nourish the soul as well.

There are several different ways that congregations with intensive food assistance programs seek to accomplish this dual task. At Faith Haven–COGIC (Church of God in Christ), the charismatic senior pastor—Elder Reeves—plays a prominent role in the distribution of food from this church's on–site pantry. Faith Haven is located at the juncture of a business district and a working–class African American neighborhood. As Elder Reeves personally distributes food to the community's poor, he offers eloquent words of affirmation, encouragement, and love to recipients of the church's benevolence. In playing such a central role in weekly food provision efforts, Elder Reeves adeptly blurs the line between religious leader (his formal church role) and community servant (his intentional commitment to hands–on food provision). By transgressing the line between leader and servant, Elder Reeves effectively removes the shame that might otherwise accompany the receipt of church benevolence. The testimony offered through this pastor's personal involvement in food distribution draws force from the countercultural facet of Christian theology that equates greatness not with self–aggrandizement and worldly achievement but with humble service to the least of God's children. And as Elder Reeves practices the humility of hands–on giving at the food pantry, aid seekers are invited to follow his lead through their humble acceptance of his servanthood to his church and the community.

Beyond the relational dimensions of intensive food provision, it is noteworthy that Faith Haven provides foodstuffs not piecemeal, but rather packaged together as an assortment of goods—again, underscoring the theme of holistic, well–rounded relief. Food items in these sacks vary greatly from basic necessities such as canned vegetables, rice, and dry cereal to other items that might, at first glance, seem rather indulgent—for example, heart–shaped boxes of chocolates on Valentine's Day. In this instance and others like it, food beyond the bare necessities is provided to relief recipients to communicate the congregation's love and concern for both the physical and spiritual well–being of the needy.

Nourishing both the body and soul is also the primary motivation of intensive food relief at the predominantly white Hopewell Church of God. Hopewell, situated in an affluent white suburb near a highway that divides predominantly white neighborhoods of privilege from largely black neighborhoods of scarcity, serves a hot meal to the local poor once per month during its food pantry's open hours. In this congregation, members assert that it is not enough to open their pantry—funded jointly by congregational contributions and USDA–subsidized food from the Mississippi Food Network—once per week for grocery sack distribution. Adding a monthly hot meal program to their pantry–based distribution efforts provides congregants and local needy persons with the opportunity to bridge racial boundaries and class divisions that are otherwise pervasive in this small Southern town. Pastor Johnson explains that one goal of Hopewell's food assistance program is to engage in "incarnational ministry—much like it was performed in the early church, in Acts of the Apostles." Incarnational ministry entails the building of relationships with the families that Hopewell serves, and stands in bold contrast to food assistance orientations that focus solely on "running people through" a pantry as quickly as possible.

Thus, compassionate giving is the stated motive underlying intensive food assistance at both Faith Haven and Hopewell. Yet, even in the context of such intensive relief, these congregations struggle to adhere to the imperative of compassion. Hopewell's Pastor Johnson says that he would prefer not to have the government paperwork and its concomitant qualification criteria associated with their food assistance program. Like other congregations that wish to disburse government–subsidized food, the church must require proof of residency (such as an electric bill), inspect social security cards for everyone in the household, and secure other identifying information from recipients. Still, Pastor Johnson is well aware that his congregation can serve more people by securing USDA–subsidized food for its pantry from the Mississippi Food Network.

Hopewell has taken many steps to offset the red tape "rigmarole" associated with food provision from the pantry. Despite the large numbers of people served within their combined pantry–meal program, Hopewell has structured food disbursement to minimize the amount of time recipients spend standing in lines. At points where recipients must provide identifying information, there are many tables staffed with volunteers to speed the process along. Slow–moving lines would smack of an impersonal, bureaucratic culture that is precisely the opposite of personalized "incarnational ministry." This identifying information is collected in a building separate from the site at which grocery sacks are disbursed and hot meals are provided.

As the procurers, cooks, and servers in the hot meal program, a coterie of highly active Hopewell women are the embodiment of intensive benevolence. While serving hot food to those coming through the meal line, the Hopewell women extend warm welcomes to the local poor—many of whom are African American. Conversational exchanges between church members and aid recipients continue as hot meals are consumed at one of about three dozen nicely decorated tables in Hopewell's multipurpose benevolence hall, tellingly named "Compassion Pantry." The hot meal program is preceded by a worship service—optional for recipients of church benevolence—that is designed to set a spiritual tone for Hopewell's food assistance efforts. Recipients in this hot meal program also have the opportunity to visit a prayer table—which program supervisors are careful to emphasize is an optional part of their food relief efforts. The prayer table features extended member-led prayers in which the congregant and relief recipient join hands, close their eyes, and seek spiritual supplication in a private, one–on–one forum. The church has chosen to fund its hot meal program solely from congregational coffers. Consequently, it is in the context of its hot meal program that Hopewell can be most compassionate and least discriminating. Quite tellingly, a leader in Hopewell's food provision effort says that while their hot meal program probably serves "a few" people who may not really need such benevolence, they "are not going to turn anyone away. We figure that's between them and the Lord."

Personalized, compassionate food assistance at the Hopewell pantry is also sought after through a disbursement structure designed to exhibit sensitivity to recipient–specific needs and life circumstances. The size and number of grocery sacks provided to a recipient take into account the number of people in that individual's family. And a group of sacks is always prepared and ready for those with special dietary needs (such as diabetes and high blood pressure). On most days, grocery sacks contain a few indulgences—in one instance, sun–dried tomato gourmet bread—along with basic necessities. Grocery sacks are disbursed through a division of labor that aims to meld efficiency with compassion. Standing in front of the sack preparation counter, several church volunteers field tickets containing household information and deliver the grocery sacks to aid seekers. Behind the counter, a separate group of volunteers busily prepares sacks to replace those that have just been disbursed. And yet another group of volunteers delivers sacks to recipients' cars. Grocery delivery is offered to everyone who receives a sack, but is most commonly accepted by parents with young children, elderly individuals, and those who receive more than one bag of groceries.

This is not to say that the countervailing moral logic of judgment is wholly absent from intensive food relief efforts. In subtle ways, premeal worship services, service–line meal provision, and prayer tables institutionalize queue discipline and may reinforce social distinctions between the givers and recipients of such gifts (cf. Berking 1999; Schwartz 1975). Like most other service organizations, congregational food pantries embrace a service priority principle—first come, first served. Consequently, those who attend premeal worship services are rewarded by being among the first to receive their hot meal and grocery sack. Moreover, those who provide hot meals in food lines are stationary servers while the recipients of such benevolence are mobile clients. In many respects, the stationary server-mobile client model ritually affirms the power of the gift–giving server over that of the gift–receiving client (Schwartz 1975:17–19). In contrast to restaurants in which customers sit at their tables and are waited on by mobile servers, this model of service has mobile clients expending resources (wait time, movement, gratitude) as they seek goods from the stationary server.

Feasting and Fasting through Intensive Benevolence

Within the context of such intensive relief efforts, then, food becomes a medium for the generation of social capital. The strategic inclusion of a heart–shaped box of chocolates or gourmet bread within a food sack, and the serving of a hot meal with grocery disbursement, aim to establish a sense of intimacy—a "feast" among basic necessities—between the concerned provider of aid and the needy recipient of such benevolence.

The faith community's holistic concern for the physical and spiritual well-being of the disadvantaged is designed to generate a denser, more enduring form of social connectedness than could be provided through spartan forms of food distribution.

And yet, pastors who endorse and practice this aid–giving strategy as a primary means of offering relief are quick to note the appreciable time and painstaking effort—a symbolic "fast" through self–sacrifice—demanded by intensive engagement. In actuality, intensive engagement with the poor places great demands on a wide range of persons—the pastors themselves, their church staff, and many of their local congregants. Yet these adherents' long-suffering for the welfare of other less fortunate individuals is not seen as a drawback. To the contrary, the collective effort marshaled to support intensive relief efforts is viewed as a transformative—and therefore crucial—aspect of sustained engagement with the poor. Apart from his hands–on engagement with the Faith Haven–COGIC food pantry, Elder Reeves makes available his home phone number on all church brochures—including those distributed at local public events—with an open invitation to be contacted at any time. This bold gesture serves as evidence of his unyielding commitment to ministry, and throws down the gauntlet to other local pastors who would prefer to draw clearly defined lines between their pastoral role and their personal family life. In the same breath, this pastor's wide distribution of his personal phone number among the unchurched poor in his community implies a critique of local religious leaders who distinguish their public antipoverty ministry from their private congregational calling.

Given the prodigious effort associated with intensive relief to those in need, some of its practitioners are explicitly critical of religious leaders who would rather avoid sustained personal engagement with the poor. At times, pastors committed to intensive relief allude to other religious organizations—"hands–off" churches or ministerial councils—that solely support "boardroom" poverty programs bereft of personal engagement with the poor. Some of these pastors even castigate groups within their own religious communities who eschew the "hands–on" approach of intensive benevolence.

One pastor who advocates intensive engagement with the poor ministers extensively to Hispanic migrant workers in the local area. In advancing his critique of hands–off congregational philanthropy, this pastor impersonates the voice of a hypothetical, detached religious leader who would opt for cash–based assistance in lieu of more sustained personal engagement: "We do a Good Samaritan program for them. But we make sure they don't come and eat with us." Then, adopting his own voice once again, this critical pastor offers his appraisal of this financial donation–only relief strategy: "So, you know, the right hand is saying, 'Here is five hundred dollars,' and the left hand is saying, 'Make sure you don't spend it around me, because I'd rather not talk to you.'" Much like critics of scientific charity during the late nineteenth century, such pastors charge that social patterns of segregation are often reinforced through boardroom benevolence.

Intermittent Relief

A second benevolence strategy utilized by many congregations entails the provision of intermittent direct relief to the poor. This aid–giving strategy is quite popular among a wide range of local congregations— black and white churches, along with working–class and middle–class faith communities. Intermittent direct relief takes many different forms, and the specific mode through which this relief is offered varies by congregational context.

At times, direct relief may take the form of semiextended support under the auspices of "adopt–a–family" initiatives. In this scenario, an affluent religious congregation or some subgroup of its members decides to remain in periodic contact with a particular family that has faced protracted hardship. Interestingly, these initiatives may emerge through informal social networks in which there is a common point of contact between the sponsoring congregation and the disadvantaged family. In one case, parents in an affluent white United Methodist congregation became aware that the family of their child's schoolteacher had run across a string of misfortunes, including serious medical problems and monthly financial shortfalls. In this instance, the child himself served as a conduit for the cultivation of social capital. The nexus of relationships in which this particular youngster is enmeshed (mother–son and student–teacher) facilitates the reciprocal bonds of trust that helped initiate the adoption of this family by the mother's Sunday school class. This discrete, grassroots adopt–a–family initiative—and its apparent success in this particular church—stands in bold contrast to the top–down "pairing" of churches with disadvantaged families wrought by former

Governor Kirk Fordice's Mississippi Faith & Families program. On the continuum of congregational aid provision, sustained efforts to adopt a disadvantaged family can blur the line between intermittent relief and intensive benevolence.

More common by far than the informal adopt–a–family scenario described above are congregations that use this aid–provision strategy to provide one–time aid in the face of a short–term crisis, or that disburse intermittent relief during particular times of the year. When individuals must unexpectedly confront the fallout from a house fire, a serious physical accident, or the death of a relative who had no savings or burial insurance, a local congregation will often step in and provide short–term material relief—typically accompanied by offerings of social support such as short–term visitation.

Intermittent Relief with Known Quantities: Mutual Aid

The provision of intermittent relief in the face of a discrete crisis is most certainly inflected by social capital considerations. One–time or short–term aid that is provided to individuals who are well known to congregants is rarely viewed as a handout. Rather, it is understood as mutual aid. Consequently, when the aid recipient is a member of the benevolent congregation, the problem of trust—that is, "Will the aid be used responsibly?"—is resolved rather straightforwardly. Active members risk a denial of access to future resource pools—and, more importantly, social ostracism—if they are found to have been irresponsible in their use of relief. When mutual aid is practiced on a broad scale, religious communities function very much like a revolving credit association in which benevolence itself is a currency that members invest regularly and withdraw in troubled times.

In some cases, congregational leaders themselves may not wait for members in need to come forward and request benevolence. Because trust is the cornerstone of dense and durable congregational networks, mutual aid may be offered—rather than requested—in a strikingly proactive fashion. Several religious leaders explained how they navigate friendship and kinship networks to discover the nature of an ailing member's "situation" and to ascertain the individual's specific needs. Those needs sometimes entail the payment of medical or prescription bills in the face of an insurance shortfall. In other cases, they involve the provision of employment contacts in the wake of a job layoff. A leader at a local mosque composed largely of university students described members as "too shy"—really, too proud—to request assistance in the face of short–term need. This religious community and many others like it respond to such reticence with mutual aid that can be offered in the dignified spirit of a gift rather than the unacceptable form of a handout.

Mutual aid of this sort offers three key advantages. First, as noted above, issues of character and deservingness are made less ambiguous through extant social networks. Prior knowledge of the person in need is viewed as a form of accountability—in a word, proof that the relief will be appreciated and used judiciously by the recipient. Second, mutual aid enables members of the congregation to witness first–hand the ways in which their benevolence can transform the lives of people they value and call their friends. In the language of social capital, such aid givers receive an excellent "return" on their "investment." The providers of aid become the recipients of renewed bonds of trust and faith within their own community—bonds that are reaffirmed by effectively meeting the needs of fellow congregants. Finally, because these momentary providers of aid may someday find themselves in need of relief, they are wise to tie their fortunes to the collective and reciprocal investment networks made possible through congregationally based mutual aid.

There are also several gray–area cases of intermittent direct relief in which benevolence is not technically mutual, but the problem of trust can nevertheless be resolved. In some instances, nonmember beneficiaries of aid are able to ride the coattails of faith–based social capital through transitive relationships with select congregants. Thus, a church member's relative or close friend may be seen as trustworthy because of this individual's relationship with a trusted congregant. In yet other circumstances, social capital between congregants and nonmembers is a product of the faith community's local tradition and the collective memory of benevolent members. Some congregations provide intermittent relief such as holiday food baskets to particular elderly persons or couples in the community because they "have always done so." The enduring character of this relationship is, of course, viewed as an asset within such congregations. Congregants build for themselves a legacy of longstanding—though still intermittent—benevolence because they take pains to remember a specific family during the winter holiday season.

Intermittent Relief with Unknown Quantities:
Managing Risk by Determining Need

Aid solicitors who are not known to members of local congregations present many faith communities with a thorny set of questions. Given limited congregational resources, how should faith communities manage the risk associated with providing relief to potentially untrustworthy parties? And in the absence of social capital, upon what basis are bonds of trust between the relief provider and the aid solicitor to be formed?

Although most pastors eloquently discussed their aversion to aid–provision standards and means tests, many of these same religious leaders conceded that limited financial resources and congregational or denominational accountability structures required the development of screening mechanisms for unknown aid solicitors or suspected "abusers" of faith–based benevolence. Aid–giving standards imposed by local faith communities vary considerably, but include:

- call–backs to verify the source and status of phoned–in solicitations for aid;
- visitation to the home of the needy person, whereby available household resources and living circumstances can be ascertained by visual inspection;
- in–depth discussions of alternative avenues for resource acquisition that an aid solicitor should explore before drawing on church benevolence funds;
- an escort to the grocery store for supervised purchases in lieu of providing cash; and
- referrals to faith–based or secular agencies that specialize in providing the type of aid that is being sought (this last option is discussed more fully as a distinct aid–provision strategy in the following section).

To be sure, few religious leaders were willing to state outright that they would deny aid to nonmembers. Indeed, most pastors said that when faced with an aid request, the membership status of the individual ("Is this aid seeker a member?" "Will he or she attend our services?") is not raised and is considered irrelevant. Yet, despite the stated irrelevance of membership status, adaptive—and sometimes exclusive—aid–giving tactics are wielded by many local congregations.

Several congregations whose social networks cascade outside the church can deny or withdraw aid if they have reason to believe that an individual will squander limited congregational resources. A pastor from a black Methodist church spoke generally about the power of grassroots social networks in this regard: "We try to find out [about aid recipients and their situation] when people call. Because this happens a lot. This is a very small town. . . . If we find out [that aid recipients] are having any kind of deviant behavior, using the money in a negative way and if they are just abusing what we give them, we just jerk back and don't give them anything else." Of course, some advocates of faith–based welfare reform such as Marvin Olasky view such sanctions as one of the most redeeming qualities of aid provision in local religious communities. From an Olaskian perspective, such sanctions promote personal accountability and moral reform among the poor.

Consequently, faith–based social capital is not solely integrative, but can serve exclusionary ends as well. The same membership circles that enable churchgoers to support one another with intermittent direct relief also provide the power, if needed, to deny aid requests to nonmembers. Some resource–poor religious communities with needy members perform very little outreach per se and instead focus on intracongregational benevolence because a failure to exclude outsiders could threaten the congregation's well–being. Monique Dees, a black religious leader at a small rural Church of Christ congregation, offered the following account of her church's ministries: "Right now, we're not offering any outreach—except during Christmas and Thanksgiving. We give out food baskets [at those times]." In fact, this church is not atypical of some small rural congregations. The provision of food baskets and gifts to local needy families during the winter holiday season is a prime example of intermittent congregational relief.

When asked how her church would respond if an increasing number of nonmembers came to the church requesting aid, Ms. Dees replies:

> That has never really happened, really. We are out in the country and no one just comes up and asks. We have a lot of little churches that people go to, and each one asks their own. But if I would have to make a comment on it, nonmembers are always welcome. And I think that there

would have to be an assessment as to need or real need, you know, in order to give. But when you come and there is a need for our members, our members will be served first. Unless there is a greater need for this person—an emergency kind of thing.

Given the scarce resources in this community, Ms. Dees defends the inner–directed relief orientation of her church. While she contends that nonmembers are welcome to solicit aid, she argues that such occasions are rare. Given the many churches nearby, local aid solicitors are expected to "ask their own" congregation when in need. For this reason, nonmembers who approach this Church of Christ congregation with needs that fail to meet "emergency" status should be prepared to defer to members' relief requests.

It is important to recognize that the term "nonmember" is often code for an array of intersecting social cleavages. Because many religious communities in Mississippi—and throughout the United States—are such homogeneous organizations, a key outcome of this help–our–own orientation entails the preservation of boundaries that insulate persons of different racial, socioeconomic, and denominational backgrounds from one another. Race was an especially salient theme in our interviews. Most pastors interviewed for this study conceded that race currently affects the way in which congregations provide aid to the needy and would likely do so into the future. Several pastors even argued that racism is more entrenched within local churches—white and black congregations alike—than outside them. Even those religious leaders who maintained that racial antagonism does not directly influence the provision of aid within their own faith communities typically recognized that such factors hold sway in neighboring congregations. This issue is explored more fully in the case studies featured in chapters 4 to 7 of this volume.

Many congregations that employ an intermittent relief strategy for ministry to nonmembers wrestle with the antinomies of compassionate giving and discerning judgment. Some of the pastors that we interviewed point to struggles within their congregations regarding who should be helped and, especially, how members' donations ought to be used for relief. And, of course, religious organizations are guided by both ethical imperatives (mandates to assist those in need) and practical considerations (obligations to maintain financial solvency). It is in confronting these vexing issues that some congregations have sought to cultivate collaborative relationships with parachurch relief agencies.

Parachurch Collaboration

A third aid–provision strategy utilized by local congregations entails the forging of collaborative relationships with parachurch relief agencies. Why would faith communities opt to refer aid solicitors to parachurch relief agencies? Several pastors commented on the fruitful and meaningful relationships they have forged with other congregations through parachurch relief agencies. In this sense, parachurch agencies provide an organizational framework for cultivating bridging capital—the establishment of network ties and normative diffusion across congregational and denominational lines. Parachurch agencies often draw together material and human resources from many different congregations and from denominations of various stripes. As such, they put religious leaders from different traditions side by side in collaborative benevolence ventures and at agency meetings. Religious leaders and congregants often talk in very positive terms about such relationships.

Beyond the bridging capital cultivated through parachurch collaborations, supply and demand considerations shape some congregations' preference for this form of relief provision. On the demand side of the aid–provision relationship, the centralized and standardized relief of parachurch agencies is believed to safeguard individual churches from aid solicitors who might advance fraudulent, self–serving, door–to–door requests for relief—which several pastors argued are quite common. Standardized and centralized relief is typically used in large towns where population density makes knowing one's neighbors difficult. Parachurch agencies employ screening procedures, often maintain a centralized database on aid solicitors and agency contributors, are open during regular hours, and are overseen by individuals judged to be competent staff workers.

In singing the praises of a local parachurch relief agency, Outreach and Uplift Relief (OUR) Ministries, one pastor offered the following account: "We have to be careful in the church—because the funds are limited—of who we help. So, there has to be a screening process, because unfortunately there are those people who are out there to make a living off of the church. Some of them do very well at it. Some of them make eighty thousand dollars a year and are not in need at all." This pastor continued by describing the critical role of OUR Ministries in light of such dilemmas:

> We [local churches] feed OUR Ministries. OUR Ministries, in turn, helps the needy. They are our screening process. If I have a question about somebody [pause]. Let me explain this to you. I am a sharp guy. I know how to read a phone book. I know how to go to the Yellow Pages under "churches." If I want to make five to ten thousand dollars in a week, I start calling every church in [the county]. If I can get into every church in [the county], thirty–eight of them, it's feasible to come up with five to ten thousand dollars worth of food or things that I could sell. . . . By taking them to OUR Ministries, there is a master file maintained there. That's one of the places I can call to check on people to see if they are abusers of the system.

These demand–side concerns about fraudulent aid solicitations are not the only reason that many congregations use parachurch relief agencies. On the supply side of the aid–provision relationship, various types of congregational dynamics make parachurch relief agencies an attractive option. Leaders in some churches comment on the time constraints faced by their members—many of whom are in dual–earner households where couples struggle to meet their own family obligations. Here the notion of "helping our own" takes on a specific meaning—members are consumed with day–to–day financial provision for their families in order to maintain a middle–class standard of living.

A religious leader from a large white Methodist church composed of middle–class members offered the following account of their membership: "We do have a lot of generous, giving people here who are very concerned about others. It is a very caring and loving church." However, when asked about the prospect of church members participating in expanded aid programs, she reacted with some caution and hesitancy: "You know, time, of course, is an issue for everyone nowadays with all of the working folks we have. We do have retirees who are very gifted and who are doing a lot of things." In light of the fact that it supports a plethora of nonprofit and interfaith relief agencies with philanthropic donations, this church often refers individuals requesting aid to these agencies. According to such reasoning, the church "already supports" aid to the needy through such donations.

Consequently, faith communities that engage in extensive congregational philanthropy value the time—and, most likely, the trouble—that they can save themselves by channeling church–door solicitors to parachurch relief agencies via referrals. Several churches that engage in this practice of outsourcing often provide a long list of local interfaith relief agencies which they underwrite through resources (such as money and clothes) donated by members and, occasionally, through temporary volunteer labor. To be sure, these churches may use other relief–provision strategies—such as intermittent direct relief—in addition to congregation–sponsored philanthropy. However, several pastors argued that, given the time constraints and lifestyles of their members, they can most efficiently provide aid to the needy through semiprofessional parachurch relief organizations rather than at their own church door.

Apart from time constraints, the contested meaning of money emerges as a salient factor in congregational alliances with parachurch agencies. Congregational monies are invested with both material value and moral value (Wuthnow 1994b; see also Lamont 1992; Zelizer 1997). As a material currency, benevolence funds in many small local churches are extremely limited. Such churches are simply not able to address "desperate, dire" aid solicitations of over three to five hundred dollars. These churches will often provide a referral to a parachurch relief agency rather than exhaust their benevolence funds completely. In return, the local church may channel small contributions of clothing, canned goods, or other resources to the parachurch agency as such items are donated.

Yet in many cases the material worth of congregational relief funds is eclipsed by their moral value. Pastoral referrals to parachurch relief agencies sometimes seem motivated by a desire to quell membership concerns about the use of congregants' donations. Of course, no pastor openly admitted to providing referrals to parachurch agencies simply because he or she feared confronting uncomfortable questions about the use of member donations. Nevertheless, a careful analysis of the complex machinations of power in local congregations makes such a scenario quite fathomable. Several pastors, especially those at Methodist and Baptist churches, stated quite straightforwardly that the church belongs more to the congregants themselves—and longtime members in particular—than to pastors. Methodist pastors serve itinerant appointments in which they are transferred from one church to another every few years. In a handful of instances, congregational power dynamics and struggles centered squarely on the use of member donations.

For example, one pastor mentioned that his church members sometimes suffered from confusion concerning the rights of "ownership" over donated monies. He stated emphatically that the moment donations touched the collection basket they were no longer the property of any individual; rather, they became "God's money." Indeed, this pastor had recently spoken to his congregation on this very point because there was debate about pastoral authority over financial contributions to the church. This same pastor recently chastened several of his senior congregants for begging out of their financial obligation to support the church's benevolence programs because they were on fixed incomes. Dismissing these excuses as "fixed income syndrome," this pastor charged that virtually all working people were on "fixed incomes"—that is, incomes in which meager raises amounted to modest cost–of–living adjustments. It is indeed possible that local skirmishes about the ownership and expenditure of benevolence donations encourage pastors to rely on parachurch relief agencies. In such cases, a parachurch aid–provision strategy lends legitimacy to pastoral relief efforts and circumvents thorny squabbles—material and moral in character—that may otherwise come between pastors and the congregations they are charged to serve.

Of course, when employed as the sole or primary aid–provision strategy, philanthropic aid giving and congregational referrals to parachurch relief agencies maintain or exacerbate social distance between local faith communities and the disadvantaged. By outsourcing the actual provision of aid, the faith community can—strategically or unwittingly—avoid offering direct assistance to the poor. Still, the parachurch strategy presents itself as an attractive option when compared with the range of vexing issues that accompany church–door relief—the deservingness of solicitors, the time constraints faced by congregants, and potential challenges regarding the appropriate use of social ministry funds. Yet, inasmuch as congregational philanthropy and referrals to parachurch agencies can bureaucratize the aid–provision process, they are precisely the opposite of the Olaskian vision in which a particular local religious community transmits valued material resources and provides intimate networks that promote personal accountability, job readiness, and moral reform among the poor.

Distant Missions

Several churches in the local area employ yet another aid–provision strategy to engage in social ministry to the poor—namely, distant missions. Through various types of distant mission programs, congregations offer their membership the opportunity to participate in pilgrimages of relief provision to a needy population that is physically removed from the local scene. Some distant mission programs utilized by local churches are centered around a proximate location in the South—typically, a one–day trip by van from the Golden Triangle Region. Several affluent churches offer a full slate of distant mission trips from which interested congregants can, in the discourse of travel and tourism, "choose their preferred destination." The plethora of relief itineraries and mission destinations offered in such churches ranges widely from weekend to weekslong excursions. Such trips may entail travel to remote areas to confront extreme rural poverty or inner–city ghettos. For the most venturesome souls, select churches offer distant mission trips of approximately two weeks to an impoverished area abroad, including Central American sites near the Caribbean. For many middle–class Mississippians, such mission trips may provide their only occasions for travel abroad and for contact with dramatically different cultures and socioeconomic settings.

Distant missions are typically paired with one or more of the relief–provision strategies described above. One large white affluent church offers a variety of missions on the domestic scene and abroad—a week's relief work at an inner–city homeless shelter in Texas; ministry to needy persons living in Appalachia; and several weeks of relief work at a Christian mission in Latin America. This church employs a distant missions strategy in combination with an array of other aid–provision programs: one–shot funds for discrete crises, a grassroots adopt–a–family initiative begun in a Sunday school class, referrals to a local interfaith relief agency that this church helped to organize, and local volunteer efforts with—among other nonprofit organizations—Habitat for Humanity.

Often, distant mission trips are coordinated through pastors or adults who work with youth groups in such congregations. Several churches in this study coordinate distant missions for their youth that involve travel to highly disadvantaged populations (for example, inner–city children, residents of dilapidated homes in cities of adjacent states). Consistent with the metaphor of religious pilgrimage, the aim of these missions is transformation and redemption in several ways. First, the relief work

performed on these distant missions is designed to yield small but per-
ceptible transformations of the disadvantaged community. Intensive relief work such as building a chapel or roofing a house performed by the
mission team is centered explicitly on this goal.

Second, distant missions can promote spiritual transformation for the
travelers whose faith and camaraderie are enriched by the extraordinary
challenges that they collectively confront on such sojourns. Distant missions programs involve relationships that gain meaning, in part, through
their social structure. Mission teams—complete with seasoned mission
coordinators—coalesce under the auspices of church leaders who oversee the slate of program offerings. Particular mission teams may develop
a repository of meaningful memories and enduring friendships by re-
turning—on an annual basis—to face the trials presented in "their" mission field. Team–specific cultural repertoires emerge through these re-
peated excursions. Mission teams develop particular strategies for re-
solving gender etiquette in the absence of private bathing facilities, and
for determining the appropriateness of eating out at well–heeled restaurants during their trip to a poverty-stricken mission field. Finally, mission teams determine the proper amount of tourism time that should be
incorporated into the mission trip. Folklore generated through
on–the–ground confrontations with "lived poverty" also emerges in the
wake of these trips. Annual meetings among mission teams provide a
forum for the recounting and dissemination of mission field folklore.
During one meeting of mission field coordinators in a local church, a
team leader recounted one of his most vivid memories from the field—
namely, the "syrupy thick black coffee" consumed by homeless men at
his inner–city mission site.

Third, many distant missions teach lessons about the cultivation of
values such as hard work, thrift, and self–sufficiency. Some youth–oriented distant missions are underwritten in part by young congregants'
fund–raising activities. In one prominent local church, mission funds are
generated by youngsters' sale of flowers to other members. Consistent
with agrarian metaphors in the Bible (blossoming grains of wheat, fruitful vineyards) and the small–town locale in which these Christian
youngsters live, the flowers used to generate these funds are said to represent the "planting" of mission "seeds." In a sense, youth who take
these pilgrimages of aid provision are being simultaneously confronted
by and insulated from poverty. Through their mission trip, they face the
stark reality of poverty. Yet through their fund–raising efforts they are

ostensibly being provided with the values—and the social capital—to protect them from personally facing such misfortune. Through contact with the poor in their distant missions, they become sharply aware of their own privilege—yet they are ostensibly protected from confronting the local structures of class privilege in their home towns.

Finally, such face–to–face ministry to the very poor serves as a get-away—a liminal break from the everyday grind—for church youth. These getaways are designed to be educational and morally challenging, with a bit of fun thrown in for good measure. Longer mission trips often include a day or so of recreational activities in which participants consume distinctive aspects of the distant culture which might not otherwise be available to them in a small Mississippi town.

Like the first aid–provision strategy outlined in this section (intensive benevolence), distant missions require close contact with the poor and can promote spiritual transformation for all parties involved. Reflecting on the impact of these types of programs at his large white, middle–class church, one pastor concludes: "[The youth] become sensitive. When they have the opportunity to work with poor people, they begin to see people and not just the situation or something they have heard. They identify with people." Such relief work can therefore subvert common misperceptions about poverty through experiential knowledge which attaches faces, bodies, and names to an otherwise abstract group of people—namely, "the poor"—who would otherwise appear foreign to those from a middle–class upbringing. However, at the same time, such outreach efforts entail a pilgrimage that propels the aid giver outside his or her own community. There is, then, no guarantee that distant–mission pilgrimages promote local activism—or even an enduring awareness of social inequality—upon the sojourner's return home.

Conclusion

This chapter began by describing the emergence of faith–based welfare reform initiatives through Mississippi's Faith & Families program. We then proceeded to explore four organizational strategies through which local congregations engage in poverty relief—intensive benevolence, intermittent relief, parachurch collaboration, and distant missions. We highlighted the practical contours of these poverty relief strategies and paid special attention to the vocabularies of motive that local pastors invoke to explain their congregations' use of them. All congregations with active poverty relief programs wrestle with the competing religious imperatives of compassion and judgment. Yet by utilizing different aid–provision strategies, religious organizations strive to navigate the Scylla of compassion and Charybdis of judgment in congregationally specific ways.

In the next three chapters of this volume, we feature a series of comparative case studies that illustrate how pastoral understandings of faith–based benevolence are shaped by the congregational context within which religious leaders are situated. By invoking the motifs of identity, memory, and destiny, pastors define the character of their congregations' relief efforts, situate these faith communities in local histories, and evaluate the future prospects for faith–based poverty relief in the post–welfare era. Throughout, these narratives are inflected with pastoral interpretations of salient features of contemporary life in the South—race, class, denomination, and nationality.

4

A Tale of Two Churches
United Methodists in Black and White

Our first comparative case study highlights key points of divergence between two churches that share the same denomination—the United Methodist Church (UMC).[1] Given their common denominational affiliation, both River Road UMC and Green Prairie UMC are situated near the cultural mainstream of Southern religious life. Methodists in Mississippi and throughout the South cannot boast the market share enjoyed by Baptists. Yet, with approximately 15 to 20 percent of Mississippi's churchgoing population reporting a Methodist affiliation (Bradley et al. 1992), the United Methodist Church is clearly a prominent force on the local religious scene. Apart from their shared denominational affiliation, these two particular United Methodist churches are situated within a common social context. They are both located in small–town rural Mississippi, a locale in which religious congregations are the central social institution for local residents.

Beyond these general points of similarity, however, River Road and Green Prairie are very different religious congregations. River Road United Methodist is an African American church, while Green Prairie UMC is a white congregation. Moreover, River Road's pastor is very favorably disposed toward charitable choice initiatives. This view contrasts sharply with the highly skeptical appraisal of church–state collaborations advanced by the pastor of Green Prairie. The narratives of poverty relief articulated by pastors in these two Methodist congregations weave together notions of congregational identity ("Who we are") and destiny ("Where we are going") in strikingly different ways.

Great Expectations at River Road

Nancy Evans, a graduate of Duke Divinity School, considers herself fortunate to serve her latest pastoral appointment as the minister at River Road United Methodist Church. River Road is a middle–class black congregation situated in a small town just outside the Golden Triangle Region. With over two hundred members, this congregation is small enough for church members to know one another quite well, yet large enough to staff many different church–run relief ventures. The preponderance of River Road's members are older adults or elderly persons who range in age from fifty to sixty–five. Members of this church are proud of the fact that their congregation has played an integral role in the local community for well over one hundred years. They are particularly proud that River Road was one of the grassroots congregations at the forefront of the Civil Rights Movement in Mississippi several decades ago.

Pastor Evans is among the most enthusiastic supporters of the expansion of faith–based social services through charitable choice partnerships. Pastor Evans was made aware of charitable choice initiatives because the United Methodist Church featured former Mississippi Governor Kirk Fordice, then a gubernatorial candidate, as a keynote speaker at a conference for its ministers throughout the state. Pastor Evans is one of many local religious leaders in our study who oversees several successful congregational relief programs based in diverse aid–provision strategies— including intensive benevolence, intermittent relief, and participation in parachurch initiatives. Optimistic ministers like Pastor Evans articulate clear visions about how new resources would be used to augment or expand specific relief programs currently sponsored by their churches. Many of these religious leaders describe in detail how they could launch new programs with public monies or would seek to reestablish initiatives that were previously dissolved because of deficient funds. Yet even these very hopeful pictures of charitable choice initiatives are laced with cautionary tales and admonitions about policy implementation that stem from years of relief–provision experience.

Taking a future–oriented tone, Pastor Evans boldly announces that River Road would pursue every one of the aforementioned avenues—program initiation, reinitialization, and expansion—if its congregation secured such funds. Members of River Road currently volunteer in a city–run drug addiction treatment program staffed by professional counselors. And given the increasing magnitude of drug addiction problems within the local community, River Road has also been instrumental in establishing the Hope Recovery House. Offering a critical counterpoint to recent laws that characterize drug abusers as hardened criminals, Pastor Evans remarks that Hope Recovery House is a rehabilitation center which, "rather than punishing people, [aims to] get them into some kind of rehabilitative services." Pastor Evans contends that faith–based initiatives targeted at drug abuse rehabilitation, which are still getting off the ground in this small town, could be augmented effectively by an infusion of new resources into local religious communities.

Moreover, as a female minister who is sensitive to the needs of women and children in families, Pastor Evans has aspirations for initiatives that would assist these constituencies. She envisions launching a new program for victims of domestic violence—ideally, begun with the assistance of a trained counselor—if resources would support such a venture. Expanded funds would also enable the church to reopen a child care center that was previously closed because it lacked the start–up money necessary to achieve compliance with local day care regulations. Front–end costs on such ventures often keep these types of faith–based initiatives from effectively getting off the ground. Even congregational programs that have heretofore been unsuccessful, such as this church's fledgling after–school tutoring program, could be provided with additional resources (such as computers, academic supplies, and a curriculum) needed to make them more effective.

When asked if her congregation would be willing to participate in relief programs that involve the state, Pastor Evans responds in an enthusiastic and affirmative tone. The "myriad of professional people in my church," she says, provide her with "a wealth of people that I can tap to oversee such programs." "People here want their church to be more involved," she contends. "They just don't want the door shut during the week. They want to be more involved. That church—they used to call it the Civil Rights church. That church has always . . . been about improving."

Whose Church? Pastoral Itinerancy, Congregational Ownership, and Poverty Relief

The language Pastor Evans uses to refer to River Road United Methodist is quite telling. When discussing River Road, Pastor Evans refers to the congregation in many different ways. In some instances, River Road is construed as an organization under Pastor Evans's charge—"my church." In other instances, River Road is depicted as a congregation owned by its members—"their church." And in yet other circumstances, this congregation is typified as an independent religious community with its own historical legacy and trajectory—"that church . . . the Civil Rights church."

The significance of these conceptualizations cannot be overstated. Language that defines the church as "belonging" to the pastor or, alternatively, to its congregants contains within it the power to define the identity, memory, and destiny of local religious communities. And at River Road, the past, present, and future come together in denominationally and congregationally specific ways. As River Road's minister, Pastor Evans is subject to the United Methodist Church's denominational policy of pastoral itinerancy. Pastoral itinerancy within the United Methodist Church grew out of the denomination's tradition of having pastors simultaneously serve multiple congregations by traveling—on horseback in the UMC's early days—from one community to another each week. With this structure in place, pastors could not become overly invested in congregations they served and the oversight of church functioning could be retained by the congregants themselves. This denominational structure reflected a distinctive Methodist commitment to the "priesthood of all believers"—the core idea on which Protestantism was founded.

Pastor Evans recognizes that this denominational policy of moving pastors from one congregation to another—now every few years, and no longer by horseback—has important repercussions for faith–based welfare reform. As a minister whose successive appointments keep her moving every three years or so, Pastor Evans argues that the effectiveness of prospective church–state collaborations depends more on the congregation's involvement than on her own efforts. Where long–term poverty relief efforts are concerned, Pastor Evans concedes that River Road belongs more to the congregants than the pastor. If and when charitable choice initiatives are implemented, she argues that government officials "need to be careful not to really allow the ministers to do everything, but allow the people [congregants] to get more involved." Referring to the United Methodist policy of itinerant preaching, she says that UMC "ministers move constantly. If you want any program to be in place, to work, and to have long–term effects, you are going to have to have the people [congregants] involved more. The people who are in the church—they are going to be there for longer amounts of time."

Given the UMC's itinerancy policy, such concerns were commonly raised by local Methodist ministers. Quick to underscore the importance of congregant support for faith–based ventures, pastors in such religious communities recognize that ownership, authority, and responsibility for church relief programs cannot rest on the shoulders of highly mobile ministers. While such pastors readily concede that successful aid programs depend heavily on congregant activism, ministers themselves are not powerless pawns of the congregations they serve. Armed with various motivational strategies that include stirring sermons and exceptional managerial skills, local ministers like Pastor Evans can—and often do—facilitate member involvement in faith–based relief programs. Yet almost invariably, a critical mass of motivated members is required to transform the inertia that can accompany nebulous aid–giving visions into the momentum of collective action. Pastor Evans says, "I am telling you there is so much they could do. There is so much they could do. And then I think they would be able to attract more people that way." With a nod toward the bridging capital that rural congregations can command through social networks that cascade outside the church proper, Pastor Evans concludes, "I have people who are in my congregation who know this community." Pastor Evans has professional–class members who are therfore able to act as mediators with dominant institutions.

Parachurch Prospects and Pitfalls: Race, Class, and Interfaith Relief Efforts in Rural Mississippi

Relief provision narratives articulated by Pastor Evans also speak to the prospective opportunities and the potential pitfalls of parachurch relief efforts under charitable choice in her small town. Pastor Evans is proud of the ecumenical spirit at River Road and in her local community. She often has the opportunity to work closely with other ministers in nearby Baptist, Apostolic, and Presbyterian churches. River Road also engages in collaborative mission work with other United Methodist churches in the area. Such interdenominational efforts are necessary, she says, "because so much needs to be done. The state and the government are taking a more hands–off approach when it comes to welfare programs. And the churches are just taking up the banner, I guess you could say."

Yet as she evaluates the results of these interdenominational partnerships and parachurch collaborations, Pastors Evans takes a somewhat somber tone. Interfaith and parachurch alliances, she says, have been "marked by some difficulties because it seems as if some people just do not want to let go of this racism–type problem that they carry around with them—that they have been carrying around for years and years." As a pastor who is not native to rural Mississippi, she expresses her dismay at the pervasiveness and persistence of racism within many local churches: "You really have [racism] much more in church than anywhere else. . . . It is a really big problem here. I don't know why. I think it just has a lot to do with ignorance or something. I don't know. But that is not just on the white side. I see it on the black side also. So that is something that we really want to work on." As an "outsider" non–Mississippian, Pastor Evans is frustrated by the politics of racism sustained through collective memory in Mississippi. Stories of discrimination in bygone years are kept alive through family folklore that transmits prejudice across generations. Pastor Evans's critique of this practice is pointed: "You know, I am not from Mississippi. I have no dealings with what happened fifty years ago to whatever's grandad!"

Despite her frustration with this issue, Pastor Evans remains optimistic about overcoming racism within local churches, and often invokes a pragmatist rationale in the hope of effecting such change: "We are trying to overcome those obstacles and just work to the higher good. . . . I just want them to get rid of these negative–type things that keep them apart. Because I think the closer they can work together, the more they will get done." In remembering the past, then, Pastor Evans encourages religious believers to use the power of positive thinking. This form of selective memory emphasizes the positive aspects of the past (including her church's civil rights legacy) while downplaying the "negative–type" antagonism of bygone years (namely, particular memories of discrimination)—and does so to foster collective action.

Yet, by Pastor Evans's own admission, racial differences among local faith communities will not be resolved by mere changes in attitude or appeals to pragmatism. When asked if she thinks that race relations would affect the allocation of block grant money to local churches, she replies, "Yes, it would." She continues, highlighting subtle structural factors that could inadvertently reify current racial and economic inequities among local congregations—some of which can afford to support a full–time minister while others cannot: "Now I am just going to tell you the way it is here. I am the only full–time black minister of an established church in this area. All the other people, who happen to be black gentlemen, are ministers—but they work on a part–time basis. And so, that would make a difference, I am sure. That shouldn't, because they have just as vital congregations. They have just as vital people working in their congregations. But the actual leader is not on–site like I am." Pastor Evans worries that policy makers might hold tacit assumptions about bivocational ministers that would lead them to "feel as if [they] are not as established." Alternatively, she wonders if government officials may erroneously think that "the money will not be taken care of as well" in congregations led by part–time clergy. Yet here too she ends on a note of optimism. Drawing once again on ideals that resonate with Methodist itinerancy and the priesthood of all believers, she concludes "That is where the people step in, I think. They just have to learn to trust the people more—not put everything on the leader." In contradiction to her own religious community's emphasis on the power of the congregation, faith–based initiatives may privilege churches with leaders who are available to represent congregations on pastoral committees and to coordinate interfaith and parachurch programs.

Notably, these types of social inequalities will not affect River Road. This middle–class black congregation has the ability to support a professional full–time minister. However, the intersection between race and class remains salient for this congregation in other, more subtle ways. Many congregants at River Road, despite their membership in the black middle class, will nonetheless be affected indirectly by welfare reform as the program's time limits begin to affect their extended kin (cf. Patillo–McCoy 1999). Such kin, Pastor Evans surmises, will place financial pressure on River Road's middle–class congregants. It is possible that resources otherwise available to River Road through member donations will be channeled instead to these needy kin. In this sense, River Road is not insulated from the effects of welfare reform.

The Winter of Despair at Green Prairie

Apart from sharing a common denominational affiliation with River Road, Green Prairie United Methodist Church also features a predominantly older adult and elderly population. Seventy–five percent of

Prairie's nearly one hundred members are over age sixty–five. However, quite unlike black middle–class River Road, Prairie is an all-white, working–class congregation. The typical household in this congregation earns around twenty thousand dollars annually.

Pastor James Holt has been a part–time minister at Prairie for the past four years. Pastor Holt is fifty-five years old and has a master of divinity degree from Emory University. There is, consequently, a rather stark disparity between Pastor Holt's educational capital and political sensibilities when compared with those of his congregation. Given the religious ecology of the rural South, it is perhaps not too surprising that Prairie's congregational culture has both Methodist and quasi–Baptist elements within it. Like many neighboring Methodist and Baptist churches, Prairie places a premium on congregational autonomy and independence. And like many Baptists, its members embrace a literal interpretation of the Bible. Prairie is Pastor Holt's first part–time appointment. Semiretirement is cherished by Pastor Holt, who has invested a great many years in the ministry. With visions of full retirement on the horizon, Pastor Holt has adjusted to saying "no" when asked to perform duties he feels are above and beyond his semiretired status as Prairie's minister.

The Downside of Democratized Congregations: Apathy and Inaction

Unlike River Road, Prairie does not have formal or sustained aid programs per se. Rather, Prairie provides aid—to members or the known needy within the community—on a discrete, as–needed basis only. When surveyed about the number of persons the church helps in a given month, Pastor Holt simply pencils in "periodic help." Within the same survey, he checks none of the response categories concerning the types of aid typically offered by congregations. Pastor Holt explains Prairie's orientation toward aid provision tersely: "This church does not have a lot of extra programs going on, except the . . . usual worship service, the men's group, the women's group." Most often, solicitations for aid are not sought at Prairie's front door. Rather, aid requests are quietly communicated to individual church members. Congregants who are approached with aid requests then act as gatekeepers, inasmuch as they choose whether or not to pass along such solicitations to church leaders. Pastor Holt recounts a recent instance when select members of the congregation became aware of a person who needed "handicapped equipment." In this case, the church stepped in to provide financial support needed to purchase the items.

Unlike Pastor Evans at River Road, Prairie's Pastor Holt is quite hesitant when asked about the prospect of church–state partnerships in social service provision at Prairie. Indeed, he positions Prairie at the opposite end of the continuum on receptivity toward charitable choice initiatives. Like Pastor Evans at River Road, Pastor Holt has discussed faith–based welfare reform with other ministers. Yet when asked for his evaluation, he states forthrightly that he is "not optimistic at all" about the prospects of such programs. Pastor Holt says that his church "should be" more involved in ministry to the poor and disadvantaged. "But," he quickly adds, "I don't think it will be."

Pastor Holt identifies several impediments at his church to poverty relief in general, and church–state partnerships in particular. To begin, he argues that lofty theological ideals about Christian service simply do not motivate his members to participate in actual ministry to the poor. Social action within this congregant–controlled church is consistently derailed by members' inability to resolve their disagreements about poverty ministry. Prairie's combined commitment to individualism (voluntary participation) and collectivism (consensual decision making) creates a congregational culture where opposition to church programs can be expressed in many ways—all of them virtually guaranteed to kill proposed initiatives. At Prairie, opposition to proposed poverty ministry programs can be exercised passively through apathetic nonparticipation or actively through a refusal to grant consensus during congregational deliberations. Given this congregational culture, Pastor Holt admits that the chances of active engagement in poverty relief at Prairie are slim to none:

> I think in one sense of the word, churches ought to be very involved in this area out of concern for other people. But at the same time, I've had some reservations about whether we will become much more involved than we already are. A lot of time at the grassroots level, people may say, "Yes, we need to be involved." But as far as really volunteering for work or increasing their giving to do so—that's where the problems usually begin. Not to mention agreeing on what those needs are that need to be met, and who those people are that need to be helped. So as voluntary as the church is in depending on a consensus rather than a mandate, it is

going to be difficult, I think, to get the churches involved in any significantly increased level.

Strikingly, Pastor Holt does not contend that his congregation's members lack the free time needed to take advantage of charitable choice: "Most of them, as I have mentioned, are retired. And other than just keeping up their home and keeping their garden and all that, they have time to do pretty much what they want to do." Moreover, his congregants do not lack the skills or talents to participate: "They have the skills and they have the time, yes, to do certain things. They don't have the skills to do a varied amount of programs or work or serving. But they do have some skills. They are rural, independent–type people who can do a number of things."

Who Are the Deserving Poor?
Race and Relief in Rural Mississippi

Pastor Holt says that "periodic" relief is offered when the church becomes aware of a problem that congregants themselves collectively define as requiring a solution. When asked if members of his congregation would be motivated to engage in a sustained relief program under the auspices of faith–based welfare reform, Pastor Holt describes his congregants' orientation: "Not unless they were challenged in a—a very." He pauses momentarily, and then continues. "At the present time? No, they would not have the motivation. The motivation would have to come. It would have to be—they would have to be challenged by something they really see as a problem. . . . A problem they care about before even the challenge comes."

Congregational definitions of legitimate problems that members care about are, in actuality, influenced by various considerations—among them, racialized perceptions of welfare recipients as well as this community's valorization of the work ethic. These considerations, according to Pastor Holt, would cause members concern about participating in charitable choice. In Pastor Holt's estimation, government standards mandating equality and a color–blind allocation of aid would be viewed as coercive within this congregation and many like it. When asked if attitudes about race and ethnicity might affect welfare service provision through local congregations, Pastor Holt replies unabashedly:

Yes, definitely. Well, it would affect it even in the beginning—if it was accepted to be—for them to get involved. That is one way it would be affected. I don't feel my church would accept [such an opportunity] because of their attitude. They would simply turn it down. I feel there might be some churches, though, that might accept it. But their attitudes about the way they handled it and who they helped individually would shape [pause]. In other words, they might consider some persons unworthy of help and kind of refuse help. Or [they might] formulate their guidelines so that these people would be excluded. And their attitudes toward race might be one of those guidelines.

According to Pastor Holt, this racially insular implementation of faith–based initiatives would simply be an extension of the way that religious aid is currently provided. He says that current efforts at faith–based relief are "most definitely" affected by attitudes about race and ethnicity. Such inequities, which Pastor Holt thinks are likely to continue under charitable choice, could manifest themselves through both overt and symbolic racism. Concerning overt racism, Pastor Holt says that there is "very much a reluctance to cross racial lines" in local churches. This form of racism, Pastor Holt contends, is present within his own congregation: "I have not seen them work across racial lines to help locally." To be sure, the letter of the law would not permit overt racism in service provision under charitable choice, and congregations would have to seek funds rather than simply be offered public money. Still, Pastor Holt's concerns remain valid, given the social context from which he articulates them.

Institutionalized racism in some local Mississippi churches gains force from racial segregation in other local institutions. Given the largely white private school system that has emerged in Mississippi in the face of court–mandated educational desegregation, ongoing school segregation may reinforce support for racial separatism among members of Pastor Holt's congregation and other local faith communities. Turning his attention to local youth and those within his congregation, Pastor Holt says that there is a "separation of, really, many of the youth in that area—along the lines of race. [Black youth and white youth] have absolutely nothing to do with each other. No contact whatsoever. And I doubt [they] would even know each other, even though it is a small rural community." Pastor Holt concedes that there is one young member of his congregation who attends public schools, but quickly adds that this girl is alone in doing so. "She would be the exception. She would know some of the other, you know, black youth in the community. The others go to private schools and really have absolutely no contact other than maybe, you know, seeing them ride the roads or whatever." The de facto segregation of schoolchildren into predominantly black public schools and mostly white "Christian Academies" in the South is itself the product of local resistance to the federally mandated desegregation of schools in the 1960s.

Apart from these overt and institutionalized forms of racism, Pastor Holt wonders if faith–based poverty relief could be affected by a more subtle and strategic form of prejudice—namely, covert racism. It is quite feasible, he says, that aid solicitors would be turned down for reasons that prima facie seem color–blind but that in fact have everything to do with racialized perceptions of African Americans. When discussing racial motivations for aid provision, Pastor Holt describes how guidelines aimed at racial exclusion might be formulated. He even specifies particular rationales that might be used to turn away aid solicitors defined as undeserving: "Whether [congregants] feel like they are willing to work or not might be the biggest one." The common misperception that all welfare recipients are African American and that African Americans lack a work ethic could therefore play a key role in aid programs at congregations like Prairie. Pastor Holt suggests this form of discrimination is already present among such congregations. So, where overt racism might be deemed illegitimate by a state agency providing a grant to a local religious community, congregations that embrace and practice racial separatism may find other ways to avoid crossing racial lines—namely, by drawing clear distinctions between those groups of poor persons that are "deserving" of relief and those that are not.

Parachurch Pessimism

Green Prairie United Methodist's antipathy toward charitable choice stems from its general suspicion of parachurch relief efforts as well. Green Prairie is not, by Pastor Holt's account, enthusiastic about parachurch programs. Failed collaborations—even with other United Methodist churches in the local area—have generated pessimism about parachurch relief in this minister. In describing his—and, ostensibly, his congregation's—position on this issue, Pastor Holt once again draws distinctions between theory and practice, as well as between theological imperatives and social action. In theory, says Pastor Holt, Methodists are supposed to work together on collaborative projects. Yet, he says: "Practically speaking and looking at reality square in the eye, local churches don't work together that well and that often. Sometimes it is even difficult to get the four or five [Methodist] churches on the [same] charge to work together on a project . . . especially when it is in the area of helping people." Why are such collaborative efforts largely doomed to fail? Among the reasons this minister names are "pride" and a host of utilitarian motivations, including the selfish desire of some churches to gain visibility and additional members through their sponsorship of community initiatives.

In the end, Pastor Holt is among the most pessimistic ministers in our study. There is little bridging capital—that is, congregational linkages for outreach to the broader community—present at Prairie. As such, Pastor Holt is not convinced that his church could help move people from welfare to work now or in the future: "I'm not sure my church could [get people off welfare]. Being a small rural church, I don't have anybody that employs people." Like many of the ministers in this study who are deeply skeptical about charitable choice, however, Pastor Holt does not wish to close the door completely. He expresses a glimmer of hope that church members could participate in faith–based welfare reform in some small capacity via counseling and mentoring, or by providing "contacts maybe" designed to equip welfare recipients with "certain skills." Pastor Holt's last word on this subject, however, has a pessimistic ring: "I have some people who have the skills to do it and can do it. Whether they would do it—be motivated to do it—I don't know."

Conclusion

This chapter has compared congregational identities and visions for the future of faith–based welfare reform at two United Methodist Churches— River Road and Green Prairie. The pastoral narratives articulated by these religious leaders underscore the importance of local congregational cultures in faith–based relief and church–state collaborative ventures. Although River Road and Prairie share a common denominational affiliation with the United Methodist Church, these churches could not be more different in their orientations toward church–based relief programs or their evaluations of charitable choice. Black, middle–class River Road has highly active relief programs, utilizes an array of aid–provision strategies simultaneously, and works with other churches (Methodist and non–Methodist) in seeking to provide relief to the local needy. Prairie, a white working–class congregation, offers relief on a highly restricted basis, focuses on periodic aid to known persons in the face of discrete crises, and eschews parachurch efforts at aid provision (including initiatives with other Methodist churches).

River Road's Pastor Evans is optimistic about faith–based welfare reform. She provides a long list of programs that River Road could expand, reinitialize, or initiate with an infusion of block grant monies. Faith communities with active relief programs often rely on congregants themselves to staff and supervise church–run initiatives, thereby giving these congregations a grassroots, democratized authority structure. But what happens when the members in congregant–controlled churches are unwilling to shoulder the burdens associated with implementing such initiatives? Pastor Holt at Green Prairie United Methodist faces just this set of circumstances. He has little faith in the ability of churches to change the face of poverty in Mississippi or elsewhere. His pessimism toward charitable choice stems directly from the apathy he has witnessed among Prairie's members, and the unwillingness of his white congregants to work across racial lines. At Prairie, the congregational culture—founded on an ethic of voluntary participation overlaid by a commitment to consensual decision making—provides many means of opposition to proposed relief programs. Prairie's members provide relief on a discrete, as–needed basis only.

Interestingly, both these Methodist pastors believe that racial inequalities currently affect the provision of faith–based aid in Mississippi, and both concede that such inequities could continue under charitable choice. Narrative motifs concerning the pronounced racism within rural Mississippi churches is crucial, given the inattention of some proponents of charitable choice to this issue. Pastor Evans says that racism is more entrenched within local Mississippi churches than outside them; and Pastor Holt can foresee congregations like his own formulating aid–provision standards that are overtly or covertly racist. Moreover, the degree of social distance between Pastor Holt's white congregants and their black neighbors suggests that the grassroots character of faith communities is severely circumscribed by established social hierarchies. In rural Mississippi, such hierarchies take the form of racial segregation and exclusion, such that black and white children have "no contact whatsoever." This state of affairs leads Pastor Holt to "doubt that [black and white youth] would even know each other." It is often said that "the children are our future." If this is the case, Pastor Holt sees a bleak future indeed.

Finally, both the churches within this comparative case study underscore the overriding significance of congregational members—as opposed to pastors alone—in implementing charitable choice initiatives. Despite the many differences between the congregations discussed above, they are both strongly influenced—in a grassroots fashion—by the beliefs and practices of local congregants who are also longstanding members of the community. The democratized character of River Road facilitates extensive member participation in congregational relief initiatives. Congregant–supervised poverty relief programs will surely outlast Pastor Evans's short tenure in this African American congregation. And yet this same emphasis on grassroots control provides Prairie's members with a structure for inaction concerning poverty relief. Prairie's limited aid offerings have not been altered by Pastor Holt, and its apathy toward poverty relief will likely persist long after its part–time minister has retired. Local empowerment does not always live up to its promise.

5

Debating Devolution
Pentecostal and
Southern Baptist Perspectives

In the previous chapter, we contrasted narratives of congregational poverty relief articulated by pastors from two small Methodist churches in rural Mississippi. We examined how aid provision practices are connected to notions of congregational identity ("Who we are"). Narratives of identity, in turn, yielded divergent visions of these churches' respective destinies ("Where we are going") with regard to forging charitable choice partnerships on the heels of welfare reform. In this chapter, we continue to examine the ways in which narratives of congregational identity influence pastoral perceptions of poverty relief and orientations toward charitable choice. And we again undertake a comparative analysis of congregational narratives emanating from two churches with different racial constituencies. However, in several noteworthy ways, the focus of this comparative investigation is different from that of chapter 4. In this chapter, we turn our attention away from small rural churches to focus instead on two large congregations located in a more urbanized milieu. Moreover, instead of analyzing pastoral imaginings of the future, we fix our attention on religious leaders' typifications of the past. Consequently, we explore how congregationally specific collective memories are produced through religious discourse while analyzing the relationship between the past experience and current congregational orientations toward aid provision and charitable choice partnerships.

While both the churches featured here share the same township in east central Mississippi, each is associated with a different denomination.[1] The first of the churches featured here is Temple Zion Church of God in Christ (COGIC). A predominantly African American Christian denomination in the Holiness–Pentecostal tradition, COGIC is among the largest African American denominational bodies in the United States, and is the single largest black Pentecostal body in the world (Baer and Singer 1992:155). COGIC, which traces its origins to the early-twentieth–century Holiness movement in Mississippi, currently boasts a total of 5.5 million adherents (Lindner 2000). It enjoys a strong presence among Southern blacks, with its headquarters located near the Mississippi–Tennessee border in Memphis.

We compare Temple Zion–COGIC with Main Street Southern Baptist Church. Main Street is a white, upper–middle-class church affiliated with the Southern Baptist Convention. The Southern Baptists are the largest denomination in the South in general and Mississippi in particular. In the Golden Triangle Region, confirmed Southern Baptist churchgoers alone account for between 39 to 46 percent of all church adherents (Bradley et al. 1992). With the Convention founded in 1845, Southern Baptists have a long history in the South and currently claim 15.7 million confirmed members nationwide (Lindner 2000). Approximately one quarter of all Southern Baptists reside in the four southeastern states of Mississippi, Alabama, Tennessee, and Kentucky (Bradley et al. 1992).

As the following accounts reveal, both Temple Zion–COGIC and Main Street Southern Baptist are favorably disposed toward charitable choice partnerships. Yet, despite this point of consensus, pastoral narratives emerging from these two local congregations are rooted in fundamentally different ways of remembering the past, understanding the present, and evaluating alternative futures. These two pastors express divergent views concerning race relations in Mississippi and the legacy of the "Old South" for black and white Mississipians today. Moreover, the congregational narratives featured in this chapter evoke very different themes concerning the relationship between the poor, religious benevolence, the local community, and the government. In the end, these pastors offer very different appraisals of political devolution in rural Mississippi.

Defending Big Government:
Tribulation and Transformation at Temple Zion–COGIC

Temple Zion Church of God in Christ (COGIC) is a large, thriving, and politically engaged African American congregation located in a Mississippi town with around twenty thousand residents. As a congregation with four hundred members—and similar figures in Sunday service attendance—this church is competing effectively in the local religious economy. In stark contrast to the mostly retired adherents at River Road (the black United Methodist Church featured in chapter 4), the membership of Temple Zion is quite young. Seventy percent of the membership is under thirty-five years old and virtually all are younger than fifty. Elder Cornelius Smith, Temple Zion's pastor of eighteen years, attributes his predominantly female membership—70 percent women—to the abundance of black males in the community "who have problems with authority due to their reaction to slavery and Jim Crowism." Despite its young and predominantly female membership, Temple Zion is a heterogeneous religious congregation in other significant ways. White-collar, skilled, and service sector employees, as well as laborers, homemakers, and unemployed persons are well represented at Temple Zion.

Temple Zion's physical facilities are impressive. The church has over fifteen classrooms for Sunday school instruction, a cafeteria that can accommodate nearly three hundred persons, and a balcony that serves them well on Sunday mornings as they attempt to grow their membership to around five hundred congregants. Temple Zion's annual budget of $300,000 is modest when compared with its slate of social service programs: rental payment assistance, temporary shelter, clothing, various types of counseling, and financial assistance to those in need of medical services. Perhaps most notably, this church runs a food pantry that, according to Elder Smith, serves over five hundred families per month and utilizes a grocery voucher system for items not stored in their pantry. In all, Elder Smith says that his church provides relief to nearly six hundred people in a typical month. Thus, in proportion to its financial and human resources, Temple Zion provides many different types of relief to a sizable number of people.

Debunking the Myths:
Blackness, Welfare Recipiency, and the Question of Fraud

Elder Smith is forty-five years old, has a high school diploma, and is one of the few pastors in our sample who is not seminary trained. Elder Smith's critical political sensibilities are clearly and unabashedly manifested throughout his discussion of state-sponsored welfare programs. "There is a myth in our country that welfare recipients are mostly black," Elder Smith asserts. This erroneous belief, he contends, has found fertile soil in the minds of both whites and African Americans—even local black pastors: "I think that sometimes black preachers hear that [welfare services are being transferred to local churches], and we think 'My God, the whole welfare burden will be on our shoulders.' That is not true."

Elder Smith also critiques what he views as other "welfare myths." He has little patience for those who assume that the allegedly all–black recipients of public assistance commonly "abuse" the system through "welfare fraud." Like several other black pastors in our sample, Elder Smith cites concrete instances in which welfare fraud—when understood in a broad, though very practical sense—has been perpetrated by privileged whites who extract benefits indirectly from welfare recipients. Among the most common examples cited are white landlords who artificially inflate rental prices for local black tenants, and small–scale merchants who keep retail prices high in order to absorb the monies of welfare recipients in nearby neighborhoods. Elder Smith, who has personally seen such abuse, deftly redefines the notion of "welfare recipiency" when he says that some local "white people will be crying [about welfare reform]. It will be the mom and pop grocery stores who have been taking the food stamps and taking the welfare checks the first of every month [that will be adversely affected by welfare reform]. They will be going broke."

Interestingly, Elder Smith's critical appraisal of such welfare myths has not spawned jaundiced resignation or political apathy in him. To the contrary, Elder Smith's vibrant religious convictions create for him an unyielding sense of confidence in his congregation's ability to minister effectively to many different disadvantaged populations. Material relief is provided at Temple Zion in many different forms—to the hungry at the church's food pantry, to the infirm who struggle with medical and prescription bills, to parents of limited means in need of dependable child care, and to those who, because of job loss or unexpected expenses, find that they cannot pay both their rent and their utility bills. Other types of sustenance—nonmaterial in character—are provided to struggling couples in need of marriage counseling, depressed persons with flagging self–esteem, or addicts requiring drug rehabilitation counseling.

If they are not already attending Temple Zion, clients of the congregation's food pantry and other relief programs are viewed unambiguously as future church members. In this sense, Temple Zion melds accountability standards—namely, the expectation of church membership—with compassionate relief. While some critics would characterize such expectations as aid provision with "strings attached," Elder Smith does not. He proclaims unflinchingly: "We hope that somehow, if we show enough love, [aid recipients] will come back to our services and be a part of our church." He continues: "In our sessions, we offer Christ many times and there are those who don't really want Christ." The church's "solution" to those who reject such efforts at proselytization is pragmatic but uncompromising—ministers "give them counseling of a secular nature also. But we let them know that we believe [in Jesus Christ], and we teach that Jesus Christ is the answer to all of our problems."

From Welfare Dependency to Spiritual Dependency: Heartfelt Connection and Social Capital

Elder Smith adamantly states that Temple Zion's distinctive approach to relief provision moves public assistance recipients from welfare into more economically productive endeavors. To discourage dependency on public assistance programs, Elder Smith critically invokes the notion of self-sufficiency from welfare discourse. However, he transforms the meaning of terms such as "handout" and "dependency" by giving them a spiritual, otherworldly cast. As discussed in chapter 3, the discourse of self-sufficiency was prominent in the Faith & Families of Mississippi brochures and in the rhetoric of those who deride prereform federal assistance programs as merely a "handout." By invoking the notion of spiritual dependency, Elder Smith argues that all believers "depend" on the grace of God for their "welfare"—broadly understood:

All I can tell you is two-thirds of our people when they came to us were on welfare. It is my Sunday morning sermon at some points [that is] on that [topic]. [I tell my congregants:] "If you are on welfare, get off as soon as you can because welfare is limiting your future. Welfare is hampering your success." That's how I teach it. I tell them this. "It is not God's will for you to be on welfare. And it insults God for Him to be our Father, [for] us to trust in Him, and we have to have a handout every day of our lives." So, therefore, I teach it is essential to us growing, to being proper witnesses, that we don't find ourselves on welfare. And I would dare to say [that] out of the numbers we called to you earlier [i.e., two–thirds of those who came to the church on welfare], I would dare to say that less than 10 percent are on welfare.

Elder Smith therefore critiques public assistance—rather than its recipients per se—because such programs are set up to undermine the believer's dependency on God. From this perspective, all believers—rather than just welfare recipients—must recognize their common state of dependency.

Through such sermons, Elder Smith charismatically champions achieving "success" and fully exploring one's "future" through means other than welfare.[2] Regardless of how terms such as "success" and "future" are interpreted by his diverse congregants, Elder Smith claims to be achieving results by preaching against public assistance programs. In a similar fashion, Elder Smith boasts a 95 percent success rate for marriage counseling with church members and estimates a one–in–two long–term success rate through the church's drug rehabilitation program.

If these dramatic success rates are taken at face value, how are we to make sense of them? Perhaps these outcomes result from the unique combination of compassion and judgment that characterize Temple Zion's relief efforts. At Temple, both compassion and judgment are seamlessly woven together. Moreover, these twin moral imperatives are practiced as personalized convictions rather than merely preached as abstract principles. Elder Smith claims kinship—literally and figuratively—with those on welfare: "My sister was a welfare recipient. Now she has a school of ministry." Redemption–from–public–assistance narratives such as these chart the move from tribulation (welfare dependency) to transformation (productive endeavors) and, ultimately, triumph (spiritual dependency complemented by proactive Christian service). Such stories mirror the retrospective accounts conveyed by former convicts or recovering alcoholics who have effectively wrestled with and scored victories over their own "demons" (cf. Denzin 1987, 1993).

Perhaps most importantly, recovery and redemption narratives at Temple Zion are personalized, autobiographical accounts of "my life" and "my family" in which the poor are understood not as "they" or "them" but as "us" and "ours." The sense of intimacy and kinship conveyed in these narratives provides fertile soil for cultivating social capital. Elder Smith recounts how some churches lament that very poor persons "clutter . . . their foyers and their lobbies." He is critical of such views, and also implicitly critiques outreach efforts that offer relief to the poor from afar: "To us, it is [the poorest people] who we want. We want to show love to the most dejected people who are nearest [to us] to help. And so we look for those kinds of folks."

It is in this spirit that Elder Smith addresses the expectation of church attendance from recipients of congregational relief. According to Elder Smith, success rates in Temple Zion's relief programs are significantly lower for nonmembers. The distinctively therapeutic interaction provided by both counseling and church attendance—the latter of which entails personal commitment and fosters a deep connection with the community of believers—is apparently the key to producing such positive results. Utilizing this "both/and" strategy of aid provision, Elder Smith says that those who seek out the most holistic forms of counseling at Temple Zion "get their lives straight with the Lord and with each other." Continuing in this vein, Elder Smith asserts: "You cannot expect to be irresponsible, cannot expect to be footloose and fancy-free, [and then] not go anywhere near the church and expect the church to always help you. You have got to get into a church and support that church."

Thus, while Temple Zion stops short of formally requiring aid recipients to join their church, recipients are strongly encouraged to join a local church or to reactivate their membership in the church they had previously attended. In fact, Temple Zion aid workers will phone a church listed by a prospective recipient and inquire about his or her status at that church. In Elder Smith's view, African American church membership in the South is not so much a question of rational choice or personal preference; rather, it is a necessity for survival: "Because truly, in my opinion, the black church is the only hope black folk have. Always was."

Consequently, Elder Smith is extremely positive about the potential for his church to expand its current slate of services with an infusion of government monies. Elder Smith contends that, when compared with government welfare, faith–based relief is far superior. Faith–based aid, he says, can "cut through the bureaucracy and get the money to the people in a much more efficient manner." In Elder Smith's eyes, the efficiency of faith–based social service delivery is due, in part, to congregations facing lower overhead costs "than they are paying downtown" in government offices. Under charitable choice, this reasoning goes, faith communities can use volunteer labor and existing congregational networks to register significant savings in wages, benefits, and operating expenses. Interestingly, the neoliberal language of efficiency is comfortably employed by pastors like Elder Smith. He says that his church will compare favorably to governmental agencies when evaluated by the economic standards of costs versus benefits. Elder Smith invokes the more modest office space in his church as a sign of its greater economic fitness. However, the salary savings that could ostensibly be yielded by his church's largely female volunteer labor force are unexamined.

Denominationalism Trumps Blackness: The Exclusionary Face of Congregational Capital

Like Pastor Nancy Evans at the predominantly black River Road United Methodist Church (chapter 4), Elder Smith also sees an important role for the funding of African American interfaith and parachurch organizations through charitable choice. However, whereas Pastor Evans focused on the many accomplishments of interfaith agencies in her small rural community, Elder Smith seems dismayed by the fact that parachurch groups have not developed strong social ties in his local township. Elder Smith argues that white churches have been working cooperatively for some time now, and he believes that black churches must begin doing the same. Taking an optimistic future–oriented tone, Elder Smith envisions black faith communities wielding significant power if they work collectively for social change. He charges that black churches in his county alone control nearly four million dollars. He laments the fact that these monies are currently spread over various financial institutions in the region.

Yet if "the Black Church"—as he uses this singular term—were to pool its resources and invest such monies collectively, it could transform supracongregational financial clout into political leverage.

> For that money, we [would] want that bank to give us a board position so that we can sit on that board and watch how that bank does business. How it makes its loans and is it fair and viable? Out of those concerns, we believe the Black Church can become [a social force] to get things done. Out of those concerns, we believe the Black Church could become a voting block that could control campaigns, that has the ability to do petitions, and to get things done as an effort to pull us together—both economically and socially—which is what has not been done in the past. The preacher in the past has made his money by amplifying differences. Your Baptist, our Pentecostal, your Methodist, our Presbyterian—

through those differences, we have kept ourselves apart. And we are the only group that does it, because even though the white brothers may be Pentecostal or Baptist or Presbyterian, they have a council of churches. They get together and they make decisions in those church meetings that coincide with the church meetings down the road. And they get things done. That is what we haven't been doing.

In connecting the collective deployment of pooled resources to would–be institutional transformations outside the congregational set-ting, Elder Smith and pastors like him offer an extremely expansive con-ceptualization of "faith–based aid." From this vantage point, churches should not simply be in the business of caring for down–and–out indi-viduals on an intermittent or even a semiregular basis. Rather, Elder Smith argues that churches can and should function as critical institu-tions within civil society—"critical" in the sense that faith communities could represent the interests of the oppressed who may otherwise be in-visible in the most powerful social institutions (including banks and lending agencies). As the community's "collective conscience," such churches could facilitate economic and political alliances through peti-tion drives and marches to advance the causes of equity and justice.

Why, then, has "the Black Church" as envisioned by Elder Smith not coalesced in his home community? His reply is short and pointed: "I think our prejudices and our Reformational racism is probably worse than the white people." It would seem that the collective interest of African Americans in local Southern communities has been undermined by denominational splintering that separates different factions of black Protestants, black Christians, and even black religious adherents in gen-eral (including Christian versus Muslim) from one another. In this way, local black congregations have found the cultivation of broad–based, bridging capital most elusive. Because these faith communities remain divided by congregational and denominational boundaries, Elder Smith recognizes that churches are complicit in producing pernicious social hi-erarchies.

Elder Smith's use of the phrase "Reformational racism" to refer to denominational divisions suggests that racism is a sort of master model for community divisiveness. In this sense, all forms of divisiveness that are hurtful to African Americans are a kind of racism. His analysis indi-cates that African American leaders carry some responsibility for hurt-ing the very people they claim to aid by promoting prejudice toward some sectors of the black population. That a COGIC pastor, ministering to a church firmly in the Pentecostal tradition, would be aware of negative attitudes from more mainstream congregations is perhaps not surprising. Indeed, interdenominational stereotypes may take a racialized form as churches with "free–form" worship styles may be perceived as "blacker" than those with more rigidly structured programs. His support for the cultivation of interfaith alliances likely stems from his own situated knowledge of how the cultural practices of more "respectable" mainline denominations (in Mississippi, Baptist and Methodist churches) may marginalize those in less powerful faith communities.

Local Empowerment in Mississippi: Redeeming Community or Resurrecting Jim Crow?

Divisions among churches, Elder Smith warns, could influence charitable choice initiatives if not implemented with sensitivity to this issue. As noted above, Elder Smith says that some of his fellow African American clergymen have come to accept erroneous characterizations of welfare as a "black issue." Questions about the accuracy of such conceptualizations notwithstanding, these notions could place the burden of responsibility for "fixing" welfare squarely—if not solely—on the shoulders of black social institutions, African American community leaders, and the alleged lack of initiative exhibited by "their" welfare recipients. Such reactions actually reinforce the idea that welfare—and, perhaps, welfare reform—is the problem of black America.

In addressing this issue, Elder Smith recounts how a white pastor from an affluent church nearby recently inquired about routing his church's aid through Temple Zion. While Elder Smith was initially interested in the idea of serving more needy persons with monetary assistance from this nearby church, upon hearing the details he found the other pastor's motivations for the proposed plan to be highly objectionable:

A while back a large white church in Mississippi came to me. [A pastor from that church inquired:] "Can we funnel our assistance programs through you?" I saw this as a great opportunity to get more money to more people. I said, "Certainly. What are you talking about putting through?" This was a large church. This church probably does three million [dollars] a year or more, so [it is] a large white church. And so I said, "What are you talking about moneywise?" And the pastor said to me,

"We will give you four thousand dollars a year." I was insulted. I stood up and walked out, and he said, "What is the problem?" I said, "I am insulted." . . . At this time, our gross income was roughly two hundred thousand [dollars] a year or a little better. I said, "We spend anywhere from $14,000 to $20,000 in helping people already. You mean to tell me you are going to offer me $4,000 a year to run all of your people through us? Your problem is you simply want to rid your lobby of a certain kind of people and put them in my lobby. You are not serious about the problem. So, when you want to spend some real money, we will talk." So I think the problem we are going to have is that if the government is going to do this, there [have] to be some real strict guidelines on how the money is appropriated at a state level so that it won't get into the wrong hands and the wrong churches [but] will get to where the people really need it.

Narratives such as these reveal the concerns that some pastors who are positively disposed toward charitable choice harbor toward the actual implementation of such initiatives. When offered a minuscule sum to perform a great deal more antipoverty work, Elder Smith realized that the pastor wishing to route that church's aid programs through Temple Zion was less concerned with assisting the poor than with maintaining a comfortable social distance between an increasingly visible underclass and the affluent congregation of his white church.

Elder Smith's last words on this subject clearly indicate his concern that pastoral and congregational motivations to help the poor be an important consideration as political devolution places the responsibility for welfare administration and work placement on local communities. Local communities—for all the merits of grassroots empowerment—are not bereft of their own stratification mechanisms, including denominational, racial, and class–based hierarchies:

Whenever I hear people in Congress and the senators say things like, "We have to make government smaller and giver power back to state governments" [pause]. To a Southern black person [pause]. Whenever I hear them say those kinds of terms, I know that means that [political power and resource control] is going to be put in the hands of the good old boys. It is going to be handled the way it was handled all the time. And the people who need [help] most won't get it. And so for that reason, I opt to say, "Let's keep the government [as is]." I too would like to see a small government. But I would like to see a more fair system to where the government could be smaller because we have rectified the problem [of] each state being able to discriminate when they want to.

Thus, while expressing his generally positive view of charitable choice partnerships, Elder Smith advances a pointed critique of pro–welfare reform discourse and a stern warning about placing too much faith in the political devolution of federal assistance programs. Here, then, is the "devil" in devolution.[3]

Praising Local Empowerment at Main Street Southern Baptist

In many respects, Main Street Southern Baptist Church is a very different religious congregation than Temple Zion. Whereas Temple Zion's Elder Smith is not seminary trained, Main Street's pastor Robert Davidson obtained his Doctor of Ministry from New Orleans Baptist Seminary. Pastor Davidson, in his late fifties, ministers to a large, affluent, upper–middle–class congregation. Main Street boasts a membership of well over two thousand persons and operates debt–free with an annual budget approaching one–and–a–half million dollars. The complex of buildings that make up this church house a chapel capable of seating eight hundred Sunday service attendees, and include fifty classrooms, ten offices, expansive kitchen facilities, and one of the largest children's playgrounds among area churches. Main Street, situated at the geographical and social center of the small Southern town in which it resides, has been housed on its current site for more than one hundred and fifty years. Pastor Davidson, an articulate minister who is well acquainted with Southern culture through his pastoral training and recent appointments, is proud that his church has "always been very strong and active locally" during his tenure there.

Nearness and Distance through Faith–Based Benevolence

Main Street, which offers church–door aid to about twenty persons in a typical month, administers a range of relief programs directly: payment of rental, utility, or medical bills; food assistance; temporary shelter; counseling. These direct forms of congregational relief are complemented by Main Street's extensive support of several local interfaith efforts. As Pastor Davidson explains, Main Street's

> benevolence program . . . is well known in the city. Sometimes too well known because of the number of calls we get, and the people who refer people to us for help. We sometimes kid about it—that somewhere out on a bridge on the outside of town is our phone number with our names. So that people who are sort of the highway bums—and that's not a derogatory term, it just is a term—[we sometimes kid that] if they come to town . . . [they can easily find out] what our phone number is and who to call for a handout, for food, for money.

Pastor Davidson adds that his church gets referrals from "just about everyone" in town, including the emergency telephone service, the police department, and various aid agencies. In addition to the list of relief efforts described above, most of Main Street's Sunday school classes have adopted needy families. These adopt–a–family relief efforts often provide the children in less privileged households with school clothes, winter coats, and other needed items over a sustained period of time.

Main Street Baptist is also involved in parachurch relief efforts. The church supports and coordinates some of its activities with Outreach and Uplift Relief (OUR) Ministries, an interfaith organization that provides select material goods (including food and clothes) to needy residents. As discussed in chapter 3, OUR Ministries commands more resources than many small churches in the area and serves as the "go to" option for small–church pastors when faced with aid requests that would deplete their meager resources. Interestingly, Main Street's connection to OUR Ministries is the converse of that of many small churches. Pastor Davidson stresses that Main Street's own aid programs are more financially robust than virtually all nearby parachurch agencies. "They probably send more people to us than we do to them," Pastor Davidson concludes, adding: "They probably have less to work with in that whole organization than our church."

In addition to these relief endeavors, Main Street has also offered assistance in opening a local emergency shelter for children. Main Street has allocated approximately one thousand dollars per month to underwrite that shelter, which is run by the local Salvation Army. Pastor Davidson refers to this cooperative partnership financed by Main Street as "great," adding: "I'm proud that we don't run [the children's shelter]. I told our church family [i.e., congregants], I said, 'You've got to look at this and say a thousand dollars a month is cheap.'" Pastor Davidson considers all Main Street's current relief efforts to be effective, and explains tersely: "Our goal is ministry, not programs." By outsourcing programs such as the children's shelter, he suggests, the church is able to keep its focus on the spiritual ministry which is at the heart of its mission. His emphasis indicates that he is keen to distinguish the goals of his church from the work of social welfare agencies and of professional social workers, who administer "programs."

Welfare Culture and the Problem of Accountability

Yet Pastor Davidson's tone takes a less than sanguine turn when he reflects on his church's experience with former Governor Fordice's Faith & Families of Mississippi program. Echoing the sentiments expressed by other pastors at affluent white churches in our study, Pastor Davidson expresses frustration with the apparent failure of program applicants to appear for their designated appointments with the church. Pastor Davidson recounts the typical scenario: "The Faith & Families office will call us and they'll say, 'We've set up an appointment for you with Ms. So–and–so to come see you at a certain time related to your involvement [in Faith & Families].' And then the person doesn't show. . . . And [Faith & Families] will try to follow up and [the applicant] can't reschedule." Pastoral frustration with this state of affairs is amplified by the fact that Main Street was among the churches who were most supportive of this program in its initial stages.

As Pastor Davidson sees it, the underlying cause of this no–show outcome is the reluctance of welfare recipients to submit themselves to the church's scrutiny. From this vantage point, these recipients have a strong aversion to being held accountable for their lifestyle and actions. Pastor Davidson contends: "We've basically raised up a culture that says, 'We really do deserve the money and you don't deserve anything from us.'" Remembering the sixties as a period of cultural decadence rather than progressive social change, he asserts: "Since the 1960s, it has been a problem because we've developed a culture to allow people who really don't want any accountability required [of them]." He links this antiaccountability orientation to the problems associated with the Faith & Families program: "I think a lot of times, if a person realizes maybe if they are going to get involved in having a church and a mentorship, they are probably going to have to change some things in their lives. And they are going to have to face some responsibilities they don't want to face."

Power, Race, and Benevolence at the Grassroots: Taking Pride in the Old South

Pastor Davidson says that longstanding public assistance programs were initially predicated on an altruistic, "want to help" mentality. But they blossomed into a "welfare system" fraught with corruption: "The welfare system basically operates in America today not for the poor person, but for the administrators." He asserts that such corruption is currently not incidental, but intrinsic to federal government programs: "What is it they say? That something like 20–something percent of all federal welfare money is gulped up in fraud. In dishonesty." In contrast to Elder Smith's selective borrowing from the discourse of neoliberalism, Main Street's pastor reviles big government and unambiguously supports political devolution: "Most of those people [in the federal government] got those jobs through political appointments. They were put there to do just what they're doing—that's to lie, cheat, and steal. . . . I don't have a lot of appreciation for [federal government workers]." As a counterpoint to federal government fraud, Pastor Davidson highlights the grassroots altruism that he says emerged in local Mississippi communities during the protracted power outage recently resulting from a winter ice storm. This storm, which left thousands without electricity and many without heat for as much as one week, was met with "neighbors . . . show[ing] up with chain saws and drag[ging] limbs and help[ing] their neighbors. And they want to help. They want to cover that roof. They want to give food."

Consistent with his celebration of local altruism, Pastor Davidson is confident that his church could figure prominently in charitable choice initiatives. When asked what type of relief programs his church could sponsor with an infusion of grant monies, he answers confidently, "Anything." However, his optimism toward charitable choice at Main Street does not translate into blanket support of such initiatives. Churches as a group, Pastor Davidson contends, are not above reproach where funds designed to underwrite relief provision are concerned. Now qualifying his optimism about charitable choice, Pastor Davidson mentions several instances in which financial partnerships between the state and local congregations have gone awry. In one instance, he says that a Memphis church "organized themselves to accept money—government money— to build public housing. And the pastor got sent to jail eventually because he spent most of the money on himself and his family, his brother–in–laws. . . . And eventually there were no houses built. The same thing happened on the Gulf Coast with a guy. . . . And so, sometimes the unscrupulous have a unique way of getting into those things."

In a striking departure from Temple Zion's Elder Smith, Pastor Davidson argues that attitudes about race and ethnicity would generally not affect service provision under charitable choice. His response is telling. It is not that charitable choice would legally prohibit race–based provision (which others concede while questioning the effectiveness of enforcement mechanisms). Rather, Pastor Davidson asserts that racism is no longer a part of contemporary Southern culture: "No, because any group involved in [providing] aid today, to anyone, has long since dealt with that one." So, whereas Elder Smith and others point to the persistence of racism within both black and white local churches, Pastor Davidson charges that racism is an issue of the distant past—the quite distant past, it would seem.

According to Pastor Davidson, blacks were previously offered help by Southern plantation owners and farmers. Pastor Davidson's views of enduring white altruism toward "the black community" are most clearly evidenced when he is asked if he thinks race affects the way in which relief is currently provided by local congregations:

> No, I doubt that [race currently affects the distribution of church aid]. In fact, see, particularly in the South [pause]. And, you know, I'm a Southerner. [I] grew up in the South, [and] have lived in a lot of other places, but [pause]. Southerners have always seen themselves as having to help, say, the black community. You know, the old plantation owner, he did it. The farmers did it. It's always been there. And so, race has—in my own lifetime—has never been a problem in relationships. Even when you had the active Ku Klux Klan and the marchers and everything, there's always been a desire to help. And I don't think that's ever been on a racial basis.

Using such language, Pastor Davidson suggests that even during tumultuous times—Klan activity and public marches supporting racial segregation and Jim Crow laws—white Southerners have "always seen themselves as having to help . . . the black community." One of the most striking features of this narrative is the way in which it portrays whites as the benevolent, compassionate agents of relief. Given this discursive memorializing of the past, white benevolence effectively trumps Klan activity and paints "old [Southern] plantation owners"—popularly viewed as a source of black oppression—in a positive light. This revisionist narrative, however, assumes a singular and homogeneously needy "black community"—claims which would likely draw criticism from Temple Zion's Elder Smith. Recall that Elder Smith pointedly criticized racialized "welfare myths" that equate neediness and aid recipiency with membership in "the black community." Of course, "not knowing" about racism is a privilege rarely afforded African Americans. But it is possible for privileged persons to be so insulated from routine practices of discrimination that they can comfortably situate racism in the past.

Pastoral Concern and Congregational Relief for Working Families

In the end, however, Pastor Davidson argues that the group about whom he is most concerned are not the recipients of welfare, but instead working poor families. The race of the hypothetical working poor family he describes is unmarked. However, the father in this nuclear family evinces an impressive work ethic, faces a heavy tax burden, and—through no fault of his own—cannot afford to provide the children he loves with the most basic forms of healthcare. Pastor Davidson explains:

> That's the man who's going out there and working every day—forty and fifty hours a week. And yet, after he pays his social security and gets his income tax taken out of this salary—his pay—he comes home and he doesn't have enough money to [look after] the basic needs of his family. And for whatever reason, the company he is working for does not provide insurance coverage or medical benefits. And he can't afford the hospitalization insurance for his family. So, his children can't go to the dentist. His children can't get their vaccinations and their check–ups. When they get a fever, they just do the best they can. That's the group now that I am most concerned about. And in our system we're destroying that family.

Although issues of "deservingness" are not addressed directly in this narrative of the struggling working poor family, one could argue that the committed male breadwinner in such families makes a compelling foil against which the stereotypical "welfare queen"—bereft of a hard–working husband/provider, and perhaps prone to shiftlessness her-self—can be counterposed (cf. Schram 2000: ch. 2). In fairness, Pastor Davidson does not draw explicitly such invidious comparisons. Yet his overriding concern for this intact working poor family hints at a decid-edly gendered vision of the deserving poor.

Conclusion

In this chapter, we have explored how two churches—Temple Zion–COGIC and Main Street Southern Baptist—engage in poverty re-lief. We have also examined their pastors' appraisals of charitable choice partnerships between faith communities and the government. Temple Zion, an African American congregation, claims to assist over twenty times more persons per month via direct church–door relief than does Main Street—where religious leaders jest that they are too well known among the local "highway bums." And while Pastor Davidson at Main Street evinces his greatest concern about working poor families whose fathers' income, after taxes, leaves them unable to meet their children's basic needs, Temple's Elder Smith argues that his relief providers con-sciously seek to aid—and, indeed, convert into active church members—the poorest of the poor within the local community.

While religious leaders at both Temple Zion–COGIC and Main Street Southern Baptist are favorably disposed toward church–state partner-ships, their pastoral narratives characterize the present and memorialize the past quite differently. Temple Zion's Elder Smith has many ambiva-lent feelings about public assistance, welfare, and charitable choice. On the one hand, he is quite critical of welfare for "limiting" and "hamper-ing" the endeavors of his church members. He argues that welfare is "in-sulting" to God, the Creator upon whom his congregants must acknowl-edge their ultimate dependency. Temple claims kinship—literally and fig-uratively—with the poor while offering redemption–from–welfare narratives that recognize the need for spiritual dependency.

On the other hand, Elder Smith worries that political devolution under welfare reform will effectively prevent the federal government from su-pervising local "good old boy" networks which historically functioned to reproduce class and race–based hierarchies in rural Southern town-ships. The federal enforcement of civil rights legislation in states such as

Mississippi may generate antipathy against "government interference" among some local residents, including white conservatives, whose enthusiasm for a new federalism may be rooted in a desire to preserve racial privilege rather than in more lofty philosophical commitments to grassroots democracy or local empowerment. Terms such as "local empowerment" raise concerns for this Southern black pastor who fears a return to Jim Crow politics in which local power structures trump federal civil rights legislation and erode gains made through federal mandates of equal opportunity and affirmative action. Yet, when faced with the expansion of social service opportunities for local congregations under welfare reform, this pastor chooses action over apathy. Given the opportunity, his congregation would vie for charitable choice funds and would strive to bring about a more equitable social order through such efforts.

Main Street's Pastor Davidson is a champion of the new federalism and political devolution. He believes that racial issues in the South have been largely resolved. In his view, Southern whites have always looked after local African Americans—even during the plantation era. Much of his support for welfare reform and charitable choice is linked to his support for grassroots empowerment which he has seen manifested most recently during harsh winter power outages in his local community. Pastor Davidson, however, also has some misgivings about church–state partnerships in social service delivery. As evidenced by his church's experiences with Mississippi Faith & Families, he argues that many disadvantaged persons would rather receive a "handout" than submit themselves to the standards of accountability that are appropriately set by local faith communities. In addition to these concerns, Pastor Davidson fears that a few "unscrupulous" ministers could attempt to pad their own pockets with monies routed through their congregations.

Interestingly, both these pastors are critical of public assistance programs that have been utilized for the past several decades—though for different reasons. Elder Smith worries that dependency on public assistance can foreclose one's future prospects in this lifetime and in the next. Long–term welfare recipiency, according to this logic, undermines a more genuine spiritual dependency on God. It is in this same vein that Temple Zion teaches aid recipients that the answer to all problems is found in an appropriate dependency on Jesus Christ. They claim high success rates in several of their service programs. For his part, Main Street's Pastor Davidson targets his critique of public assistance programs at both the "supply side" and the "demand side" of welfare administration. He argues that fraud within the federal government stems from the bureaucratic implementation of public assistance programs, as well as the political practice of cronyism. On the "demand side" of public assistance, he is critical of the self–serving, entitlement–based mentality that welfare ostensibly produces in many recipients of public assistance.

Finally, the relationship between this pair of churches and parachurch relief agencies is opposite of that evidenced in the previous comparison of two United Methodist churches featured in chapter 4. In the case of the United Methodist churches, the African American River Road congregation was highly involved in interfaith relief efforts, whereas the white Green Prairie congregation was quite removed from such parachurch agencies. Yet, in this second comparative case study, Temple Zion's Elder Smith laments that black churches in his area do not collaborate more closely with one another—in part because of "Reformational racism," which divides local black churchgoers along denominational lines. By contrast, Main Street Baptist is so large and prosperous that its relationship to the area's most active interfaith relief agency is inverted when compared with smaller congregations. Rather than referring cases of formidable need to the local interfaith relief agency, Main Street often finds itself being the target of referrals and requests from this interfaith organization as well as other nearby congregations. In its search to balance the moral imperatives of compassionate and accountable social ministry, Main Street outsources a number of its relief efforts to such parachurch agencies when opportunities arise. Doing so has provided Pastor Davidson's church members with a respectable return on their benevolent investments.

6

Invisible Minorities
Transnational Migrants in Mississippi

Our final comparative case study pairs together two religious communities composed of groups who are ethnic and religious minorities in east central Mississippi. The first case examines a local Catholic ministry to disadvantaged Hispanics dispersed over several churches. These Hispanic communities in rural Mississippi are served by the same pastor—an itinerant priest. The second case investigates an Islamic association composed primarily of students and established university professors. The Islamic Center, based in a small city proximate to several local universities, is run by a local president.

We focus on these communities for several reasons. To begin, religious life and poverty relief in both these religious communities speak directly to issues of cultural diversity. Each of these two cases offers important insights into the marginal position of nonmainstream religious communities when compared with dominant faith traditions on the local cultural landscape. Cultural diversity emerges as a salient feature of religious life within these populations not only via their nonmainstream religious convictions, but also through their distinctive ethnic identities. Taken together, the cases presented in this chapter highlight how the religious convictions held by persons of Hispanic, Middle Eastern, African, and Southeast Asian origins are shaped by a social order in which racial identity and ethnic stratification are often understood in the polarized terms of black and white.

The double marginality—that is to say, the religious and ethnic exclusion—of these populations in the cultural landscape of Mississippi sheds new light on the intersection of religion, race, and poverty relief. Regional social hierarchies and patterns of marginalization are closely linked with the aid–provision processes that are preferred and utilized by these religious communities. Their views of public welfare and appraisals of charitable choice are also influenced by their doubly marginal status. The invisibility of nonmainstream religions composed of transnational (nonindigenous, geographically displaced) populations provides a critical corrective to charitable choice discourse that effaces the role of religious and racial marginality in faith–based poverty relief (Olasky 1992).

A Pickup Truck Ministry:
Itinerant Catholic Advocacy for Hispanic Migrants

Father Dejean is the religious leader of a wide–ranging ministry that spans six dispersed rural congregations in northern Mississippi. Four of the six churches Father Dejean serves are composed of working poor and working–class Hispanic migrants. The other two congregations, by contrast, are composed of middle–class white parishioners. Father Dejean, who holds a master of divinity degree, has extensive experience working with Hispanic populations. In a previous ministry, he worked with Hispanics in the southwestern United States. This priest's rather reserved demeanor immediately falls away when he begins speaking about his congregants. Father Dejean's carefully chosen words show him to be a passionate and articulate advocate for the Hispanic migrants he serves. By Father Dejean's own account, the Hispanic population to which he ministers is quite young. Nearly half of his Hispanic congregants are between twenty and thirty–four years of age. These demographics are likely related to the fact that a large proportion of Mexican workers who have moved to Mississippi are first–generation migrants. Upon their arrival to the United States, these migrants are often employed as agricultural or unskilled workers. A typical household in Father Dejean's Hispanic congregations earns between ten thousand and twenty thousand dollars annually.

Given the high level of need in these migrant Hispanic communities, aid efforts in Father Dejean's ministry span a wide range. They include offering assistance with utility bills, as well as the provision of low–cost housing, clothing, medical services, transportation, and counseling. This itinerant priest helps parishioners to secure home loans and provides immigration counseling. Given the cultural—and especially the linguistic—marginality of this vulnerable population, Father Dejean often serves as a liaison between Hispanic migrants and the native, English–speaking Mississippians who staff most community and government agencies in

the local area. Although his survey response indicates that Father Dejean's ministry provides aid to about twenty persons per month, the limitations of survey–based measures are clearly evidenced with this itinerant ministry.

Father Dejean takes care to explain that most of his ministry is not
centered on the provision of discrete, measurable, quantifiable relief.
One of the most meaningful facets of his ministry, he suggests, is "not direct financial help, like handouts. It's more a solidarity, friendship, and
an emotional support to connect people. [Support] to help them survive,
to help them to make sense of life." Much of Father Dejean's social ministry therefore entails his persistent physical presence among migrant
families and individuals as they negotiate the vicissitudes of everyday life
in this country. "It's a very rural, almost primitive way, you know, of
being around the campfire—but now the campfire has become a pickup
truck—that kind of ministry."

Most of Father Dejean's Hispanic parishioners are recent migrants
from Mexico. Many of them were part of their nation's underclass before emigrating, and came to the United States in the hope of improving
their lives.[1] Many of these individuals have, at most, four or five years of
formal schooling. They are not fully literate in Spanish, much less in
English. Many of them speak enough English to communicate on the job
or at the grocery store. However, they lack the language proficiency
needed to communicate effectively with government officials or case-
workers who are likely to be monolingual speakers of English. Consequently, much of Father Dejean's ministry involves mediation between
these migrants and assorted agencies or contacts—particularly schools,
but also occasionally landlords and employers—in which English proficiency is assumed. Father Dejean explains his role as a multifaceted me-
diator: "That kind of help means [getting them] a driver's license, getting
them to jobs when they lose a job; taking them to agencies, to hospitals,
to child care, to the WIC [Women, Infants, and Children] program; providing transportation. A lot of our work is with the schools—you know,
talking with the principal, with the teachers. Making sure that there is a
better understanding."

In one sense, then, new arrivals into this migrant community need assistance orienting themselves to their new locale. Yet at the same time
local educators and government officials require help in communicating
with immigrant children—many of whom enter the school system without speaking English. Thus, Father Dejean spends a great deal of time

accompanying adult migrants and their children to school or the doctor's office, as well as to motor vehicle agencies, welfare offices, and the local immigration agency. Father Dejean also assists his congregants in finding stable employment that will provide them with a very meager, but survivable, standard of living. "There are no 'hours of operation' in my ministry," comments Father Dejean. "I do a lot of it by phone. A lot of these are referrals—you know, seeking jobs, interviewing for jobs, trying to find the right people, or tell them about [the requirements for a] driver's license here. . . . It's a lot of information–giving, you know."

Father Dejean's churches sponsor aid programs that will provide small loans. However, Father Dejean is quick to explain that his Hispanic congregants rarely accept money in this way: "They are a very proud people. They don't ask for money." Still, he says that those who do take advantage of the church–based loan program "always repay." For similar reasons, Father Dejean contends that members of this community are reluctant to use the local food pantry located in a nearby town. Despite the fact that this food pantry feeds four hundred families a month, he says: "Hispanics don't like to be subsidized. They don't like to have the handouts."

Adopted Migrant Families and the Catholic Legacy: Godparenting as Bridging Capital

Pastoral mediation takes other forms as well, often involving the negotiation of boundaries between members of different ethnic groups and social classes. This type of mediation has been bolstered by new laws that permit the sponsorship of undocumented migrants by U.S. citizens. Father Dejean facilitates these sponsorships, tellingly describing himself as "the bridge" in such arrangements. Given the fact that Father Dejean serves both migrant Hispanic and middle–class white churches, he has sought to elicit interest in this immigration sponsorship program among his two primarily Anglo churches. In this way, Father Dejean himself seeks to become a conduit for bridging capital, essentially aiming to eradicate the cultural, economic, and geographical distance between these white middle–class churches and his four Hispanic congregations.

Father Dejean's efforts to cultivate bridging capital between migrant Hispanic families and white middle–class congregants is structurally facilitated by a distinctive tool in the cultural repertoire of Catholicism— the practice of godparenting. Within Catholicism, the godparent–godchild relationship is sacralized through sponsorship—a covenant of a sort—at the child's baptism. Catholic tradition even charges godparents with raising their godchildren in the event that the child's natural parents die before their son or daughter reaches the age of adulthood. Godparents make promises to raise the child in the Catholic Church, and enjoy an esteemed status when compared with other relatives and friends of the family. The godparent–godchild relationship therefore has both spiritual and material dimensions.

Father Dejean explains how this unique element of Catholic tradition has been transposed into the godparenting of migrant Hispanic families by some of his white middle–class congregants via this new immigration policy: "Sponsorship with the new law is fostering, you know, godparenting." This relationship, too, has both spiritual and material dimensions. "People sign on behalf of the dependants," says Father Dejean. "That has done miracles." The commitment on the part of the sponsor requires not only faith in the migrant family, but also "quite a bit of money. . . . Some of the Anglos have it, and they are willing to sign."

Those most likely to serve as sponsors, Father Dejean explains, are well–educated Anglo women who have themselves experienced some form of struggle and hardship. Within these migrant communities, interracial families with young children—those in which "she's American, he's Hispanic, and there is a baby or two already"—are most likely to gain sponsorship. These sponsorship patterns underscore the importance of the aid provider's empathy with the poor and personal identification with social disadvantage as a motivating force behind relief efforts. At the same time, they suggest that race remains a primary consideration in determining the type of family a sponsor chooses to provide with assistance. Despite these racial and nationalistic biases, Father Dejean is optimistic: "You never know who is going to sponsor, who is going to take the risk."

Pride in cultural distinctiveness can also hinder bridge–building efforts. Potential sponsors who, in the end, shy away from the program often do so because their shared religious convictions (Catholic) have been superceded by racial differences (Hispanic versus Anglo). Father Dejean points out that some migrants are wary of the sponsorship program based on a desire to protect their distinctly Hispanic brand of Catholic heritage. Such wariness of sponsorship, he says, is typically defended using the following rationale: "We are very Catholic—protective of our tradition. We are proud to be Catholic. And so we are going to be proud as Hispanics, and we are not going to talk to the Anglos."

These trepidations about the sponsorship program, however, are rooted only partly in cultural pride. Father Dejean admits that some Anglo congregants fetishize the immigration sponsorship initiative as a cultural exchange program. This cultural–exchange approach to sponsorship exaggerates social distance between white sponsors and the Hispanic beneficiaries of such sponsorship while subverting any opportunity for both parties to discover what the priest calls their "common humanity." According to Father Dejean, these types of Anglo congregants say, "Well, you know, we tolerate you [Hispanics]. We like the kids. We like to have them come in. But do we really believe that they belong to us? No. They're still outsiders."

Despite these setbacks, the godparenting initiative has been generally successful, due in large measure to the tireless—though intangible—efforts of Father Dejean. Such efforts, which amount to persistent and strategic networking between migrant families and Anglo sponsors, help to cultivate social capital—again, outreach–oriented bridging capital—between these two disparate groups. This program, designed to safeguard the future of migrants and their children, is generally effective despite such social distance. Father Dejean concludes, "It's very delicate. But it works."

Despite the overall success of this godparenting program and many of his other ministerial efforts, Father Dejean admits to less than stellar results with some of his other endeavors. Among the programs that have left this itinerant priest most dissatisfied are literacy classes aimed at building English proficiency. Father Dejean assesses the program's outcome: "Tough, oh tough. . . . They come and go, you know. They come three or four times and drop out." In fact, Father Dejean concedes forthrightly that his attempts to elicit sustained participation in many church activities have been disappointing. In a society without clear rites of passage from one social status to another, many of his migrant Hispanic parishioners have become sacramental Catholics. Father Dejean laments that too many Catholics come to church for the sacraments only— Catholic "transitions in life [such as] First communion, Baptism, and so forth." In the Catholic tradition, the sacraments are thought to confer grace and, as such, are viewed as crucial to spiritual salvation. Yet this theological orientation has not worked in favor of long–term church participation among the Hispanic migrant communities Father Dejean serves. He says that sustained church activities are "not too successful. We bring them in and we never see them again."

A Globalized Workforce

Although these migrant workers are likely to withdraw from church participation and congregational literacy programs, they are diligent workers above all. In contrast to dominant images of the poor as lacking a work ethic, these migrant workers are poor in spite of their strong belief in hard work. Indeed, Father Dejean locates the causes of poverty among Hispanic migrants in a complex mix of domestic and international economic factors. Depressed economic conditions in Mexico are intertwined with a global economy that encourages transnational migration from poorer to wealthier countries (see L. Chaves 1998:3). These factors, in turn, produce a docile workforce with few options other than enduring long workdays for meager wages.

Father Dejean explains that many of the migrants come to the United States to work and send money back home. In the United States, these migrants can earn seven to ten times the income they could command in Mexico. Father Dejean remarks forthrightly: "The number one priority is work, not school." He continues: "They're here to work and send money away. [This situation] creates a cycle of more poverty. Because once you make a salary and you send 70 percent of it away, not only are you poor here—because you don't earn much money—but you're poor because you don't have much money to live on. So it's a double whammy." In fact, if young men are successful in bringing their families to the United States to live with them, their economic condition often worsens. These men's meager wages are stretched extraordinarily thin when they support those same dependents in the United States rather than in Mexico. "It's great to see them," says Father Dejean, referring to migrants' families that are able to reunite in the United States after months or years of separation. "But," he adds, "they are not better off. They are better off familywise [because they are together]. Healthwise they are better off. They are happier. But they won't make a decent living." Significantly, most migrants have very little trouble finding work: "Many of the bosses are highly in favor of Hispanics. They seek them out. Furniture plants, lumberyards, sweet potato farmers. There's a commitment to hire them. Now, they are not treated okay, you know. But at least [these employers] want them."

Implied in Father Dejean's aside—"they are not treated okay"—is the well-documented exploitation of migrants in the global economic marketplace. Less likely to have the legal, cultural, and linguistic competence to challenge exploitative labor practices, transnational migrants make the "ideal" docile workers for industries that pay extremely low wages accompanied by precious few benefits. In addition, the linguistic and cultural diversity of work crews divided among Anglo and Hispanic workers is likely to be a benefit to employers who seek to avoid the complications of a unionized workplace.

Ambivalent Sentiments about Charitable Choice

Can faith communities participate effectively in welfare reform through charitable choice programs? Father Dejean has mixed sentiments on this score. His enthusiasm for such programs stems from his belief that faith–based relief can motivate relief providers to embody scriptural teachings more fully than is currently the case. He says that faith–based welfare reform can promote "the realization [that] the Christian message and the Gospel mean something. And we can take charge—as a body of believers—we can take charge of our well–being and the well–being of the poor." This perspective is noteworthy because it fixes responsibility for the success of faith–based relief not with changing the poor, but rather with effecting a transformation among the providers of aid—what Father Dejean calls the "body of believers."

What types of programs does he envision being implemented effectively under charitable choice? Father Dejean can foresee organizing "some government–sponsored programs for gardening," including food cooperatives that would help the "little people" who are most disadvantaged: "You don't have to carry the food for miles and miles. It's right here. Subsidize coops and gardens for good and reduce for the little people all these costs." Father Dejean also hopes that current church relief programs can be expanded. Consistent with recent priest recruitment strategies employed by the Catholic Church in the United States, Father Dejean says that such programs might even be advertised so that they could reach more people. Among the programs Father Dejean views as most ripe for expansion are initiatives for single mothers with children, as well as skills–based classes in bilingual education, self–esteem, cooking, sewing, parenting, and money management. Father Dejean optimistically foresees an abundance of volunteers nearby if public funds were forthcoming to help underwrite materials costs. He asserts that individuals in rural locales "have a greater sense of community than [their counterparts] have in larger churches in urban areas."

In the eyes of this pastor, such funds could be used to transform some faith–based antipoverty initiatives from intermittent direct relief to intensive engagement with the poor. Father Dejean cites holiday food distribution as the perfect example of an intermittent effort that needs to be expanded to include the whole year: "Why can't we do that on a more regular basis? You know, so it's not just things in a basket—seasonal help. But it would be a year–round thing." He continues: "There is a certain pride at Thanksgiving and Christmas, when we see all these people coming and saying, 'Here Father, for the poor,' or 'For your Hispanics,' as they say. But I say, 'My Hispanics have to become your Hispanics.'" Thus Father Dejean sees his work as one of constant intervention, not only with the disadvantaged, but also with the privileged members of his congregations. He challenges each of his constituencies to become involved with one another, to develop actual relationships across boundaries of class, ethnicity, and in many cases, nationality. In this way, he seeks to foster a sense of citizenship in a moral community that transcends national boundaries.

At the same time, however, Father Dejean envisions potential difficulties in the implementation of charitable choice initiatives. His many years of experience in the local area have contributed to these misgivings. Even as Father Dejean proudly endorses the community spirit evidenced in rural areas, he also recognizes that "isolation" and "lack of transportation" in such locales could hinder faith–based welfare reform. He cautions, "It's a lot harder to coordinate in rural areas, you know."

Moreover, given the prejudice and discrimination against Hispanic migrants witnessed first–hand by Father Dejean, he worries that racial, economic, and cultural divisions could influence the implementation of charitable choice on the local scene. Without pointing fingers, Father Dejean says that many Mississippi religious communities unfortunately adopt a help–our–own orientation when confronted with solicitations for poverty relief. He laments that the all–too–common response, "We help our own people," is evidenced across all racial groups. Religious insularity—which, in much of Mississippi, simultaneously entails racial exclusion—is closely linked, in Father Dejean's eyes, to a blame–the–victim orientation toward poverty and the poor. Father Dejean charges that these depictions of the poor are often racialized and stem, most fundamentally, from disparities in power:

> We hear people . . . say, "Why can't they be better off? Why can't they manage their money better? Why can't they get out of poverty? Why do we have to provide subsidies? Why do we have to help them?" You know, the prejudice and the racism is so ingrained. [As I define it] racism is prejudice plus power. And it's a lot harder to let go of the power than to let go of the prejudices. So even though I may be helping them . . . I'm still powerful, because I have not let go of my wealth. . . . It's only when they have begun to share in their common humanity that the power stops, and the higher and lower people begin to be equal, [which is] the message of the gospel.

Quite notably, Father Dejean's critical interpretation of the gospel rejects pastoral discourse that stresses personal conversion (individual piety) over social change (structural transformation). From Father Dejean's standpoint, the individualistic discourse of personal responsibility is trumped by a quintessentially Catholic notion of collective responsibility that is rooted in the "common humanity" of disparate groups. The goal of his Hispanic ministry is, quite significantly, not saving "one soul at a time." Rather, Father Dejean seeks a more thoroughgoing transformation of locally embedded power structures that stratify whole groups of people by class and race. This critical hermeneutic suggests that faith–based alliances rooted in the message of the gospel can help all persons to recognize their shared interests. In doing so, such alliances could ultimately unmask and negate the two facets of racism—prejudice plus power—that provide it with such force.

Father Dejean's last words on this topic, however, underscore his profound ambivalence about religious congregations' ability to dissolve such forms of stratification simply through the receipt of block grant monies. "Money can be a two–edged sword," says Father Dejean. "Giving money's real easy." In the end, Father Dejean fears that increased financial expenditures will erroneously convince religious communities and the public that the country is doing all it can to eradicate poverty and inequality. In this pastor's eyes, poverty will never be eradicated unless the well–off come to recognize their privilege—and the gross injustice of such privilege—through sustained contact with the poor. Given his years of ministry around the campfire and alongside the pickup truck, Father Dejean is convinced that the difficulties experienced by poor Hispanics stem only partly from financial sources. The more formidable task, he argues, resides in redressing the ways that long–term poverty assaults the dignity of migrants while effacing their personhood among those who are more privileged. Father Dejean concludes that it is "not so much the financial difference, but the human [difference]. How do we raise people up? . . . They're courageous and all that, but there is a spirit of defeat."

Relief Work and Religious Conviction at an Islamic Center

"I don't like to be isolated," says Dr. Amir Hamman. "I would like to work with other religious communities." Dr. Hamman is the president of a local Islamic Center in east central Mississippi. This religious center has a membership of approximately two hundred. Dr. Hamman is a part–time leader of his religious community. A spry man in his forties, he has over twenty years of education and is employed full–time as a university professor. Like him, all of the leaders in this local Islamic community are volunteers. Composed mostly of international students, this Islamic association has the most ethnically diverse population of any religious congregation in our study.

A sizable contingent of members within the association are students currently in the midst of their university degree programs. As students, these members command meager resources. On average, households in the association earn between ten thousand and thirty thousand dollars annually. Yet, unlike the poor Hispanic migrants featured in the previous case study, the large group of students at the Islamic Center are on the path of upward mobility made possible by the eventual completion of their university studies. For the most part, students within the association feel confident that their economic hardship—although deeply felt— is temporary. They have the aspiration of gaining access to a middle–class lifestyle—whether in the United States or in their home countries—upon the completion of their professional degrees here in small town Mississippi.

The association is currently focusing its energies on completing the construction of their new mosque. As they approach the final stages of constructing the mosque, the association has effectively resolved a dispute about the status of women in their congregation. To promote respect between the sexes, some members are committed to the preservation of social distance between men and women in public space. These members—whose commitment to gender difference resonates with traditional gender ideologies in the Deep South—wanted to have the mosque constructed with separate entryways for men and women. Association members who eschew gender segregation, by contrast, desired a single entryway for male and female members. With association members originating from Islamic countries marked by different local religious practices, association leaders thought it wise to placate both groups. The mosque was constructed with two entrances—a large entryway for use by men and women, along with a side door for use exclusively by women who opt for a segregated entryway. As they waited for the mosque to be completed, members of the Islamic Center performed their daily prayers in a neocolonial–style house. This house formerly served as the home of a university fraternity.

Beyond Black and White:
Negotiating Legitimacy at the Religious Margins

The local community within which the Islamic Center is situated has two separate ministerial organizations. The town's Ministerial Council is composed of predominantly white congregations. The Ministerial Council was initially formed to combat door–to–door aid solicitations perceived to be abusive by many of the white area churches. This town also has a parachurch group that calls itself the Ministerial Coalition. The Coalition is composed of black congregations. Both of these ministerial organizations are composed almost entirely of Christian churches—with the lone exception of a representative from the local Jewish community who, like Dr. Hamman, is a part–time religious leader. When asked about whether the Islamic association participates in either of these local ministerial organizations, Dr. Hamman responds, "I have heard about it. But still we haven't got an invitation to participate or contribute to that." In this way at least, the Islamic Center is not on the "official list" of local religious organizations.

To be sure, Dr. Hamman does not charge local Christian pastors with anti–Islamic prejudice. However, he is acutely aware of the marginal status of the Islamic Center in Mississippi's overwhelmingly Christian and predominantly Baptist religious landscape. Dr. Hamman belongs to a faith community that is widely misunderstood and even feared in some parts of the United States—and throughout much of Mississippi as well.[2] The Iran hostage crisis of the late 1970s and the Gulf War of the early 1990s exacerbated anti–Muslim and anti–Arab sentiments that became pervasive in the wake of the Islamic resurgence in the Middle East.

When the Oklahoma City bombing occurred in 1995, it was initially suspected to have been staged by "Muslim terrorists" before investigators moved on to explore other possible motives. These charges caused deep concern among Muslims on the local scene, who feared that they could become victims of retaliatory hate crimes. Dr. Hamman recounts the Center's instructions to its membership in the wake of the Oklahoma City bombing. Students and professors were instructed not to leave their homes unless absolutely necessary. They were admonished to take every possible precautionary measure until the Muslim terrorist thesis was proved false or the case was resolved.

The religious marginality of the Islamic Center in small–town Mississippi was boldly evidenced when it sought a city permit to build a new mosque. That permit was denied on the grounds that the mosque was being constructed in a residential area rather than a commercial zone. The Muslim community hired a lawyer and sued the city. Dr. Hamman remembers this series of incidents: "The Muslim community lost in the city court, lost in the state court, and then later—after five years—they took it to the appeals court in New Orleans. And they came out with a segregation case—religious segregation—and [ruled that] the mosque should be opened."

During the long series of trials, the antagonism that led to the suit gradually receded and was replaced by city officials' respect for the local Muslim community. Ironically, then, the conflict and antagonism initially behind this legal battle ultimately yielded social capital for the Islamic Center. By fighting the city's discriminatory practices within the system, Dr. Hamman suggests, city officials developed a greater sense of civility toward the Muslim association. Dr. Hamman comments, "So after that things went very smoothly with the city. [We] can understand each other after that. . . . We have, very much, a kind of understanding with the city. They help us a lot." As it turns out, the lawyer for the Muslim association won the suit by determining that there were several Christian churches within a quarter mile of the proposed site of the mosque. This discovery indicated that city officials who initially denied the permit were responding to neighbors who specifically did not want a Muslim religious institution in their residential area.

Bridging and Bonding: Islamic Networking in Mississippi

As non–Christians, Muslims in the rural South are likely to be situated at the margins of local religious life. They may be directly subjected to anti–Muslim sentiment or, at least, may confront pervasive misperceptions about Arab Americans, Asians, and Africans. And they are likely to feel alienated from a public religious discourse characterized by the hegemony of Christianity and, more specifically, Protestant variants of the Christian faith. Muslims on the local scene, however, do not passively accept their marginal status and have done much to change it. A central form of outreach within this community entails not poverty relief per se, but education. Leaders at the Islamic Center earnestly seek to educate a public that is, at best, ignorant of Islam and, at worst, hostile to it. As part of this outreach effort, students at the Islamic Center often travel to elementary and high schools in the area when instructors teach on the subject of culture. Such forums provide members of the Islamic association with the opportunity to educate local youth, who might otherwise uncritically accept the negative portrayals of Islam they hear on the evening news or even in their local churches.

Like Jews living in predominantly Christian areas, the Islamic Center's public speakers gain a proficiency in bridging discourse that emphasizes similarity and downplays cultural difference (that is, "We recognize Jesus as a great prophet. We share much of our scripture with Christians.") Dr. Hamman himself describes Islam in largely ecumenical terms: "Islam is actually a continuation of the message carried since Adam, by all the prophets—including Abraham and Jesus Christ and the Prophet of Islam. The message of Islam is just coming to complete the message after Jesus Christ. We believe in all of them and we believe in all of the prophets since Adam until Jesus Christ. . . . That is the concept which is misunderstood by many, especially in America here. But it is the same Lord we worship and it is the same message."

The civil and ecumenical tone of such language notwithstanding, bridging discourse is a strategic reaction to a dominant culture (Protestant Christianity). In the context of rural and small–town Mississippi, this dominant culture can effectively marginalize explicitly non–Christian religions (for example, Islam, Judaism, Hinduism, Buddhism) and those it perceives to be not "truly" Christian (for example, Catholicism, Mormonism). Of course, such religious differences run deeper than a mere acceptance or rejection of Jesus Christ as the savior of the human race. Consistent with the evangelical notion of deliberate conversion ("accepting Christ as one's personal Lord and Savior"), Protestantism in the rural South casts religious conviction largely as a matter of personal choice and consumer preference. This individualistic, deliberative approach to religious conviction stands in bold contrast to faith traditions—like those at the Islamic Center and among Hispanic migrants—in which religious conviction is commonly inherited through ethnicity and nationality.

As noted, the Islamic Center is not on the official list of the town's local ministerial organizations. In the absence of such interfaith connections, the Islamic Center has developed networking strategies that gravitate between bonding (inreach) and bridging (outreach) capital. The Center has recently begun networking with other Muslim associations in the region (e.g., Memphis, Tuscaloosa). These types of linkages involve simultaneous bridging and bonding. These interassociation networks bridge geographical distance while cultivating intimate bonds among fellow Muslims in a region where the *ummah* (community of believers) is a dispersed minority.

Dr. Hamman cites another instance in which the bonds of Islam are building geographical bridges for this increasingly visible Muslim association. A chaplain at Parchman State Penitentiary—who is himself a Muslim—had recently contacted the Islamic Center. As Dr. Hamman explains, the Muslim chaplain at the prison wrote to the Islamic Center and said, "Can you help me? I have too many Muslims in jail and would like to teach them about the religion so . . . they will become righteous individuals [who] will contribute to the community." The Islamic Center has accepted this request and will begin a new jail ministry program, despite what Dr. Hamman calls the "long, complicated procedure" of ministerial certification and the protracted orientation program at the penitentiary.

The building of these bridges with Muslims elsewhere in the region seems to have provided increasing visibility and newfound opportunities for this burgeoning religious community. The Islamic Center recently applied for and received money from the state's Tobacco Settlement Trust Fund to sponsor an antitobacco youth education program. It is one of over a hundred faith–based initiatives across the state that is being sponsored by the trust fund.

Marginality, Respectability, and Faith–Based Relief

As the Islamic Center begins to move away from its marginal status and into its newfound role of respectability, great care is taken to ensure that its poverty relief efforts are directed toward those who Dr. Hamman calls the "truly needy." Like his religious ecumenism, Dr. Hamman's views of public assistance programs prior to welfare reform employ the discursive tactic of bridging with the mainstream. As such, his standpoint on public assistance is strikingly consistent with that of many local pastors: "I believe . . . the government should actually help people who cannot work. And the system should strongly force individuals to be productive. . . . But I am against giving support to people who are not productive and [yet are] capable of producing. . . . Most strongly. Because that will take away the motive of working. . . . I am against giving to anybody according to the income without studying the case of individuals."

Dr. Hamman therefore echoes the received view that perpetual "handouts" are unhealthy and unreasonable. And the Islamic Center's practices are governed by these very sensibilities. When confronted with an aid solicitation, the Muslim association requests references from relief seekers. Because the mere request for references does not itself stave off abusive solicitors, the leaders of the Islamic Center take pains to check these character references. Dr. Hamman recounted a recent solicitation that was denied because the leaders felt they were not receiving the "whole truth" from this solicitor.

The great value placed on productive labor within this community has had some intriguing implications. Relief at the Islamic Center is tailored to meet individual needs as they arise. Therefore, the Center opts overwhelmingly for a strategy of intermittent relief, albeit overlaid by robust social support. Yet, given the antihandout mentality at the Center, members facing economic difficulties or personal crises are somewhat reluctant to accept material assistance from the association. Consequently, leaders within this community must proactively use their social networks to discover who is in need. They then discretely route aid in the direction of that needy person or family. Dr. Hamman explains:

> Most of the people who are needy in attending the masjid or prayer, actually, they don't come and ask [for aid]. These are the people who we really help. We know that some individuals, for example, have certain

problems. But he is too shy or whatever. It is not part of what he was raised up to [pause]. He is too shy to ask for help. So we will go ask his friends: "Okay, did you think that that individual paid for school [tuition]? If he did not pay, why did he not pay?" If he is in the hospital, we will ask his friend or her friend, "Does he or she have insurance?" Then if they say, "Yes," we will say, "Okay, does the insurance cover all of it? What is left over? Is he or she capable of doing that?" We go through friends and we ask.

Dr. Hamman argues that racial dynamics in his own religious community do not affect the distribution of aid. "The composition of the members is very diverse. You can find every nationality. You'll find every race in there represented. And most of the judgment is done on a need basis and not on a racial basis." Yet, when considering relief programs administered in other local religious organizations, Dr. Hamman says that theological ideals that mandate a color–blind administration of relief may often be at odds with entrenched patterns of prejudice and discrimination on the local scene. Dr. Hamman concedes "that there is no religion in the whole world that says, 'Give to somebody because he or she is that.'" At the same time, he worries that churches might discriminate against some factions of the poor "if they acted according to [the desires of] the members attending that church and they forgot about their religious teaching." Indeed, the Muslim association experienced religious discrimination first–hand through local opposition to the construction of its mosque. Dr. Hamman says that if such patterns of discrimination were to mark aid provision in local congregations, the United States would simply have traded one form of corruption (the graft of government welfare) for another (discriminatory faith–based aid).

In general, though, Dr. Hamman believes that religious communities can effectively fight poverty because religion can "wake up individuals" and give them a sense of "responsibility." Dr. Hamman charges, "Most of the time, the motivation [problem]—if linked with religion and connected with responsibility—can be solved." He argues that religious involvement can provide valuable social networks through which individuals can seek out economic opportunities and improve their life situations: "The churches . . . and masjids and temples, they can help individuals find work. They can use some of their money or their savings also to take some individuals off welfare. There is a lot of money [in religious communities] most of the time. . . . [Religious congregations can] easily locate who is truly needy. It can solve a lot of problems [and can] . . . turn all the members of that family into a very productive family."

Like many of the religious leaders in this study, Dr. Hamman argues that another advantage of faith–based relief is the strict standards of moral accountability that religious organizations can impose on aid applicants. As evidenced by the Islamic Center's reference–checking networks, religious communities can demand that aid solicitors "be real. Tell the real story. And that is not what is available to the government agencies. So they make the individual conscious of what he or she is going to say. The faith community can also bring to the individual's attention the religious issues which are relevant to the person's experience." From this vantage point, then, religious communities couple accountability standards (demanding "the real story") with compassionate sensitivity (making religion "relevant to the person's experience"). Despite his generally positive view of faith–based welfare reform, Dr. Hamman concedes that religious congregations have not totally fulfilled their responsibility to the poor thus far: "If every church took care of the members and the people who attend that church, I don't think there would be that much for the government to do."

Dr. Hamman's final appraisal of charitable choice, however, highlights one clear point of cultural distinctiveness that separates his views from those of other local pastors. When queried about the separation of religion and the state under charitable choice, Dr. Hamman evinces little concern. Indeed, he rejects this dichotomy, one that produces one–sided fears among some pastors about "government intervention" into "religious business." Dr. Hamman explains, "Well, the religion of Islam does not separate this. [It] says an individual is an individual. I mean, you cannot be religious in the church and not–religious in the office. It is the same individual, so . . . we believe that the whole thing is one thing."

Conclusion

This chapter has compared narratives of religious identity and poverty relief articulated by leaders in two marginal Mississippi faith communities—an itinerant Catholic ministry to working poor Hispanic migrants and an Islamic Center composed primarily of professional-class university students and professors. The collective identities of these religious communities, along with their distinctive relief efforts, underscore the overriding influence of social marginality on congregations situated outside the cultural mainstream. Within the context of rural and small–town Mississippi, the Hispanic migrant congregations and the local Muslim association are twice marginalized—first by their religious distinctiveness (non–Protestant, non–Christian), and then by their racial difference (nonwhite, nonblack). Because these communities are situated well outside the religious mainstream, both Father Dejean and Dr. Hamman utilize bridging tactics to connect their otherwise marginalized congregations to the religious center. Within the context of these two religious communities, such bridging tactics are motivated by divergent concerns, assume culturally distinctive forms, and yield decidedly different social outcomes.

For Father Dejean, bridging tactics take two key forms. First, Father Dejean advocates a critical hermeneutic of the Christian gospel that invites all persons to recognize their "common humanity" with their brothers and sisters. His critical interpretation of the gospel emphasizes the fundamental equality of all persons, including this itinerant priest's disparate congregational constituencies—working poor Hispanic migrants and middle–class whites. Utilizing this hermeneutic, Father Dejean casts social inequities as an affront to the radical message of egalitarianism contained in the gospel. Quite significantly, his critical reading of the gospel places the ultimate responsibility for "fixing" poverty on the privileged—not the poor. The problem with poverty, from this standpoint, is not the shiftlessness of the poor, but rather a system of structural inequalities that confers privileges on the chosen few. "Racism," says Father Dejean, "is prejudice plus power." Consequently, Father Dejean uses the Christian gospel to both engage and, ultimately, transform the cultural center of religious life in Mississippi. He eschews the managerial discourse of welfare reform—through which the privileged know "what's best" for the poor (Schram 1995)—in favor of a language that casts privilege as taking unfair (even un-Christian) advantage of the less fortunate.

Second, in a more practical sense, Father Dejean himself serves as a bridge between his disadvantaged Hispanic communities and the more privileged strata of Mississippi society—including congregants in the two white middle–class churches under his charge. Armed with the distinctive Catholic tradition of godparenting and new immigration sponsorship laws, this priest mediates "adoptive" relationships between migrant

Hispanic families (typically, those with young children with one natural-ized parent) and his middle–class white congregants.

To be sure, such efforts are not a thoroughgoing solution to the long-standing inequities Father Dejean sees quite regularly. Considerations of race, gender, and nationality retain currency within the sponsorship pro-gram. Migrant Hispanics, persistently marginalized in the cultural land-scape of Mississippi, face ongoing exploitation in the global labor mar-ket. And the bonding capital that ties Hispanic migrants to their cultur-ally distinctive brand of Catholicism often undermines this priest's most diligent bridging efforts. Yet this itinerant priest retains a commitment to the gospel's messages about the common humanity of all God's children. Through his relief efforts, he remains optimistic about the transforma-tive power of extended contact between the privileged and the poor.

As another marginalized religious community, the Islamic Center also utilizes bridging tactics aimed to connect local Muslims to mainstream Mississippi culture. The Islamic Center's president, Dr. Hamman, fre-quently employs bridging discourse to highlight the commonalities be-tween Islam and Christianity. Cultural difference is downplayed when speakers from the Islamic Center travel to elementary and high school classes to speak about Muslim culture. In light of American caricatures of Islam, the Center's outreach efforts entail the melding of select relief initiatives (e.g., intermittent relief, a burgeoning jail ministry) with a great deal of cultural education. These educational outreach efforts are aimed at debunking stereotypes about Islam, and infusing this maligned religious tradition with respectability.

Indeed, respectability is a key theme in aid efforts undertaken by this religious community. The Islamic Center is an achievement–minded, middle–class community that has fought doggedly against its religious marginality—most recently by suing the city for a permit to build its mosque in a residential area in which several Christian churches are situ-ated. Paradoxically, the Islamic Center's lawsuit against the city revealed its commitment to work within established institutions (i.e., the court system), a strategy that generated respect for the Muslim association among city officials.

As a religious community that seeks engagement with the cultural mainstream, the Islamic Center uses outreach and mutual aid strategies that show its commitment to core components of American culture. The Muslim association, composed largely of established university profes-sors and degree–seeking students, takes great pains to emphasize the value of "productive" labor and self-sufficiency—to the point where the association's own members are reluctant to accept intermittent assistance in the face of short–term financial crises. And where poverty relief is concerned, the Islamic Center is careful to ensure that it provides aid only to the "truly needy" by securing and carefully checking references from those outside the fold.

In the end, both of these religious communities are forced to contend with their social marginality. Hispanic migrants and Muslim internationals in rural Mississippi are doubly "other"—made potentially invisible by their non–Protestant religious affiliation and their nonblack-nonwhite racial identities. Narratives of religious identity and poverty relief articulated by leaders in each of these communities demonstrate that they utilize different cultural resources to meet the challenge of their marginal status. The distinctive sets of bridging tactics and poverty relief efforts they manifest have given each of them decidedly different future trajectories. Whereas Father Dejean's Hispanic migrants are likely to remain invisible in the cultural landscape of northern Mississippi despite his best efforts at mediation, the Islamic Center has emerged as a respectable and increasingly prominent religious community on the local scene.

7

Street–Level Benevolence
at the March for Jesus

In this chapter, we step outside the confines of Mississippi congregations to join in a performance of street–level benevolence at the 1999 Golden Triangle Region March for Jesus. The March for Jesus is an international event celebrated annually in late spring. In recent years, event organizers have dramatically changed the March for Jesus to center on benevolence and outreach within local communities sponsoring a march. In what follows, we explore the planning and execution of this one–day event in the Golden Triangle Region. We draw on first–hand observations of the march, as well as the reflections of a pastor who served as an organizer for the event. This ethnographic foray enables us to draw detailed comparisons between religious benevolence undertaken at this event and congregational relief initiatives discussed in preceding chapters. The 1999 march challenged two significant dimensions of denominationally based faith–based initiatives in the Golden Triangle Region: the emphasis on spiritual supplication rather than material ministry and the racialized cleavages that are embedded in the religious landscape.

Reinventing the March for Jesus: Christian Faith in Action

The March for Jesus in Mississippi's Golden Triangle Region has long given public expression to the spiritual convictions of area Christians. Initially conceived in London in 1987 by leading evangelicals who wished to recapture the bygone practice of street–level evangelism, the March for Jesus was designed to promote public prayer through massive, revivalistic marches in local communities on the Saturday before

Pentecost (see <www.gmfj.org>). On "Jesus Day," as the March for Jesus is dubbed by its organizers, sponsoring communities take their prayers to the streets and literally sing God's praises in the public square. The year 1998 marked a sea change in the March for Jesus. No longer content to have public prayer and worship as the sole focus of the event, leaders redefined the march to make community service its centerpiece. The March for Jesus executive committee first introduced the shift in focus from worship to benevolence at its national planning conference in Atlanta, Georgia. This national conference, complemented by multiple regional conferences, provided the ideal forum for broadcasting the change and enlisting local religious leaders as community–level organizers of the march. With these goals in mind, the conferences treated pastors from across the United States to panels of religious activists who talked passionately about the plight of the poor, the nature of effective social ministry, and the Christian mandate to provide relief to those in need.

In Mississippi's Golden Triangle Region, Reverend William Cummings became one of the event's local organizers. An African American pastor at a prominent black Baptist church in the local area, Reverend Cummings explains the rationale for redefining the aims of the march: "The previous March for Jesus really had a focus on the community and prayer. Whereas this year, the March for Jesus had a focus on the community not only praying, but serving. You know, prayer is vitally important and is central. But if we only pray, we don't do the job right. Because it takes putting feet on your prayer, putting prayer in action, becoming a servant to the community, and being sensitive to the felt needs of people in the community."

By integrating community service—and, specifically, hunger relief— into the march, organizers have become more hopeful about bridging the longstanding divide between Christian faith and action. As Reverend Cummings explains:

> One of the things that happened in evangelical Christianity after the sixties and seventies was a sort of divorce from social action. They had some real lean years of the church being concerned singularly about the salvation of people, which is not bad. That's not a bad thing. But what I've seen happen across the country, in the last two years especially, is that they've realized [that there is a problem with] being concerned about souls and not being concerned about a life. . . . They're so intertwined.

> The social role of the church, and the religious evangelistic role in the church need to be brought together as a single prayer, and not two separate prayers.

Thus, although the March for Jesus remains a day of prayer, Reverend Cummings defines prayer broadly to include both devotional worship and social activism. When defined in such holistic terms, prayer seamlessly unites public hands–on ministry ("being concerned about a life," in Reverend Cummings's words) with private spiritual conviction ("being concerned about souls").

To underscore the problems with privileging souls over lives, Reverend Cummings describes the 1980s—the decade that marked the apex of cultural dominance by the New Christian Right—as "real lean years of the church." Unlike the positive gloss commonly given to the term "lean" in American corporations and government (see Martin 1994), Reverend Cummings uses this word in a distinctly pejorative sense. Here, leanness is a state of want, incompleteness, and unrealized potential in the Christian church. Accordingly, it is only through the provision of direct relief to the hungry—and to all those suffering hardship and penury—that the church itself will "fill out" and thereby realize its complete potential.

Apart from bridging the chasm between Christian faith and action, the integration of hands–on ministry into the Golden Triangle Region march is designed to transgress boundaries rooted in race, class, denomination, and local geography. To achieve these ambitious ends, Jesus Day organizers intentionally plan a marching route that traverses affluent white neighborhoods and low–income black neighborhoods in the Starkville area. (Starkville is one of three county seats in the Golden Triangle Region. The others are Columbus and West Point.) This route will bring marchers through the center of Starkville—parading for several blocks down Main Street—and then will have them proceed out to the town's periphery. Because the march is designed to enlist the participation of church members across the denominational spectrum, the route will take marchers by several different local houses of worship. In planning the march, special efforts are made to contact a wide variety of local Protestant churches, along with the town's only Catholic Church, to ensure participation across denominational lines. Guided by the notion of religious pilgrimage, organizers strategically plan the route to remove marchers from the comfortable confines of their home neighborhoods and thrust them into unfamiliar settings throughout town.

The climactic destination of the marching route is J. L. King Park. The park, named after a prominent black social activist from the area, is located in an economically depressed, predominantly African American part of Starkville. In choosing King Park as the final destination of the march, organizers intend to mark a significant departure from previous Jesus Day events. Traditionally, such marches ended with a praise and worship service at the Mississippi State University Amphitheater. But as Reverend Cummings explains, the new route "requires [marchers] to leave their home and come on out to the park"—thereby transforming neighborhood boundaries by staging the event in public space that is itself situated in a black, working-poor part of town. As if borrowing a page from the late-nineteenth–century Salvation Army's street–corner revival and benevolence ministries (Winston 1999), the plan then calls for the staging of an open–air worship service alongside relief work undertaken collectively by local churches and march participants. Organizers tell prospective marchers to bring canned food items with them to the event. These food items will be collected and given to the needy at the park.

Within days of the march, however, organizers realize they might be facing a serious problem. In light of a front–page newspaper article promoting the new focus of the local march, word reaches organizers that residents in the projects are wary of the "help" to be offered in their neighborhood park. Hearing of this resistance, march organizers quickly mobilize Jesus Day volunteers in a door–to–door campaign through the projects. At each doorstep, volunteers explain the intent of the march and invite project residents to the event. Reverend Cummings is pleased to see that this eleventh–hour mobilization "got a response from the neighborhood," adding: "I don't really want them to see it as coming into your neighborhood to have something, but coming into your neighborhood and having something with you—and you're a part of it." Wishing to avoid this problem in future marches, Reverend Cummings says that in the future doorstep invitations will begin in earnest several weeks before such events: "We will do a better job of working the community itself within the three weeks prior to the [next] March for Jesus—knocking on doors, and letting people know that we want them to be a part of what's going on in the park that day."

Even more significantly, this problem convinces Reverend Cummings that the structure of the march's organizing committee needs to be changed. Reverend Cummings vows to put residents who live in the projects on the March for Jesus planning committee from this point forward. No longer simply recipients of Christian charity, these working-poor residents will themselves become agents and shapers of community benevolence. Reverend Cummings's discussion of this initial shortcoming of the march dramatizes the dynamism of his ministry—its ability to transform an obstacle into an opportunity, to turn an outsider into a participant, a member, and an activist.

With this issue resolved, organizers again focus all their energies on final preparations for the march. They are motivated by one key goal—taking the unbound spirit of religious benevolence created by this one-day liminal event into the everyday lives of committed Christians and community residents. With long-term compassionate ministry as their goal, organizers aim to set up "care groups" at the park. Care groups are intended to promote long-term partnerships through which middle-class residents, in the words of Reverend Cummings, "volunteer to be part of an ongoing ministry [offered] through different churches to really minister to people" in need. Reverend Cummings asserts that long-term care groups fill in the many gaps left by more restrictive forms of relief, including mutual aid within Christian churches and benevolence during the Thanksgiving and Christmas holidays. While choosing his words carefully, Reverend Cummings contrasts the vision of care groups with holidaytime benevolence binging:

> A lot of what happens during the holidays at local churches is with their members, and it's not really communitywide. What we try to do with the March for Jesus is almost to make it possible every day to help people in need—not just a holiday kind of thing. My concern was that people don't just get hungry Thanksgiving Day. They get hungry all the time. It's always been terrific about Thanksgiving and Christmas. Churches at this time will adopt hundreds of families, and provide them with a Christmas. But there's more to life than Christmas Day. An ongoing food pantry ministry would help families suffering in ways that last. Help during the holidays is like putting a band-aid on [a bad sore].

Christmastime benevolence, then, ritualizes giving and ties it to a particular time of the year. The problem with this model, however, is that poverty is a year-round predicament for many of the community's most disadvantaged residents. The march takes as its goal the provision of long-term care for people whose needs know no season. As the band-aid metaphor suggests, seasonal benevolence and a myopic focus on mutual aid do little more than lightly salve the serious wound that is poverty.

Taking It to the Streets: The Jesus Day Pilgrimage

After much planning, Jesus Day finally arrives on a Saturday in late May. The march itself begins shortly after eight-thirty on Saturday morning. Canned goods in hand, the marchers wander into the community center parking lot from which the event is to be launched. The community center is located near the downtown area, where several prominent houses of worship—Methodist and Baptist churches, black congregations and their white counterparts—are situated. The fast-tempo praise and worship music blaring over a loudspeaker in the community center parking lot serves as a wake-up call, at once physical and spiritual, to the marchers. Over the blare of the music, participants visit with one another, exchanging pleasantries and fellowship, before falling in parade-line formation. Part prayer march and part parade, this year's Jesus Day includes an impressive cavalcade of vehicles along with the traditional marchers in its procession. Staging the march, which requires the securing of sound equipment and will conclude with a communal meal in the park, is not an inexpensive venture. As marchers proceed to the registration table, they are made aware that "free-will donations" used to defray the cost of the event are being accepted there.

Given the heat and humidity of late-May Mississippi, the march itself gets under way soon after nine o'clock. After pouring out onto the road in successive waves, we proceed to Main Street. Marchers and participants number in the hundreds, and may total as many as one thousand. With people moving about on the streets, it's difficult to pin down any precise number. Considering that Starkville's total population hovers around twenty thousand, this is not a bad turnout. Black and white, men and women, young and old—marchers run the gamut. Those capable of enduring the one-hour march on this sultry Saturday morning will walk the route. Others unable to walk but willing to brave the heat sit on deck chairs arranged on a decorated flatbed trailer. This trailer, protected from the sun by a makeshift roof, is pulled behind a large, slow-moving pickup truck. Parents in the march push strollers or pull wagons that serve as the primary mode of transportation for their children. Here and there, an adventurous father walks the full route with a toddler straddling his shoulders. Kids of all ages sport helium–filled balloons—green, blue, orange, and yellow—floating gently in the breeze above them. Clusters of pedestrian marchers are interspersed with processions of slow–moving vehicles. Some church groups carry banners that proclaim their Christian—and, quite often, their evangelical—religious convictions. One reads: JESUS IS LORD!

It quickly becomes clear that this will not be a silent, solemn march. The partylike atmosphere of Jesus Day—billed as "a day of heaven on earth"—requires music. A spate of upbeat contemporary Christian songs are on the bill. Laced with hopeful messages of evangelical renewal and undergirded by penetrating bass lines, this music is broadcast into the open air by a set of portable loudspeakers. The loudspeakers are ferried along the route in the bed of a pickup truck that accompanies the procession of marchers on their pilgrimage through town. Much of the music features upbeat call–and–response choruses that cue marchers to echo melodic chants with such reprises as "Jesus Is Lord" and "Praise Him." The blaring music and the collective chanting it evokes make a public statement to all within earshot: Christians speak with one voice and will not be silenced in praising their God. Residents living along the march route peer out their windows in an attempt to determine the source of all the commotion. Some of them emerge from their homes for a time to watch the makeshift parade go by. Invariably, onlookers are greeted with a smile and friendly wave from the marchers.

As marchers approach busy intersections, police halt traffic and give our Jesus Day cavalcade the right of way. Motorists have no choice but to yield. Given the exhilaration of turning the normal state of affairs on its head, a sense of collective effervescence wells up at the busiest of intersections. On any given day, cars own the streets in downtown Starkville and, as in most American towns, pedestrians cross busy intersections at their peril. Apart from the very center of downtown, most of the town's streets have no sidewalks and pedestrians observed walking on narrow shoulders are usually marked as international students, local eccentrics, or as truly disadvantaged people who cannot get a ride from a neighbor or relative. But today is no typical day. On Jesus Day, a motley crew of marchers enjoys the rush of taking back the streets for the common folk—we are pedestrians in every sense of the word. Having obtained the proper permits and enlisted the police in their cause, otherwise law–abiding citizens are empowered to disregard stoplights and confidently stride by motorists who remain halted until the procession passes (cf. Regis 1999).

On the final leg of its journey, the marchers cross Highway 82. Where it runs through the predominantly African American part of town, Highway 82 is called Martin Luther King Drive. This highway is the busiest street on our route. Where we cross the long straightaway, motorists regularly exceed its speed limit of forty–five by as much as fifteen miles per hour. This highway is also one of the most prominent boundary lines dividing the city's better–off from their disadvantaged counterparts. At the behest of police holding off traffic, we cross the highway and head into the projects. Rarely frequented by the town's more privileged residents, the projects are home mostly to working poor African American residents.

After walking for another half–mile or so, we reach King Park. The dedication frontispiece at the park entrance reads:

J. L. KING, SR. MEMORIAL PARK
A WARRIOR FOR JUSTICE AND A SOLDIER FOR PEACE
MAY HIS LIGHT ALWAYS SHINE
THROUGH HIS CONTRIBUTION TO HUMANITY
Reverend J. L. King, Sr. (1890–1966) raised the standard by preserving the past, serving the present, and preparing for the future.

As the final destination of our journey and the climax of the Jesus Day celebration, the park greets marchers with music blaring so loudly that it easily drowns out the tunes still being broadcast from the portable loudspeakers in the pickup truck. The song bursting forth in the park's open air, "Lord, I Lift Your Name on High,"[1] is provocative in its message and sweeping in its rhythm:

> You came from heaven to earth to show the way
> From the earth to the cross my debt to pay
> From the cross to the grave
> From the grave to the sky
> Lord, I lift Your name on high

Unusual sights are also part of the Jesus Day celebration. One church has decorated the park's restroom building with a large violet banner. The banner features an oversized golden crown and the bespeckled word, JESUS, beneath it. As marchers move into the park area proper, they notice the large plumes of smoke billowing from atop a hill about one hundred yards away. A pavilion is situated on this hill, the highest point in the park. Under the pavilion is a banner that identifies the congregation on top of the hill—Faith Haven Church of God in Christ. The smoke drifting heavenward from just outside the pavilion is emanating from a series of large grills. The grills are cooking hot dogs and hamburgers that, when paired with potato chips and soda, will comprise our communal lunchtime meal. The March for Jesus planning committee had arranged in advance for relief workers from Faith Haven COGIC, an African American church, and Hopewell Church of God, a white congregation, to oversee the collection, sorting, and distribution of food offerings at the park. These two congregations also agreed to cook the hot meal partaken by parkgoers after the open–air worship service and outreach activity.

This portion of the event is organized to feature two congregations that are leaders in area churches' antihunger efforts (see chapter 3). It is noteworthy that of the two congregations featured in the park, one is white and one is black. It is also quite significant that these two congregations represent different denominations—Church of God and Church of God in Christ. Thus, while two key motifs of Jesus Day are racial reconciliation and interdenominational fellowship, organizers contend that it is not enough merely to speak out—or even to sing out—against racism and denominationalism. Social practices must facilitate actual collaboration across racial and denominational lines, thereby providing a public demonstration of the way that Christian benevolence transforms entrenched social boundaries.

After the marchers enter the park, they make their way up the hill and under the pavilion to surrender their food offerings to Faith Haven's relief workers. With a smile, these workers accept the offerings brought forward by marchers and busily incorporate the canned goods into food sacks that have been lined up for the taking. Each sack is brimming with canned and dry goods, as well as a sizable frozen ham or roast. Street–level food relief has already begun in earnest. Given the lack of parking space nearby, a slew of vehicles—including station wagons and vans—are parked on the grass adjacent to the pavilion. As each sack is filled, relief workers ferry it to one of the vehicles on the grass. These sacks are then delivered to the homes of those who, while unable or unwilling to make it to the park today, are nevertheless hungry.

The liminal character of this public celebration is underscored by a large sign that features the park's insignia and specifies its rules. The insignia and the park rules, both in bright red, stand out from the sign's white background. The insignia appears above the rules in the sign's top left corner. It is the outline of a house with three human figures of different sizes—ostensibly a mother, father, and child—etched inside it. This insignia is intended to make it clear that King Park is a family–friendly public space. The standard regulations of the park are listed in a bullet–point fashion below the insignia as follows:

RULES AND REGULATIONS
1. NO ALCOHOLIC BEVERAGES
2. NO UNAUTHORIZED VEHICLES ON GRASS
3. NO PROFANITY OR FOUL LANGUAGE
4. NO LOUD MUSIC/NOISE
5. NO LITTERING
6. PARK HOURS: DAWN UNTIL 10 PM
7. REPORT VANDALISM OR PARK PROBLEMS
   TO SPC OFFICE 323–2294

While the regulations forbidding alcoholic beverages, profanity, littering, and vandalism are respected by the marchers, those that prohibit parking on the grass, loud music, and noise are clearly being waived on Jesus Day. And, although cloaking the park's restroom building with a large banner might be viewed as a "park problem" on any other day, a complaint to the Starkville Parks Commission (the "SPC" mentioned in rule 7) would likely meet with inaction today. Jesus Day in small–town Mississippi is no normal day.

After all the marchers file into the park and turn over their food offerings, they congregate around a stage on which several local ministers— black and white, from various Protestant denominations, all male—have gathered. The music blares, with the crowd echoing: "King of Peace," "King of Peace," "Jee–sus," "Jee–sus," "Lord of all," "Lord of all," "Jee–sus," "Jee–sus." After a while, the music fades. Then, one of the black pastors on the stage steps forward to offer an opening prayer. "Let us all take someone by the hand," he says. He then proceeds to lead the gathering in prayer, praising God for the days He has given this "united people" who have gathered in the park. We, in turn, have given the Lord this day—Jesus Day.

Seconds after this formal prayer closes with shouts of "Amen," "Alleluia," and "Thank you!" from the crowd of parkgoers, Reverend Cummings steps forward and launches immediately into a free–wheeling, spirited exposition about the real meaning of Jesus Day. With his every pause, parkgoers clap, cheer, and shout "Amen!" loudly.

Amen! In our world, there are a lot of problems. . . . There are a lot of issues—a lot of things that are wrong. But there is something that is right. Jesus is who he said he was. He can do what he said he could do. And it's time for the church to stand up and just say so. . . . It's time for the church to stand in its proper place—to go beyond denomination, to go beyond culture, to go beyond class, and to stand up for the cause of Jesus Christ! To God be the glory!

Pausing momentarily to gather himself amidst the shouts of parkgoers, Reverend Cummings continues:

We have gathered together today from every church in our city. From every denomination. From all racial groups. It's a statement to the devil that we no longer accept the stuff that the world has said is normal. Racism isn't normal. That's abnormal behavior. Normal is being what Jesus was, when he included everybody and said that the ground at the foot of the cross was level. That there was no Greek, no Jew—no bond, no free—no black, no white—no Mexican, no Native American. There is one flesh! And that flesh must come by way of Calvary and be washed in the blood of the Lamb!

The crowd now breaks out into raucous cheering, after which Reverend Cummings proceeds:

This is a statement today that we no longer tolerate, we no longer live according to the lines drawn by man. Yes, they drew a circle and drew us out. But we drew a larger circle and drew them in. I believe that this is what God loves to see. Heaven is having a party! Right now! Hell is mad, but who cares! Heaven is having a party!

Again, loud clapping whips through the crowd, and many holler out, "Whoa, yes! Alleluia!" Moments later, Reverend Cummings picks up:

This is Jesus Day. And we are getting ready. We are moving from this day and we are going to walk together to June of next year, when we will have Jesus Day again. But we can't just stop it today and pick it up next year. We got to keep it going. We got to keep the word of Jesus alive! We got to keep the vision alive! And there are some concrete things we can do. We can make sure that nobody in our city is lonely. We can make sure of that. We can go to where people are lonely—to the nursing homes and the hospitals—and we can make a difference. We can make sure that those who have no father in their home have somebody to care for them. Not so they can have something added to their résumé but so they can be listed with Jesus as someone who cares. We can make sure that nobody goes hungry. We have the resources, we have the ability to make sure that nobody in our community that we know of goes hungry. We can make sure of that. We can make sure that the name of Jesus is declared. Now I know that's a whole lot to do. But just think about what he's already done for you. You remember where he found you? . . . We need to ask God to help us in several areas as we face this year of moving from this experience to making this more practical in the way we live our lives, and in the way we run our businesses, and in the way we do church. I think we need to ask God's help.

With that, Reverend Cummings introduces two different white pastors who lead local Southern Baptist congregations, each of them taking his turn to testify to the reality of racism in Mississippi and the reconciliation that God can bring to Mississippi despite its sinful past. One of these ministers, Pastor Hogan, reminds the crowd that the last known lynching in Mississippi took place not way back in the 1950s but as recently as 1970. Pastor Hogan then proceeds to pray that:

God will make Mississippi the state that leads our nation in racial reconciliation and healing [so that] when people hear of Mississippi, they'll say, "That's where the move of God is taking place." . . . We thank you, Lord, that our destiny is greater than Toronto, that it's greater than Pensacola. It's one of the greatest moves of God in healing that has ever taken place. . . . Father, we come walking in humility, bowing our heads asking forgiveness . . . for our long legacy of racism, prejudice, pride, and idolatry—for setting up the Confederacy as an idol. . . . Father, we ask forgiveness for that flag that still rules over our place. And we thank you, Lord, that we today are replacing the Confederate flag, Lord, with the flagship of the Lord Jesus Christ. . . . And we are declaring here today, Father, that the Golden Triangle Region will lead this state in racial healing and racial reconciliation.

Then, after defining racism as a "problem of sin, not skin," Pastor Hogan unifies the crowd by leading them in a cheer—albeit one with an evangelical twist. He begins by admitting that Baptists such as himself have for too long defined religion as a private matter "of the heart." Pastor Hogan recalls the aphorism from his seminary training, "It's what's in your heart that matters." He now rejects this view. We live in a time, he says, when Christians must publicize their convictions. With that, he launches into a cheer:

Pastor Hogan: Give me a J!
Crowd: J!!!
Give me an E!
E!!!
Give me an S!
S!!!
Give me a U!
U!!!
Give me another S!
S!!!
What's that spell?
Jesus!!!
Who's Lord over Starkville?
Jesus!!!!
Who's Lord over Columbus?
Jesus!!!!!
Who's Lord over West Point?
Jesus!!!!!!
Who's Lord over Mississippi?
Jesus!!!!!!
Who's Lord over all bald–headed men?
Jesus!!!! [With this, many in the crowd laugh.]
Amen! And the Lord over men that have hair?
Jesus!!! [Smiles now break out across the crowd.]

Moments later, Reverend Cummings steps back up to the microphone. He enjoins the crowd to take personal responsibility for the sin of racism, to seek redemption, and to demonstrate our spirit of reconciliation with one another. Here he borrows a page from the Promise Keepers, an evangelical men's movement committed to promoting racial reconciliation among Christian men (Bartkowski 2002).[2] As it happens, Reverend Cummings sports a Promise Keepers polo shirt that has become fully drenched with his sweat in the noonday sun. Telling us that we personally need to be forgiven for our sins of prejudice and racism, he urges us: "Find someone who is not your own color. Put your arms around them and say, 'Forgive me. I want to be healed. I want to be made better.'" As the crowd follows suit, members of the crowd mill through the park and begin embracing one another—black to white, white to black—while trading words of contrition and forgiveness.

With that, Reverend Cummings tells everyone that we will conclude with a blessing of the food and a benediction that will serve as our closing prayer. After these prayers are offered, he tells us that this "is when the *real ministry* starts." He encourages us to form partnerships with people that we have met today and to keep those relationships alive throughout the coming year until we meet in the park next summer for Jesus Day again. "It's when you can really reach out from your heart to other people that are here so you can walk together throughout this year into next year when we will fill up the whole park. So, we can make a day on earth look like a day in heaven. And it will be what Jesus said it ought to be." As small groups form, we all head up the hill. Parkgoers of all kinds picnic together. After sharing the meal, some of the adults lend their assistance to the relief workers. Together, they distribute bags of food on the spot and ferry sacks to nearby vehicles. The children enjoy a puppet show. The real ministry had begun. We had put feet on our prayers—at least for today.

Conclusion

In this chapter, we examined faith–based poverty relief undertaken outside the congregational setting. Specifically, we highlighted the place of hunger relief and community outreach in the planning and execution of the March for Jesus, a one–day event staged locally in Starkville and simultaneously throughout the world on the Saturday preceding Pentecost Sunday. In rendering this portrait of "Jesus Day," as it is commonly called by its organizers and marchers, we compared the street–level benevolence undertaken here with the everyday congregational relief discussed in the preceding chapters. We also offered this snapshot of revivalistic relief to highlight the circumstances under which congregations work together to provide aid to disadvantaged persons in the local community.

It is noteworthy that many American Christians, and Jesus Day marchers throughout the world, stage the March for Jesus in their local communities on the day before Pentecost Sunday. On Pentecost, Christians celebrate the day in which Jesus Christ's original followers (the Apostles) received the Holy Ghost to keep his spirit alive in them after he had left the earth. The story of the original Pentecost reported in the Bible's second chapter of Acts of the Apostles recounts how, upon receiving the Holy Ghost, the Apostles quickly converted thousands of people to the nascent Christian church. Despite the fact that these new believers shared neither national heritage nor language in common, they became one in their newfound faith in Christ. In fact, the biblical account asserts that the new converts all sold their possessions and gave the money to the poor. As the story goes, the Apostles were able to accomplish this miraculous mass conversion because the Holy Ghost manifests itself through extraordinary gifts such as the ability to heal, prophesy, and speak in tongues among those who receive it.

As recounted here, the sharing of spiritual gifts through community outreach and material benevolence is now a central feature of Jesus Day. For the 1999 event, organizers decided to refocus the March for Jesus so that it included not only public worship but street–level displays of religious benevolence—namely, hunger relief. As pointed out by Reverend Cummings, one of the event's local organizers, ministry on Jesus Day is decidedly different than the religious gift–giving that takes place during Christmas. The seasonal character of Christmastime benevolence does not recognize or address the stubborn, year–round persistence of need among those who are most disadvantaged. For residents whose need knows no season, holiday food baskets and angel trees are little more than a "band–aid" on a festering wound. What's more, Christmastime gift–giving often takes the form of mutual aid. Because such relief is provided to fellow church members who are in need, it insulates Christians from uncomfortable confrontations with those outside their own congregational circles.

By contrast, the March for Jesus draws directly on the untamed spirit of the Pentecost. Jesus Day aims to move beyond seasonal giving by creating long–term relationships between the privileged and the needy. These "care groups" are designed to be sustained throughout the year, as leaders urge marchers to "walk together" in compassionate ministry from one Jesus Day to the next. Moreover, the March for Jesus takes Christian unity and collaborative outreach as its explicit goals. Both the Jesus Day march and the ministry in the park are designed to bridge boundaries rooted in denomination, race, class, and neighborhood segregation.

A great deal of the open–air preaching at King Park on Jesus Day focused on these issues, as did much of the benevolence work undertaken there. Pastor Hogan, for example, spoke explicitly of racist practices as a sin and chided contemporary attachment to the Confederate flag as idolatry, thereby implying that there is a direct contradiction between Christian living and Southern nostalgia for the Confederacy. Later, in his Jesus cheerleading, he humorously implied that differences in race and culture are as insignificant as those between bald–headed men and those who have hair—Jesus is Lord over all. This humorous reference evoked laughter with redemptive power while forging a sense of shared fellowship among the black and white Christians assembled in the park that day.

So, as they cooperate to carry off this event, Mississippi churches collaboratively redefine themselves relative to their past while imagining futures that have yet to coalesce. Local ministers critically engage the looming shadow of the Old South, and pray for a future marked by sanctification and revival. In this way, the March for Jesus is a vehicle by which congregations collectively confront and seek to transform the legacies for which Mississippi is notorious—poverty and racism. And in seeking to overcome denominational divisions, these congregations strive to address fundamental questions facing them all—those concerning the substance of religious identity, appropriate relations among Christians of different stripes, and the role of religious believers in remaking the local histories they have inherited from previous generations.

Of course, the 1999 March for Jesus must be understood within a historical context that is itself undergoing rapid change. It is likely no coincidence that the March for Jesus was refocused on religious benevolence and community outreach just as debates about charitable choice rose to the forefront of American politics. In many respects, the March for Jesus provides a public forum through which Christian groups across the country can dramatize their concern for the disadvantaged and demonstrate an ability to work across social boundaries for the betterment of their local communities. Critics of charitable choice have raised questions about denominational rivalries and racial divisions that might be exacerbated by the mad rush for public funds the policy might incite. But events such as the March for Jesus—in which congregations collaborate across denominational, racial, and economic lines—serve as a forceful rejoinder to such criticisms. As a public performance, Jesus Day makes a strong statement about the resolve of Christian denominations to work together in providing for the material needs of the least of God's children.

In these respects, the march offers local Christians a mountaintop experience. On Jesus Day, Mississippi's racist history and entrenched denominationalism are at once repudiated for their evil and embraced as a profound opportunity for God to work the most compelling miracle of all—one in which the last can truly become the first. Buoyed by this mountaintop view, local religious leaders argue that Mississippi—notorious for lagging behind all other states in progressive causes—can emerge as the nation's leader in eradicating racial inequality, denominational division, and economic disparity. From this vantage point, the ground at the foot of the cross is indeed level.

Yet, exhilarating as mountaintop views can be, climbing and descending mountains are treacherous endeavors. Jesus Day is a liminal event whose power resides in turning everyday life upside down and inside out. This is a day when pedestrians take back the streets through which they march; when Christ's followers blare evangelical tunes at their neighbors; when pastors of various denominations pray alongside one another; and when Christians of different colors tearfully embrace and forgive one another in the park. Mirroring the forceful reentry of evangelical Christians into the American public sphere during the 1980s, the March for Jesus takes Christ–centered worship outside the four walls of the traditional church. But the formidable structures that the marchers seek to scale—racism, denominationalism, classism, and the everyday practices of segregation inside and outside the church—are not so easily trampled underfoot. As the March for Jesus organizers readily concede, the greatest challenge is to take the new sensibilities from the mountaintop of Jesus Day down into the valley of the believer's everyday life.

Moreover, although Jesus Day is designed to transgress social boundaries, the very nature of this Christian event excludes members of many faith communities. How might Jewish residents of downtown Starkville might react upon hearing boisterous Jesus Day marchers flanked by loudly amplified Christian songs and repetitive chanting of "Jesus! Lord of all" on this particular Saturday (read, Sabbath day)? Jesus Day leaders wish to move the Christian church beyond denomination, culture, and class while exclaiming that "we have gathered" from "every denomination" and "all racial groups." Yet these very claims to inclusiveness efface the absence of some on Jesus Day—most notably, those from faith traditions for whom Jesus is *not* Lord, and those who stand outside the binary racial discourse that is so prominent in American society. Inasmuch as these discourses divide populations into Christian/non–Christian and white/nonwhite, they marginalize the religious convictions of Muslims, Hindus, Buddhists, and Jews and obscure the social experiences of American Arabs, Asians, and Hispanics. Large and inclusive circles are indeed drawn during the March for Jesus to foster interdenominational collaboration and antiracist activism. But other, more exclusive circles are simultaneously drawn by the very performance of Jesus Day at the center of a culturally diverse town. These circles reinscribe social cleavages, particularly those between Christians and non–Christians. Interdenominational initiatives can reinforce interfaith boundaries.

8

Charitable Choice
Promise and Peril in the Post–Welfare Era

Our volume has scrutinized the prospects for charitable choice through the lens of faith–based poverty relief in east central Mississippi. The substantive portion of our volume drew on in–depth interviews collected from a diverse sample of local pastors, as well as ethnographic data culled from five area congregations with active social service programs. We also explored street–level benevolence undertaken collaboratively by local Christian churches at the Golden Triangle Region March for Jesus. Throughout, we have been especially attentive to the influence of racial asymmetries, denominational cleavages, and regional culture on religious benevolence. Readers might justifiably ask what meaningful insights about faith–based poverty relief and charitable choice can be gleaned from an intensive examination of religious benevolence in small–town Mississippi. What, in general, do we learn about faith–based initiatives from a study with such a pointed focus? In our view, we learn plenty.

We have argued that Mississippi is the ideal locale in which to study religion, race, and poverty. Mississippi led the nation in forming church–state partnerships through its Faith & Families program two years prior to the passage of federal welfare reform in 1996. There is also entrenched poverty and a profound commitment to religion in the state. Mississippi is by most measures the nation's poorest state, and is arguably the buckle of the Bible Belt. A state known for its history of racialized oppression and violence, Mississippi is widely considered the "most Southern place on earth" (Cobb 1992). At the same time, Mississippi was also the site of important civil rights activism during the 1960s. Many of the lesser–known grassroots organizers who made the movement possible were local Mississippians who first cultivated traditions of resistance in their homes, churches, and local communities

(Marsh 1997; Payne 1995). Hence, the tendency to view the South as a cultural backwater is belied by the advancement of many local initiatives—from civil rights to charitable choice—that ultimately became national policy. The ideological underpinnings of welfare reform—personal responsibility, states' rights, and local empowerment—have long been defining elements of Mississippi culture (Breaux, Duncan, Keller, and Morris 1998). In many respects, it is fair to say that the seeds of welfare reform—and even those of charitable choice—were initially sewn in Mississippi.

Consequently, the insights generated from our study should not be dismissed simply as artifacts of social and religious life distinctive only to Mississippi. Mississippi does not have a monopoly on economic and racial inequality. These forms of stratification are present throughout the United States. Throughout America, as many sociologists of religion regularly point out, Sunday morning is the most segregated time of any given week. And, of course, there are other parts of the country—the Midwest, Mountain West, and much of the South—that evince a strong commitment to conservative Christianity. Although the Bible Belt is marked by the dominance of Southern Baptists, deeply held religious convictions inform the public culture of many local communities throughout the United States. In short, although our investigation focuses pointedly on religious benevolence in Mississippi, our findings clearly illuminate broader structures—including congregational, denominational, and racial dynamics—that are central features of contemporary American culture.

In this concluding chapter of our volume, then, we summarize the core insights that emerge from our study and discuss their broader implications. We do so with attention to three key issues. First, we weigh the relative merits of the poverty relief strategies through which congregations engage in benevolence work. We argue that each of the four poverty relief strategies utilized by religious congregations is marked by advantages and limitations. These same prospects and pitfalls are likely to be manifested regardless of the social context within which such congregational benevolence strategies are employed. Next, we explore the influence of faith–based social capital on religious service provision. We discuss how religious congregations cultivate social capital by engaging collectively in boundary work, and highlight a key paradox associated with this process. The cultural boundaries used to create faith–based social capital are at once integrative and exclusionary. Finally, we discuss the relationship between structural asymmetries and faith–based service provision in the post–welfare era. In particular, we evaluate the prospects for transforming racial hierarchies through faith–based poverty relief and the expansion of charitable choice partnerships. When treating each of these issues, we remain sensitive to both the promise and the peril of charitable choice (Bane and Coffin 2000). Hence, we articulate neither a naive acceptance nor a wholesale rejection of charitable choice. Instead, we complicate the broad–brushed portraits of American religious benevolence often articulated in social debates over charitable choice by attending to the nuances and contradictions of faith–based poverty relief.

Congregational Poverty Relief: Holistic Ministry and Benevolence Strategies

Like many of the quarter–million or so congregations throughout the United States, the religious communities featured in our study trumpet the merits of providing holistic relief to the poor. Indeed, terms like "holistic" and "whole person ministry" were used by many pastors and program volunteers who described for us the work they do. At its most basic level, congregational ministry is designed to address both the material and spiritual needs of the poor. Often, public assistance programs and state welfare policies serve as a foil for holistic ministry. One minister succinctly stated that the focus of his church is on "ministry, not programs." Others called attention to benevolence work—including a personal grooming service for the imprisoned and a mobile "pickup truck ministry" for Hispanic migrant workers—that fall well outside the scope of traditional government programs. In this way, religious leaders seek to redefine the terms by which "faith–based social services" are commonly conceived by politicians and pundits.

Likewise, most leaders define spiritual needs quite broadly to include explicitly religious forms of social support, along with an attunement to psychological and emotional needs. Congregations typically offer material relief interlaced with less tangible forms of aid such as counseling, prayer, and social support. Beyond this broad and pervasive commitment to holistic ministry, however, religious communities in our study adopted particular strategies for undertaking poverty relief. In chapter 3, we discussed four congregational relief strategies in detail—intensive benevolence, intermittent relief, parachurch collaborations, and distant missions. In what follows, we examine their broader implications and evaluate each in light of the others.

First, intensive benevolence fosters sustained interpersonal contact between local congregants and the poor. Intensive benevolence is manifested in congregations that have active on–site food pantries—often in conjunction with a hot meal program. Other congregations utilizing this strategy offer weekday child care, sponsor jail ministry programs, provide work referral networks, and offer drug and marital counseling on a regular basis. Whatever its form, intensive benevolence aims to build sustained, meaningful relationships between the providers and recipients of congregational relief services. One pastor whose congregation opts for intensive food assistance referred to this approach as "incarnational ministry," and many others used terms that dovetail with this portrayal.

Hence, congregations that are engaged in intensive benevolence value not only the quantity of services offered but their quality as well. The fresh, home–cooked food served through faith–based hot meal programs expresses compassion and concern for the poor in a way that prefabricated canned and dry food alone cannot. This is not to say that canned and dry food is an inferior form of faith–based food assistance, because such goods can be used over a long period of time. However, given the cultural significance of the home–cooked meal, hot food personalizes faith–based hunger relief while building social bonds and emotional attachments between aid providers and recipients. Thus, intensive benevolence programs offer services that are impressive in terms of both their quantity and quality. Because intensive benevolence entails the provision of sustained relief, it can help to address persistent forms of poverty. At the same time, this poverty relief strategy can build enduring relationships of trust between congregants and the poor—creating a space where compassion toward the disadvantaged trumps the judgment of the poor. However, because such programs require a great deal of human and material resources, they generally do not thrive at congregations where donations are scarce and volunteer staff are in short supply.

Some congregations that are already engaged in intensive benevolence would no doubt be able to expand their service offerings with an infusion of public funds. As discussed in chapter 4, River Road United Methodist Church was in the process of starting a child care center, but had to abandon the effort because it could not muster the front–end resources needed to meet the state's compliance standards for such facilities. In cases such as these, charitable choice partnerships could make it possible for congregations to overcome the sizable start–up costs associated with the launching of some programs. Given the large quantity of foodstuffs needed to engage in intensive food assistance, several congregations in our sample are already partnering with the government—specifically, the USDA–supported Mississippi Food Network—by purchasing publicly subsidized food at a discount rate. But because public–private partnerships require participating organizations to collect household and personal information from program users, congregations engaged in intensive benevolence take steps to avert the bureaucratic cast that might otherwise result from such data collection procedures. Several congregations structure their food programs to minimize queuing—that is, waiting in line—by expediting the collection and processing of such information. In many cases, such congregations also provide comfort foods, such as gourmet bread and chocolates, beyond the bare necessities. Several also show sensitivity toward dietary restrictions by preparing special sacks for those with high blood pressure, diabetes, and other physical conditions.

As discussed in chapter 3, Hopewell Church of God enlists such tactics, and purposefully provides hot meals in the comfortable climes of its Compassion Pantry. Each of the two dozen large circular dinner tables in Hopewell's pantry is adorned with decorative tablecloths and flower centerpieces to create a homey atmosphere. Here again, then, quantity and quality are carefully balanced. With the passage of charitable choice, religious organizations that practice intensive benevolence and vie successfully for state funds are likely to engage in a range of creative service delivery tactics that "bargain with bureaucracy" by balancing compassionate ministry with the data–collection procedures and program performance measures mandated by the government.

A second aid–provision strategy commonly utilized by local congregations is intermittent relief. This strategy is employed by congregations that provide direct relief to the poor, but do so over a bounded period of time. This benevolence strategy assumes a wide variety of forms. The provision of holiday food baskets to needy families during the Christmas season is one of the most pervasive forms of intermittent relief, as are the short–term adopt–a–family initiatives common during the winter holidays. Congregations that employ frequency–of–use restrictions in their food pantry programs by imposing a monthslong waiting period on recipients also provide intermittent assistance. Mutual aid—that is, relief provided by congregants to fellow members—most often takes the form of intermittent relief. When congregants are victims of a house fire, lack burial insurance, or incur a large medical bill, they can often count on their coreligionists to see them through these discrete crisis points in their lives.

Given its bounded time frame, less volunteer support and fewer material resources are needed to undertake intermittent poverty relief. For some congregations, economies of scale figure prominently in their support of intermittent relief. Several Christian ministers stated quite forthrightly that their congregants would not support more sustained benevolence work than that done on an intermittent basis through mutual aid or during the Christmas holidays. Among congregations with many dual–income couples and few retirees, religious leaders often noted the time constraints faced by their members. Several others pointed to a lack of material resources in their congregations, while a few noted their members' prior reluctance to engage in more expansive service programs.

This is not to say that intermittent relief is dominated by stinginess, self–interest, or a desire to provide relief only in ways that are convenient. Many congregations pair the provision of intermittent relief with other benevolence strategies. And there is a great deal of good that is done in the name of intermittent relief. Thanksgiving Day dinners feed the hungry. Revival–based clothing drives assist children in need. New parents have dinners delivered to their homes during the difficult time of early postpartum. The homeless are given short–term shelter in local hotels at church expense. And a family whose primary wage earner takes ill for a time can be seen through the economic shortfall such misfortune brings.

Yet in many congregations intermittent relief overwhelmingly takes the form of mutual aid. Why is this the case? If the aid seeker is situated squarely within a congregation's social networks, bedeviling problems of trust (that is to say, questions about the deservingness of the solicitor and the responsible use of aid) are solved. However, when intermittent relief is sought by nonmembers, such problems are not so easily resolved. Given their limited resources and fears of being exploited by "abusers" of the system, many congregations engaged in intermittent relief develop screening mechanisms to judge the worthiness of nonmember aid solicitations.

As demonstrated quite clearly in chapters 4 to 6, however, such screening mechanisms—and even the rank ordering of criteria that comprise them—vary dramatically from one congregational context to the next. Some ministers prefer to evaluate requests for relief at their church office, often in tandem with other pastors or congregants in their faith community. A few stand in the shadow of the nineteenth–century scientific charity movement by engaging in home visitation—that is, traveling to the aid solicitor's place of residence to inspect household food supplies, evaluate lifestyle habits, and ensure that children are actually present in the home before providing relief. Several congregations have even set up innovative "church check" programs with local grocers who can themselves be trusted to scrutinize the purchases of relief recipients at checkout lines to ensure compliance with program rules.

It is noteworthy that when pastors at such congregations discuss their screening procedures, dramatic tales of abuse commonly follow. Those that we heard included the food request of a cigarette–smoking mother who had the bad judgment to purchase brand–name Coke rather than generic cola; the attempted purchase of candy bars and other extravagances with church checks at the local grocery store; the craftiness of skilled abusers who made up to eighty thousand dollars per year "living off" local churches; and the unscrupulous actions of a man who tried to sell church program laundry detergent as cocaine. Whether factual narratives or far–fetched yarns, such tales are always memorable. And while the specifics of these stories vary, the overriding motif within these discursive representations of abuse is invariably the same. All abuse narratives underscore the need for screening, a practice typically described in more delicate terms such as "taking care," or exercising "judgment" and "discernment." Most importantly, screening procedures and evaluative criteria that would appear to be objective and commonsensical to those who create them are often shot through with assumptions about class, race, gender, and family propriety, as well as "appropriate" consumption habits. In a word, they are inflected by culture.

This is not to say that all forms of intermittent relief are characterized by the rigorous screening and surveillance of the poor. Much intermittent relief, particularly that offered during the winter holiday season, is not an exercise in moral policing. A great deal of these initiatives are genuinely motivated by compassion and are offered without condition. But where screening for intermittent relief is concerned, there is often no escaping the pernicious power of cultural distinction and the taken–for–granted norms of propriety it assumes. Several pastors whose congregations engage in intensive benevolence spoke out against such practices. When the

March for Jesus organizer, Reverend Cummings, asserts that "there's more to life than Christmas Day," he is at once critiquing the free–spirited benevolence binging that takes place *only* during the holiday season and its more cautious counterpart—means–tested forms of intermittent relief that are common during the rest of the year.

A third poverty relief strategy utilized by many congregations entails collaborative benevolence work under the auspices of parachurch initiatives. Many congregations in our sample couple this relief–provision strategy with intensive benevolence, intermittent relief, or distant mission trips. Quite commonly, large resource–rich congregations provide financial support to underwrite the services of parachurch agencies, while small resource–poor congregations rely on such organizations to keep from exhausting their meager benevolence funds. Participating congregations of all sizes periodically hold food and clothing drives to replenish the resources of parachurch agencies, and some offer volunteer support. In this respect, parachurch organizations can effectively redistribute the material resources of faith communities and promote a form of social leveling. Apart from this redeeming characteristic of parachurch agencies, several pastors are quick to recount the meaningful interdenominational relationships that are often forged through such umbrella organizations. Because this relief strategy facilitates collaboration among local religious communities, parachurch benevolence work can generate new forms of connectedness among congregations and denominations whose members would otherwise remain unacquainted with one another.

Many pastors who strongly prefer parachurch relief praise its efficiency and champion the one–stop centralization provided by parachurch agencies. These same ministers express anxiety over door–to–door relief requests by unscrupulous aid solicitors, and see centralized disbursement through parachurch organizations as the solution to solicitations about which they are wary. In fact, one local ministerial association was initially formed as a parachurch entity with precisely this goal in mind—namely, to coordinate the benevolence work of local congregations so they could ferret out door–to–door seekers of aid.

Despite the apparent merits of social leveling and interdenominational bridging achieved through parachurch initiatives, there is an inherent limitation associated with this relief–provision strategy. Because parachurch agencies often serve as a liaison between local congregants and the poor, they can reinforce social distance between aid providers and relief recipients. In some cases, the creation of such organizational barriers may keep poverty at a comfortable distance from privileged churchgoers. If this poverty relief strategy is used in the absence of any other, the providers and recipients of benevolence may never meet in person. Social distance can indeed reinforce the notion that "poverty," "hunger," and "the poor" are abstract concepts divorced from the everyday experiences of privileged churchgoers.

Finally, several congregations utilize a poverty relief strategy we call distant missions. By sponsoring these pilgrimages of relief provision, congregations enable their members to travel to a distant locale to undertake relief work that is at once intensive in character and limited in duration. The destinations of such ventures vary. Distant missions most frequently entail traveling to another town or state—the Mississippi Delta, inner–city Memphis, or rural Appalachia. A few congregations coordinate mission trips to countries outside the United States, including relief shelters in Central America. Such mission fields, at once terribly impoverished and culturally exotic, are attractive only to the hardiest of sojourners. Whatever their destination, mission trips are typically planned for a predetermined period of time, ranging from a long weekend to two weeks in the field.

While in the mission field, congregants are immersed in poverty relief of various sorts—providing food in a soup kitchen, constructing a relief shelter, or renovating dilapidated housing. This relief strategy often challenges and transforms congregants' preconceptions about hunger and poverty with direct hands–on exposure to economic deprivation. Distant mission teams often develop a heartfelt sense of togetherness by undertaking collaborative relief work and a deep trust in one another because they commonly live in "primitive" conditions during their sojourn. Invariably, mission teams emerge from the field with vivid memories of lived poverty and a deep sense of camaraderie. They commonly recount folklore from the field at mission team gatherings subsequent to their trip.

The power of distant missions stems in large part from the timeworn practice of religious pilgrimage. In religious parlance, the pilgrim is a believer who intentionally travels away from his or her home environment. Having been thrust into unfamiliar and uncomfortable surroundings, the pilgrim emerges from the sojourn transformed by a revivified sense of religious mission and spiritual conviction. Heartfelt testimonials from many area congregants who have participated in distant missions give credence to the profound personal transformations that can occur on such pilgrimages. And because of the coordinated team effort often exhibited in the mission field, there is reason to believe that distant missions effect discernible transformations in the communities that receive these sojourners. However, given the distant locales and bounded time periods around which such mission trips are centered, this strategy of relief provision risks leaving such missionaries with the idea that genuine poverty is far removed from the local scene rather than right in their own backyard.

Congregational Relief and the Subtleties of Social Capital

Our study of faith–based poverty relief has been informed by social capital theory. Given the dominance of this perspective in social research and the sociology of religion, it is worth evaluating this theory through the lens of our ethnography. As discussed in chapter 1, social capital is conceptualized as networks, norms, and trust that foster cohesion within groups (bonding) and connectedness among them (bridging) (Putnam 2000). Our investigation highlights both the advantages and limitations of social capital theory as a means of understanding the contours and motives of religious benevolence.

To its credit, social capital theory highlights the various dimensions of congregational connectedness that are necessary to undertake poverty relief. Social capital theorists conceive of networks as durable relationships through which social groups—large and small—are formed. We have shown that religious networks dedicated to poverty relief come in many forms, including congregations, Sunday school classes, and distant mission teams, as well as parachurch and denominational relief agencies. Norms, the second component of social capital, are the cultural rules that govern social interaction within and among groups. Where faith–based poverty relief is concerned, such rules commonly encourage the stepping up of benevolence work during the winter holidays, or mandate the application of specific congregational procedures to field aid solicitations. Even liminal relief work conducted through the auspices of distant missions is rule–governed. Mission teams are typically led by seasoned members who have served on a number of missions themselves. And particular teams develop thumbnail rules governing the appropriateness of fine dining and the use of communal bathing facilities in the mission field.

Trust, the third dimension of social capital, is forged through accountability structures that enforce standards of reciprocity and fairness when resources are exchanged. In the language of social capital, reciprocity and fairness manage the "risk" associated with any "investment" in social relationships. Trust therefore minimizes potential "transaction costs" and provides "insurance" that individuals will receive an appreciable "return" on their investment of time, energy, and material resources in the pursuit of group goals. The screening of aid solicitations through home visitation or reference checks reflects an attempt to manage risk in the absence of existing social networks (a "low–trust" environment), whereas the provision of mutual aid with no apparent strings attached is more common within durable networks of exchange (a "high–trust" environment). Parachurch agencies that maintain records on the contribution of resources (investment) by area congregations while tracking the receipt of relief (divestment) by aid seekers serve as liaison managers of risk between religious organizations and the poor. Given these illuminating findings, our study is enhanced by social capital theory and is informed by scholarship that has identified the diverse forms of social capital produced by religious collectivities (Ammerman 1997; Baggett 2001; Cnaan and DiIulio 2002; Putnam 2000). Our unique contribution is found in demonstrating how religious networks, norms, and trust mechanisms combine to influence the practice of faith–based poverty relief.

Our use of social capital theory, however, should not be interpreted as a blanket endorsement of this perspective. Indeed, our study provides several correctives to this widely popular theoretical perspective. First, the conceptual framework of social capital risks reducing congregational benevolence to a self–interested entrepreneurial endeavor by imposing an etic (or outsider) interpretive framework on faith–based poverty relief.[1] In privileging economistic constructs such as self–interest and utility maximization—along with metaphors of investment, insurance, and transaction costs—social capital theory is squarely at odds with the compassion and altruism that many religious persons say is their primary motivation for relief work. Of course, we have demonstrated here that faith–based poverty relief is not a wholly compassionate and altruistic enterprise. But neither is it a practice in which economizing efficiency is the paramount consideration. Social capital theory lacks a language for analyzing moral motivations for social action—apart from conceptualizing morality as a form of trust and then reducing trust to reciprocity or mutual obligation.

A fine–grained understanding of faith–based poverty relief demonstrates that congregational benevolence is motivated largely (if not primarily) by moral concerns. We have identified various moral underpinnings of religious benevolence, but have focused most pointedly on compassion (caring for others), judgment (doing the right thing), and covenant (divinely ordained responsibilities inherent in human relationships). Religious actions motivated by these moral considerations vary across historical periods (see chapter 2) and congregational contexts (see chapters 3 to 6). These moral frameworks are also acted upon differently in revivalistic movements designed to challenge "organized religion" as it is practiced within the confines of established congregations (see chapter 7). This breathtaking diversity notwithstanding, attention to the moral bases of religious action is central to understanding faith–based approaches to poverty relief (Coffin 2000).

To the degree that charitable choice is predicated on contractual logic—competitive bidding for government funds, service provision to clients, performance–based program evaluations—it runs the risk of obscuring the covenantal impetus and moral bases underlying faith–based poverty relief. Given the opposition to public funding for faith–based organizations expressed in some quarters, the language of contract is undoubtedly the safest and most expedient way to allay fears voiced by critics of charitable choice. In our view, however, the pervasiveness of contractual rhetoric risks undermining substantive democratic discourse in favor of more superficial forms of procedural democracy that are little more than "market populism" (Frank 2000; see also Aune 2002). If moral values are defined broadly to include ethical imperatives that are both religious and secular, both public and private, then morality and the obligations it entails should be part of the debate about charitable choice (Coffin 2000; Hehir 2000). In highlighting the moral underpinnings of faith–based poverty relief, we have sought to call attention to these issues. Yet, in an even broader sense, a spirited discussion of moral issues should be central to the debate over welfare reform itself, rather than being sidelined by the marketplace myopia embedded in the contractual language of competition, outsourcing, privatization, capacity, and performance.

The clash between covenantal and contractual responses to poverty cannot be reduced to mere philosophical differences. This clash of ideologies has real–world implications. Some of the most well–connected congregations in our study have mastered the distinctive jargon and complicated procedures that govern public–private partnerships under welfare reform. Others, including many that count the poor among their membership, clearly have not. Among those in the know, hunger is now called "food insecurity" and welfare recipients are "clients." What's more, religious congregations with connections to the legal community and social work professionals know that they can become incorporated as private service providers by securing "501(c)(3) status." Those with close ties to local universities can readily decode cryptic government–speak with, for example, the ready awareness that "RFP" means "request for proposals." These same congregations can draw on the talents and grant–writing experience of knowledge workers in higher education. Hence, the vocabularies and practices of contractual governance do not ensure fairness. Moreover, the discourse and procedures of contractual governance cannot be reduced, respectively, to linguistic convention and technical proficiency. These subtle but powerful cultural markers distinguish insiders who are intimately familiar with the distinctive contours of contractual governance in post–welfare America from those outside the loop.

Our investigation also underscores a second problem with current conceptualizations of social capital and, more broadly, with contractual approaches to governance (the contemporaneous hegemony of these two frameworks is no accident). The economistic rhetorics of capital and contract fail to interrogate the social asymmetries that mark the landscape of American religion. We have argued that these asymmetries come in a variety of forms—historical legacies, cleavages between denominations and faith traditions, and racial stratification. True enough, religion is an integrative institution that facilitates cohesion and connectedness. However, while taking care to acknowledge the power of religious belonging, we have argued that faith communities are also a site for cultural distinction, exclusionary practices, and the reinforcement of social hierarchies. How can we make sense of this paradox? Far from being a static social object, faith–based social capital is dynamically produced—and, at times, reconfigured—through the myriad forms of boundary work that are undertaken in religious communities (cf. Lamont 1992, 2000). It is the quintessential paradox that religious boundary work—and, hence, faith–based social capital—is both inclusionary and exclusionary, consensual and coercive. Most crucial for our purposes, religious boundary work and the differential stocks of social capital it yields may create uneven opportunities for faith communities in this era of government contracting. Our study suggests that the haphazard expansion of charitable choice could reinforce structured forms of inequality among faith communities while undermining religious pluralism and racial justice. Apart from the stratification mechanisms already mentioned, other inequalities among religious communities might be exacerbated by charitable choice. Some of these are fairly obvious, while others are quite subtle.

As we have noted in chapter 2, the centralized structure and theological moorings of the Catholic Church have contributed to the rise of Catholic Charities as a valuable poverty–fighting ally of the government. The longstanding relationship between Catholic Charities and the government is likely to be a tremendous asset to the Catholic Church as charitable choice opportunities are expanded. While these organizational and historical factors might privilege the Catholic Church in the post–welfare era, they may leave other denominations at a decided disadvantage. Among the congregations in our study, United Methodist churches could find themselves in just such a position. As noted in chapter 4, Methodism has a historical legacy of itinerant ministers who move often and bivocational pastors who, in addition to their pastorship, hold down a regular "day job." Congregations with this organizational structure may find it difficult to compete for government funds with religious organizations headed by professional, full–time clergy who also enjoy the privilege of leading local ministerial boards. It is significant that many ministerial boards and parachurch organizations hold their business meetings during normal workday hours. This seemingly mundane practice has significant implications for religious pluralism. Weekday meeting times preclude representation by congregations (including some Methodists, as well as Muslims and Mormons) that are run by bivocational religious leaders who spend their weekdays working at their day job.

These subtle forms of denominationalism in faith–based poverty relief are compounded by racial and class–based differences among congregations. A large proportion of bivocational ministers in the local area lead black churches whose members have limited economic resources. Given the fact that wealthier congregations can support full–time pastors, one leader of a middle–class black Methodist church explained that she was the only black pastor from her denomination on the community ministerial board (chapter 4). This board, like so many others, tacitly viewed full–time pastorship as the only legitimate model of congregational leadership and structured its organizational activities accordingly. The pastor admonished government officials not to assume that parachurch groups with only full–time clergy are genuinely representative of the broad swath of denominations, racial groups, and social classes in an area. In another case, a prominent Church of God in Christ pastor (chapter 5) discussed how denominational infighting among black Mississippi churches has left them lagging behind their white counterparts in partnering with one another to form parachurch organizations and with other local institutions (such as local banks) to press for economic justice. Here, the tight–knit bonding brought about through what this pastor dubbed "Reformational racism" precludes broad–based bridging across denominational lines. In yet other cases, the racialized contours of faith–based social capital are hardly so subtle. In one of the communities that we studied, there are two separate parachurch organizations. Both these organizations are interdenominational, but the Ministerial Council is composed largely of white churches while the Ministerial Coalition is made up mostly of black churches. Of course, not all communities are marked by such stark racial cleavages, but that is not the point.

The point is that a careful inspection of religious benevolence in Mississippi—and, we suspect, elsewhere—reveals that the inclusionary facets of faith–based social capital are intermeshed with cultural asymmetries. Cohesive social practices that promote bonding and bridging simultaneously serve exclusionary and divisive ends. The very same ties that bind invariably create boundaries that cordon off some groups from others. Given the subtle and contradictory workings of faith–based social capital, the creation of a genuinely level playing field is most difficult to imagine.

Race and Religious Benevolence

Such tensions and contradictions are quite apparent where race is concerned. Our examination of racialized discourses and practices in local faith communities leaves us with a mix of optimism and pessimism concerning charitable choice. Here in Mississippi, and we suspect elsewhere in the nation at large, ethnographic studies of race and religious benevolence yield both success stories and cautionary tales.

In several instances, racialized barriers have been effectively overcome through faith–based poverty relief. The March for Jesus united black and white Christians in pursuit of street–level benevolence (chapter 7), while local Muslims have gained widespread respect for their outreach efforts in the local community (chapter 6). Moreover, several of the pastors featured in our study use their public visibility and the tools of their faith tradition to talk back to racism—both in Mississippi and in America at large. Elder Smith challenged racialized perceptions that paint all welfare recipients as black and reversed the stigma of welfare dependency by arguing that all good Christians recognize their dependence on God (chapter 5). And the adoptive "godparenting" program initiated by Father Dejean, an itinerant Catholic priest in the area, has met with a great deal of success (chapter 6). This program connects Catholics who are American citizens with Hispanic migrants seeking to formalize their immigration status. Among its most noteworthy accomplishments, this initiative has built bridges between the Hispanic congregations and Anglo churches he serves, thereby challenging linguistic and cultural modes of exclusion as well as class and ethnoracial divides.

But success stories that catalog the transformation of such boundaries through faith–based relief work are tempered by cautionary tales that emerge right alongside them. Apart from the racial divisions already discussed in the previous section, the congregational case studies featured in chapters 4 to 6 lend credence to the claim of many pastors that racism and racial segregation are as entrenched within area faith communities as they are in other local institutions. Among the few religious leaders who denied the existence of racism within Mississippi congregations, one waxed nostalgic about the merits of white–to–black benevolence on plantations in the Old South (chapter 5). And, of course, the fact that the local Islamic community needed to go to court to secure a permit to build its mosque—where it was then proved that neighborhood churches were common—says a great deal about the prejudice initially faced by this multihued religious community (chapter 6).

Despite the many successes of Father Dejean's Catholic godparenting program, the adoption of migrant Hispanics by well–off whites ran up against the durable social hierarchies of race and nationality. Privileged Catholic families are prone to adopt interracial couples where "she's American, he's Hispanic, and there is a baby or two already." Moreover, Father Dejean admits that white sponsors of Hispanic families can easily misinterpret the initiative as a cultural exchange program. Hence, the exoticness of godparenting across racial lines can fetishize the program—reducing it to an exercise in feigned multiculturalism—without challenging the deeper social hierarchies that keep Hispanics defined as "other."

Finally, the March for Jesus, while exemplifying an impressive determination among Protestant pastors to transcend the history of racism, also reproduced other forms of cultural exclusion (chapter 7). Jesus Day, as the march was dubbed, took nothing less than the transcendence of racial, ethnic, denominational, and geographical boundaries as its goal. However, members of non–Christian faith communities—including Muslims, Hindus, Buddhists, and Jews—were not included in this explicitly Christian collaboration in street–level benevolence. Not coincidentally, many members of non–Christian faith communities in the local area are people of color—Arabs, South Asians, Africans, Malaysians, Jews, and East Asians. Their exclusion from such explicitly antiracist events can unwittingly reinforce the binary matrix of American race relations (white-nonwhite) while effacing the experiences of those who are neither white nor African American.

If events billed as communitywide demonstrations and relief agencies portrayed as broadly representative organizations are going to realize their potential to build alliances among faith communities, people of color, and the poor, then serious consideration needs to be given to how religion and race are defined—and by whom they are defined—in local areas. Interdenominational movements and parachurch initiatives that take poverty relief as their goal are at once inclusive (integrating Christians) and exclusive (marking those affiliated with non–Christian faith traditions as other). After September 11, 2001, it is all the more important to draw distinctions between interdenominational and interfaith religious fellowships dedicated to poverty relief and community outreach. The former represents Christian ecumenism while the latter, spanning non–Christian and Christian faith traditions, is more broadly inclusive. In the wake of September 11, interfaith movements may have more potential to counter the harassment and racialized violence aimed at Arabs and Muslims—and that directed at persons who, in the eyes of many Americans, resembled them (including Hindus, Sikhs, and Hispanics mistaken for Arabs and Muslims).

Our portrait of race and religious benevolence therefore complicates romantic images that portray local communities as bastions of social solidarity. It also challenges damning portrayals that vilify rural communities and the South at large as a cultural backwater. A careful inspection of race and religious benevolence in the rural South shows that neither of these broad–brushed portraits is accurate. Lived religion, racialized practices, and the actual work of faith–based benevolence defy such tidy categorizations.

Last Words: Choice Begets Ambivalence

In our interviews with religious leaders and fieldwork in local congregations, we found that many pastors and program volunteers were enthusiastic about expanding their poverty relief initiatives with government monies. But even the most ardent advocates of charitable choice partnerships voiced serious concerns about how these programs might be implemented. Their concerns were informed by their denominational identities, political ideologies, and class location, as well as their positioning in the racial/spatial order. Our in–depth conversations with leaders of many faith communities also reveal that their concerns, critiques, and moral visions are connected through discourses that transcend congregational contexts. Indeed, these pastors are engaged in a call–and–response dialogue with one another, their local culture, and the dominant values of post–welfare America. What is remarkable, given the broad diversity of viewpoints articulated by these pastors, is that all of them must grapple with the ideology of neoliberalism—devolution, new federalism, and choice. Despite the many new "freedoms" attributed to the welfare revolution, the hegemony of these values in post–welfare America is paradoxically not open to choice.

As we have suggested, charitable choice springs from a political discourse steeped in economistic metaphors. This discourse invites faith communities to imagine the world and the work that they do through the lens of the market. Would–be congregants are consumers in the marketplace of American religion, seeking the best religious firms at which to invest their financial and human resources. Similarly, governments that award block grants to nonprofit providers are bound to consider secular and faith–based organizations as worthy adversaries in competitive bidding for service provision contracts. And of course America's poor have not been left out of the welfare revolution. As clients of the state, economically disadvantaged citizens can now consume government services as befits their personal taste—that is, with or without faith.

In the post–welfare era, all of us are implicated in the discourse of choice. Such new freedoms may "unleash innovation," as promoters of neoliberalism charge. However, iour volume has suggested that the rhetoric of choice obscures a more complicated reality. Religious benevolence in Mississippi, like that undertaken throughout much of America, is structured by social milieu. As such, faith–based poverty relief reinforces some social hierarchies even as it transforms others. As elsewhere, religious relief in Mississippi is the product of historical legacies, cultural determinations, and social forces that—while often resisted and sometimes transformed—are conferred more than they are chosen.

Appendix: Milieu and Method

The first portion of this appendix discusses the social context within which the congregations featured in this study are situated. The second portion outlines the research methodology used to conduct our study and provides the questionnaire used to conduct in–depth interviews with local religious leaders.

Social and Religious Ecology of Study Site

The Golden Triangle Region (GTR) connects three Mississippi counties (Oktibbeha, Lowndes, and Clay), and their respective county seats (Starkville, Columbus, and West Point) in east central Mississippi. Columbus is the largest of these communities, with a population of approximately twenty–four thousand residents. Starkville has about eighteen thousand residents, while West Point has a population of just over ten thousand (Mississippi Population Data Sheet 1993). Mississippi is overwhelmingly populated by whites (63 percent) and blacks (36 percent), complemented by very small Asian and Hispanic populations (1 percent nonwhite/nonblack) (Mississippi Population Data Sheet 1993).

Within the Golden Triangle Region, Clay County is the most rural area and has the highest percentage of blacks when compared with its two GTR counterparts. Clay County is 53.3 percent black, whereas Lowndes (37.2 percent black) and Oktibbeha (34.3 percent black) conform more closely to the ethnic composition in the state. As the most rural of the three counties, Clay County is 48 percent farmland. In Lowndes and Oktibbeha counties, 39 percent and 28 percent of their geography is composed of farmland. By way of state–level comparisons, 34 percent of land in Mississippi is used for farming; 53 percent of Mississippians live in rural areas. Oktibbeha County is the site of a large state university (Mississippi State), which has an important effect on the county and provides it with a distinctive local economy and land–use structure. Oktibbeha and Lowndes counties have more robust middle-class households than does Clay County, whose income distribution is skewed toward the very low and very high ends of the income spectrum.

A wide range of statistical indicators underscore the pervasiveness of poverty in Mississippi. The state ranks last among its peers in per capita money income ($16,531) (Statistical Abstract of the United States 1996). Along with several other southern states, Mississippi is among the nation's leaders in food–insecure households (Bickel, Carlson, and Nord 1999; Nord, Jemison, and Bickel 1999; Rowley 2000). Recent data reveal that 14 percent of all households in Mississippi are characterized by food insecurity—compared with a national rate of 9.7 percent food–insecure households and a generally stable rate of 11 percent in the South at large. Mississippi is also among the nation's leaders in the percentage of all families facing persistent hunger (4.2 percent in Mississippi, compared with the national rate of 3.5 percent). Nearly 20 percent of all Mississippians and 32 percent of all children in the state live in poverty (Statistical Abstract of the United States 1996; Kids Count Data Book 1998). About 15 percent of Mississippi children live in extreme poverty. Such youngsters reside in households whose income is less than half the poverty level. This indicator of extreme poverty is significantly greater than the national rate (9 percent) (Kids Count Data Book 1998). Mississippi has the highest child mortality rate in the nation (10.5 deaths per 1,000 live births), often considered to be an important indicator of child well–being and a marker of social inequality (Kids Count Data Book 1998). Mississippi has long led the nation in female–headed families with no spouse present (15.57 percent) (1990 Census data). It is for such reasons that Mississippi is often described as the poorest state in the nation. Although the Golden Triangle Region is not the poorest region in this poorest of states, it closely reflects the general patterns of impoverishment found throughout Mississippi. (Census data analyses supporting this point can be found in Bartkowski and Regis 1999.)

It is perhaps not surprising, then, that Mississippi features one of the highest rates of public assistance use in the country. In 1992 and 1995, respectively, Mississippi led the nation in receipt of public assistance (AFDC and SSI) (11.8 percent) (1995 Statistical Abstract) and in receipt of Food Stamps (19.26 percent) (Statistical Abstract of the United States 1997). Public assistance use rates in both Mississippi and the Golden Triangle Region—which, again, closely parallel one another—often registered at well over twice the national average (see Bartkowski and Regis 1999). Given these unusually high rates of public assistance use, caseload declines of approximately 70 percent in Mississippi (from 1994 to 1999) have exceeded those in most other states. Yet, because scholarship on the job quality and economic security of persons leaving Temporary Assistance for Needy Families is only just surfacing, such dramatic declines make it all the more imperative to understand the dynamics of faith–based service provision in Mississippi and other states boasting such overwhelming "success" in implementing welfare reform.

Religious institutions have long played a central role in Southern culture, and Mississippi is no exception to this general pattern. In rural locales such as the Golden Triangle Region, congregations are the key institution through which local communities define themselves and forge social bonds. Throughout the Golden Triangle Region, congregations—mostly Protestant and, particularly, Baptist and Methodist churches—dot the landscape. On average, Southern Baptists account for well over 40 percent of all church adherents in the Golden Triangle Region, while United Methodists attract over 15 percent of the churchgoing population in this tricounty area (Bradley, Green, Jones, Lynn, and McNeil 1992). Taken together, nearly 40 percent of GTR's total population—that is, both religiously affiliated and unaffiliated residents—identify with one of these two denominations (Bradley et al. 1992). Although both these denominations are predominantly white, United Methodists have several thriving African American congregations in the local area.

When compared with Southern Baptists and United Methodists, all other predominantly white Protestant denominations in these three counties attract meager percentages of the total churchgoing population—typically, under 3 percent of all churchgoers. The Catholic presence is quite weak in Clay and Lowndes counties—attracting under 2 percent of the churchgoing population. Catholic adherence is significantly more robust in Oktibbeha County, where this church claims 7.6 percent of all adherents (Bradley et al. 1992). Given the university nearby and its eclectic mix of non–Protestant churchgoers, the Oktibbeha County Catholic Church has one of the most racially diverse congregations in the local area.

In light of the history of racial oppression throughout much of the South and in Mississippi (see chapter 2 of this volume), black churches in the South are known to foster especially close bonds of collective solidarity and serve many vital social and economic functions for local African American residents (Lincoln and Mamiya 1990). Many black Mississippi churches mobilized African Americans for the Civil Rights Movement. These same churches often sponsored voter registration drives and emphasized the importance of political participation. As a hotbed for political activism, local black churches provided the institutional means through which African American candidates could be nominated for—and, given the support of an organized constituency, elected to—political office. To this day, many African American churches throughout the South—including Mississippi—celebrate their civil rights legacy and continue to provide a forum through which local African Americans strive to advance reformist and radical politics (Lincoln and Mamiya 1990; Marsh 1997).

Black Baptists represent the most formidable African American Protestant denomination in the Golden Triangle Region. Black Baptists, typically affiliated with the National Baptist Convention, account for between 16.6 percent (Oktibbeha County) and 32.5 percent (Clay County) of the total churchgoing population in the Golden Triangle (Bradley et al. 1992). The Church of God in Christ (COGIC), the world's largest Pentecostal denomination, traces its historical origins to early-twentieth–century rural Mississippi. Statewide and regional membership figures on the Church of God in Christ are not readily ascertainable. Worldwide membership in this denomination is estimated to range from 5.5 to 6.5 million adherents (Lindner 2000; Mead 1995), and COGIC has as many as 15,300 churches worldwide served by over 33,500 clergy (Lindner 2000).

Given its Mississippi roots, COGIC continues to enjoy prominence in many Southern states. COGIC is a predominantly black denomination whose original followers were rejected by Black Baptists because of their emphasis on sanctification (holiness) and speaking in tongues (Mead 1995). COGIC churches enjoy a distinguished civil rights legacy in the local region (see Lincoln and Mamiya 1990:224). Although Black Baptists are clearly the numerical majority among local African American churches, several thriving and civically engaged COGIC congregations are present on the local scene as well.

Research Design

Pastors representing thirty different faith communities participated in the in–depth interview portion of our study. (One pastor in our sample served two churches. Consult Bartkowski and Regis 1999 for a review of congregational profile data.) Congregations sampled for this study were selected on the basis of several criteria. First, given the significance of race relations in Mississippi, we sampled religious congregations for racial diversity. In light of racial demographics in Mississippi, our inter-view sample was composed primarily of pastors from predominantly white [n=16] and black [n=11] congregations. We also interviewed reli-gious leaders [n=2] who minister to two very different transnational populations—upwardly mobile Muslims at a local university and disad-vantaged Hispanic migrants—in the surrounding area.

Second, our sample of local religious leaders balances a concern for denominational diversity with a recognition of the predominance of Baptist and Methodist churches in this region of Mississippi. Conse-quently, a substantial proportion of our sample was composed of Baptist [n=9] and Methodist [n=9] congregations. Apart from these leaders, we also interviewed local Catholic priests [n=3]; pastors from the Church of God in Christ (COGIC)[n=2], Presbyterian congregations [n=4](both the theologically conservative PCA and the more theologically liberal PC–USA), a Latter–Day Saints (Mormon) religious leader [n=1], and (as noted) a leader of a local mosque [n=1] that serves Muslim students in a Golden Triangle Region community. Finally, we interviewed leaders from faith communities that vary considerably in membership size (ranging widely from twenty–six to eighteen hundred total members) and that differ in locale (small and midsized towns as well as remote rural areas).

After religious leaders (pastors or experienced congregational officers) completed a preinterview survey, in–depth interviews were conducted with respondents by one or, in some cases, two members of our research team. (Our in–depth interview questionnaire is displayed at the end of this appendix.) To preserve the anonymity of our subjects, pseudonyms have been substituted for the actual names of persons and organizations featured in this study. While specific religious organizations are not iden-tified by name, denominational affiliation has been preserved. These in-terviews, most of which took place in 1998, were conducted using a semistructured format. Semistructured interviewing provides all respondents with the opportunity to answer the same set of questions, but also permits probing outside the scope of the formal interview instrument as needed. Interviews were audiotaped, transcribed, and then analyzed.

Our analysis of over seven hundred pages of interview transcripts was guided by the theoretical issues discussed in chapter 1. Consequently, we were especially attuned to pastors' narratives of poverty relief and the poor, as well as the moral motivations underlying congregational benevolence strategies. Our theoretical approach also sensitized us to pastors' allusions to what we would call social capital—that is, social networks, cultural norms, and trust mechanisms related to faith–based aid provision. Analyses of these transcripts were also guided by a series of sensitizing concepts that emerged from our primary research questions, including pastors' theological views and practical experiences concerning faith–based poverty relief; ministers' understandings of the nature and causes of poverty; religious leaders' appraisals of charitable choice partnerships; and pastoral references to race, cultural difference, and social inequality. Additional themes that emerged during the course of this analysis were noted as well.

In collaboration with two research assistants, the authors also conducted on–site participant–observation research in a select subsample of five congregations—a white United Methodist church; a black Baptist congregation; a white Southern Baptist church; an African American Church of God in Christ congregation; and a white Church of God faith community. Our understanding of faith–based poverty relief efforts undertaken by local congregations was greatly enriched by this fieldwork, which was conducted over a six–month period. Data collected through participant–observation generally included attendance at worship services, observation at mission planning meetings, and participation in congregational service activities. This field research enabled us to observe the planning, execution, and outcomes of faith–based relief programs in action. Participant–observation research also facilitated interaction with a wide range of persons within each of these faith communities, thereby enabling us to compare pastoral viewpoints with those of congregational benevolence workers and laity. Additional field research was conducted outside congregational settings at an area March for Jesus event that focused on establishing relationships between local congregations and the poor. Those field data, complemented by a follow–up interview with the local pastor who coordinated the event, are the subject of chapter 7. In sum, the account articulated in this volume draws on triangulated data to provide a holistic, multidimensional rendering of local faith–based poverty relief efforts.

In–Depth Interview Questionnaire

As noted, we conducted semistructured interviews with pastors representing thirty local faith communities. Interviews were conducted in 1998 and early 1999, prior to the election of George W. Bush to the presidency and before extensive national debates over charitable choice. We adapted the wording of the interview questionnaire to fit the congregational context. The interview questionnaire was structured as follows.

1. To begin, tell me a bit about the history of your congregation and what your congregation stands for.
2. How is your congregation organized? What positions does your congregation have, and how are decisions made in your congregation?
3. What type of social service programs (e.g., outreach, mutual aid, relief or missionary work) does your congregation currently offer? How active are these programs? At whom are they targeted and by whom are they staffed? Is your congregation involved in any community based or interfaith relief programs? Have you heard of Mississippi Faith & Families? If so, what has been your experience with that program?
4. Which of the congregation's outreach or aid programs have been successful and which have not? What factors have contributed to their success or failure?
5. What do you think of government–sponsored public assistance that is currently in place in our society? Do you think congregations might be able to provide aid in ways that the government cannot? How do congregations provide aid differently than that provided by the government? (PROBE: Do congregations provide *different types* of aid? Do congregations use *different means* for delivering assistance to the needy?)
6. Have you heard of the idea that congregations might become more involved in the restructuring of public welfare? What do you think of that idea? What do you think would be the outcome of such a

program? Do you think the members of your congregation would or could support such a program?

7. Suppose your congregation was given a grant from the state to provide additional aid to the needy in the community. What types of aid could your congregation provide with such a grant? How would the congregation use those funds? Who do you think should make decisions concerning how that money is used?

8. What standards do you use when deciding to give aid? Would those standards change if public money were used to expand your aid programs?

9. If welfare services were to be routed through local congregations, do you think attitudes about race or ethnicity would affect the way in which such aid is distributed? Do you think that race currently affects the distribution of aid provided by Mississippi congregations?

10. In deciding to take people off of aid, what rules do you currently apply? Do you think these rules would change if you had additional funds at your disposal to provide aid?

11. Do you think your congregation, or religious congregations in general, can help people get off welfare? Do you think a joint effort among congregations would be effective in seeking this goal?

12. Many people living in poverty are single mothers and their children, as well as the elderly. Do you currently provide aid or services to these types of individuals? If so, how effective have these programs been? Would additional funding enable you to initiate or expand the aid provided to these groups of people?

13. If your congregation were to cooperate with the government in providing welfare services, would you have any concerns about such an arrangement? Would members of your congregation support this arrangement?

14. How will members of your congregation be affected once welfare support is no longer available to current recipients?

15. Suppose an increasing number of nonmembers came to your congregation seeking aid. What do you think would be the reaction of your congregation to these nonmembers' efforts to seek aid?

16. What are your views concerning the separation of church and state? If congregations did play a role in providing welfare services, how might your views about the separation of church and state affect the program?

17. Thinking back over the past several years, what has been the single biggest change in the way you minister to your congregation? What has brought about this change?
18. Do you think that religion is more or less important in this country today than it was twenty years ago?
19. What programs does your congregation offer youth? In what ways, if any, does your congregation minister to the youth in your congregation?
20. Finally, I am curious about your general impressions of religion in America today. What do you think are the most important issues that are influencing religion at the national level? How do you think religious communities should respond to the issues and challenges you have identified?

Notes

1. It is worth noting that Olasky's plan for faith–based welfare reform is informed by an explicitly evangelical Protestant vision of the human condition as fundamentally depraved and in need of moral reform through personal religious conversion. The historical role of evangelical poverty relief efforts is discussed in chapter 2 of this volume.

2. With greater autonomy and choice for states comes increased risk. Under 1996 welfare reform, block grant allocations were not to be raised until 2002 at the earliest. Consequently, states that failed to move poor citizens from temporary assistance into the paid workforce risk facing exhausted welfare coffers for a period of time.

3. The unpopularity of welfare during the 1980s led to the passage of the Family Support Act of 1988. The Family Support Act took initial strides away from an entitlement–based welfare system by requiring recipients with no children under age three to undergo a job training program, to actively seek employment, and to accept a job offer or face losing a portion of their AFDC benefits. Because many employers of low–paid personnel do not offer healthcare coverage, the Family Support Act also mandated that states provide child care and Medicaid funds for the first year of the former recipient's employment. However, as 1996 welfare reform legislation indicates, fears of welfare dependency were not allayed by the Family Support Act.

Notes to Chapter 2

1. In this chapter, we are selective in our use of in–text citations to primary historical sources. To be sure, all consulted sources are cited here; moreover, we are careful to acknowledge the works of authors on whose ideas we draw to support specific arguments. However, readability dictates against long string citations and the repetitive referencing of the same sources within particular sections.

2. Readers interested in more detailed treatments of many themes addressed in this chapter are encouraged to consult the following historical essays and vol-

umes: Beito 2000; Berkowitz and McQuaid 1992; Cnaan 1999: ch. 6; Gamm 2001; Gordon 1994; Hall 2001; Katz 1989, 1995, 1996; J. Schwartz 2000; Skocpol 1992, 2000; Trattner 1999; Wineburg 1993; and Winston 1999. Although we are not historians, we join other scholars (e.g., Bane and Coffin 2000; Skocpol 2000) who have thoughtfully debated many of the assertions offered in Marvin Olasky's (1992) popular work, *The Tragedy of American Compassion.* The arguments advanced here are intended both to provide a context for our empirical investigation in the chapters that follow and to push forward these ongoing debates—with particular attention to the influence of race, denomination, and community locale in the history of American religious benevolence and social welfare policy.

3. The last chapter in Trattner's (1999) outstanding historical volume, *From Poor Law to Welfare State,* describes the most recent efforts at welfare reform and is tellingly entitled "Looking Forward—or Backward?"

NOTES TO CHAPTER 3

1. The "Faith & Families of Mississippi—'What Is it?'" brochure, for example, asked its target population of local pastors pointedly: "WHY DO FAMILIES STAY ON WELFARE?" and quickly followed up:

TO RECEIVE THESE BENEFITS
(BASED ON HOUSEHOLD OF 3 WITH ZERO INCOME)

AFDC	$120.00
FOODSTAMPS	304
HUD (BASED ON APT.)	350
UTILITIES VOUCHER	84
MEDICAID	??????
*TOTAL WITHOUT MEDICAID	$858.00

*MEDICAID BENEFITS ARE BASED ON THE FAMILY'S NEEDS
POSSIBLE BENEFITS AVAILABLE:
- 5 Prescriptions per Person per Month
- 12 Doctor's Visits per Year
- Free Eyeglasses
- Free Dental Work
- Hospital Bills Paid for Mother and Children at 100%
(Based on Per–Diem and Maximums)
(FFM–a:11).

2. These accounts concerning the demise of Mississippi Faith & Families were drawn from contact with government officials whose names are withheld to protect their anonymity.

3. Such fieldwork lasted, on average, six months and typically included participant–observation in congregational service programs, observation of social ministry and program planning meetings, unstructured field interviews with program

volunteers, and worship service attendance. The appendix at the end of this volume discusses the study's research design in greater detail.

4. All pastors and religious organizations discussed throughout this book are identified by pseudonyms to keep their actual identities confidential.

NOTE TO CHAPTER 4

1. Consistent with the case study approach to social research on religious communities (Ammerman 1997; Bartkowski 2001), we do not seek to generalize the findings of this comparative investigation to all United Methodist congregations. Rather, this comparative case study featuring River Road and Green Prairie United Methodist churches highlights the overriding influence of congregational context—despite a shared denominational affiliation—on faith–based relief efforts and pastoral orientations toward charitable choice.

NOTES TO CHAPTER 5

1. Once again, we provide denominational demographics simply to provide contextual data and background information on the affiliated congregations that serve as our case studies. We do not assume that these congregational cases are representative of other churches in their respective denominations. For detailed analyses of various evangelical orientations toward current racial controversies, see the work of Emerson and colleagues (Emerson and Smith 2000; Emerson, Smith, and Sikkink 1999).

2. At the same time, it is also possible that Elder Smith's strong antiwelfare sermons and these startlingly high welfare-to-work success rates have driven long-term welfare recipients—perhaps fewer now due to benefit time limits—away from his church. It is plausible that those who continually "find [themselves] on welfare" feel ostracized by a preacher telling them that such a lifestyle amounts to needing "a handout every day of [their] lives." Such pastoral rhetoric, and the organizational culture it helps to sustain, may discourage long-term welfare recipients from becoming part of the sizable membership in this thriving congregation, thereby producing artificially high welfare-to-work success rates.

3. We credit Bob Wineburg with exploring the connections between devolution and what he calls "devilution" (Wineburg 2001: ch. 1).

NOTES TO CHAPTER 6

1. Although we cannot speak to these Hispanic migrants' motivations for emigrating to the United States, research conducted by Leo Chavez (1998) suggests that many undocumented Mexican migrants are "target earners" who work in the United States to earn a specified sum of money. Contrary to the no-

tion that immigrants enter the United States to start a new life, the migrants in Chaves's work emigrated to accomplish particular tasks back home—for example, to build a house, get married, accumulate starting capital for a small business, or support a family. The accounts provided by Father Dejean certainly resonate with the motivations outlined in Chaves's work.

2. Given the focus of this section, it bears reiterating that our interview with Dr. Hamman took place in 1998, well before the events of September 11, 2001. In the fall of 2001, public reaction to the World Trade Center and Pentagon terrorist attacks resulted in violence directed at many persons mistaken for Muslims or Arabs in a pervasive spate of racial and religious profiling cases.

NOTES TO CHAPTER 7

1. Rick Founds wrote the words and music to "Lord, I Lift Your Name on High." Christian music giant Maranatha! owner of the song's copyright, has popularized it among American evangelicals.

2. For broader treatments of American evangelical perspectives on race relations, see Emerson and Smith (2000); Emerson, Smith, and Sikkink (1999).

NOTES TO CHAPTER 8

1. In anthropological parlance, etic accounts are imposed on cultural groups by outsiders. They are often ethnocentric inasmuch as they show an insensitivity to the stated motivations of the persons whose life experiences are scrutinized by social scientists. Emic accounts take seriously the vocabularies that actors themselves use to describe their own social practices and underlying motivations. The account we provide engages the stated motivations of religious leaders and benevolence workers, while striving to relate their experiences to the theoretical perspectives discussed in chapter 1.

Bibliography

American Civil Liberties Union. 2001. "ACLU Says Bush Initiative Represents Faith–Based Prescription for Discrimination." American Civil Liberties Union Freedom Network. <www.aclu.org/news/2001/n012901a.html>.

Americans United for the Separation of Church and State. 2001. "The Bush 'Faith–Based' Initiative: Why It's Wrong." Washington, D.C.: Americans United for the Separation of Church and State. <www.au.org/press /pre220001.htm>.

Ammerman, Nancy T. 1990. *Baptist Battles: Social Change and Religious Conflict in the Southern Baptist Convention.* New Brunswick: Rutgers University Press.

—— 1994. "Telling Congregational Stories." *Review of Religious Research* 35:289–301.

—— 1997. *Congregation and Community.* New Brunswick: Rutgers University Press.

—— 1998. "Culture and Identity in the Congregation." Pp. 78–104 in *Studying Congregations: A New Handbook*, edited by Nancy T. Ammerman, Jackson W. Carroll, Carl S. Dudley, and William McKinney. Nashville: Abingdon.

—— 2001a. "Doing Good in American Communities: Congregations and Service Organizations Working Together." Hartford Institute for Religion Research. <www.hirr.hartsem.edu>.

—— 2001b. "Still Gathering after All These Years: Congregations in U.S. Cities." Pp. 6–22 in *Can Charitable Choice Work?* edited by Andrew Walsh. Hartford: Leonard E. Greenberg Center for the Study of Religion in Public Life.

Anderson, Benedict. 1991. *Imagined Communities.* New York: Verso.

Aune, James Arnt. 2002. *Selling the Free Market: The Rhetoric of Economic Correctness.* New York: Guilford.

Baer, Hans A., and Merrill Singer. 1992. *African American Religion in the Twentieth Century: Varieties of Protest and Accommodation.* Knoxville: University of Tennessee Press.

Baggett, Jerome P. 2001. *Habitat for Humanity: Building Private Homes, Building Public Religion.* Philadelphia: Temple University Press.

Bane, Mary Jo, and Brent Coffin. 2000. "Introduction." Pp. 1–17 in *Who Will Provide? The Changing Role of Religion in American Social Welfare*, edited by Mary Jo Bane, Brent Coffin, and Ronald Thiemann. Boulder: Westview Press.

Bane, Mary Jo, Brent Coffin, and Ronald Thiemann, eds. 2000. *Who Will Provide? The Changing Role of Religion in American Social Welfare*. Boulder: Westview Press.

Bartkowski, John P. 2001. *Remaking the Godly Marriage: Gender Negotiation in Evangelical Families*. New Brunswick: Rutgers University Press.

——— 2002. "Godly Masculinities: Gender Discourse among the Promise Keepers." *Social Thought and Research* 24:1–35.

Bartkowski, John P., and Helen A. Regis. 1999. *Religious Organizations, Anti–Poverty Relief, and Charitable Choice: A Feasibility Study of Faith–Based Welfare Reform in Mississippi*. Arlington: PricewaterhouseCoopers Endowment for the Business of Government. <www.endowment.pwcglobal.com /pdfs/bartkowski.pdf>.

Becker, Penny Edgell. 1997. "What Is Right? What Is Caring? Moral Logics in Local Religious Life." Pp. 121–145 in *Contemporary American Religion: An Ethnographic Reader*, edited by Penny Edgell Becker and Nancy L. Eiesland. Walnut Creek: Alta Mira Press.

——— 1999. *Congregations in Conflict: Cultural Models of Local Religious Life*. New York: Cambridge University Press.

Becker, Penny Edgell, and Nancy A. Eiesland, eds. 1997. *Contemporary American Religion: An Ethnographic Reader*. Walnut Creek: Alta Mira Press.

Beito, David T. 2000. *From Mutual Aid to the Welfare State: Fraternal Societies and Social Services, 1890–1967*. Chapel Hill: University of North Carolina Press.

Berking, Helmuth. 1999. *Sociology of Giving*. Thousand Oaks: Sage.

Berkowitz, Edward, and Kim McQuaid. 1992. *Creating the Welfare State: The Political Economy of Twentieth–Century Reform* Rev. ed. Lawrence: University of Kansas Press.

Berrien, Jenny, Omar McRoberts, and Christopher Winship. 2000. "Religion and the Boston Miracle: The Effect of Black Ministry on Youth Violence." Pp. 266–285 in *Who Will Provide? The Changing Role of Religion in American Social Welfare*, edited by Mary Jo Bane, Brent Coffin, and Ronald Thiemann. Boulder: Westview Press.

Bickel, Gary, Steven Carlson, and Mark Nord. 1999. "Household Food Security in the United States, 1995–1998 (Advance Report)." Food and Nutrition Service, USDA.

Boston, Rob. 1998. "The 'Charitable Choice' Charade." *Church and State* 51:7–12.

Bourdieu, Pierre. 1984. *Distinction: A Social Critique of the Judgment of Taste*. Cambridge: Harvard University Press.

Bradley, Martin B., Norman M. Green, Jr., Dale E. Jones, Mac Lynn, and Lou McNeil. 1992. *Churches and Church Membership in the United States 1990.* Atlanta: Glenmary Research Center.

Breaux, David A., Christopher M. Duncan, C. Denise Keller, and John C. Morris. 1998. "Blazing the TANF Trail: The Southern Mind and Welfare Reform in Mississippi." *American Review of Politics* 19:175–189.

Bremner, Robert H. 1988. *American Philanthropy* (second edition). Chicago: University of Chicago Press.

Bromley, David, and Bruce Busching. 1988. "Understanding the Structure of Contractual and Covenantal Social Relations: Implications for the Sociology of Religion." *Sociological Analysis* 49:15–32.

Brown, Dorothy M., and Elizabeth McKeown. 1997. *The Poor Belong to Us: Catholic Charities and American Welfare.* Cambridge: Harvard University Press.

Burger, Stephen E. 1996. "New Hope for Gospel Missions? Devil's in the Details." *USA Today,* September 3.

Bush, George W. 2001. "Rallying the Armies of Compassion." January 29. <www.whitehouse.gov/infocus/faith-based>

Cammisa, Anne Marie. 1998. *From Rhetoric to Reform? Welfare Policy in American Politics.* Boulder: Westview Press.

Carlson–Thies, Stanley W., and James W. Skillen, eds. 1996. *Welfare in America: Christian Perspectives on a Policy in Crisis.* Grand Rapids: William B. Eerdmans.

Cavendish, James C. 2000. "Church–Based Community Activism: A Comparison of Black and White Catholic Congregations." *Journal for the Scientific Study of Religion* 39:371–384.

Center for Public Justice. 1994. *A New Vision for Welfare Reform: An Essay in Draft.* Washington, D.C.: Center for Public Justice.

Chavez, Leo. 1998. *Shadowed Lives: Undocumented Immigrants in American Society.* New York: Harcourt Brace.

Chaves, Mark. 1999. "Religious Congregations and Welfare Reform: Who Will Take Advantage of 'Charitable Choice'?" *American Sociological Review* 64:836–846.

——— 2001. "Religious Congregations and Welfare Reform: Assessing the Potential." Pp. 121–139 in *Can Charitable Choice Work?* edited by Andrew Walsh. Hartford: Leonard E. Greenberg Center for the Study of Religion in Public Life.

Chaves, Mark, and Lynne M. Higgins. 1992. "Comparing the Community Involvement of Black and White Congregations." *Journal for the Scientific Study of Religion* 31:425–440.

Cnaan, Ram A., with Robert J. Wineburg and Stephanie C. Boddie. 1999. *The Newer Deal: Social Work and Religion in Partnership.* New York: Columbia University Press.

Cnaan, Ram A., and John J. DiIulio. 2002. *The Invisible Caring Hand: American Congregations and the Provision of Welfare.* New York: NYU Press.

Cobb, James Charles. 1992. *The Most Southern Place on Earth: The Mississippi Delta and the Roots of Regional Identity.* New York: Oxford University Press.

Coffin, Brent. 2000. "Where Religion and Public Values Meet: Who Will Contest?" Pp. 121–143 in *Who Will Provide? The Changing Role of Religion in American Social Welfare,* edited by Mary Jo Bane, Brent Coffin, and Ronald Thiemann. Boulder: Westview Press.

Coleman, James S. 1990. *Foundations of Social Theory.* Cambridge: Belknap Press.

Connolly, Ceci. 1999. "Gore Urges Role for 'Faith–Based' Groups." *Washington Post,* May 25.

Cruikshank, Barbara. 1997. "Welfare Queens: Policing by the Numbers." pp. 113–114 in *Tales of the State: Narrative in Contemporary U.S. Politics and Public Policy,* edited by Sanford F. Schram and Philip T. Neisser. Boulder: Rowman & Littlefield.

Davis, Derek H., and Barry Hankins, eds. 1999. *Welfare Reform and Faith–Based Organizations.* Waco: Baylor University, J. M. Dawson Institute of Church–State Studies.

Denzin, Norman K. 1987. *The Alcoholic Self.* Newbury Park: Sage.

Denzin, Norman K. 1993. *The Alcoholic Society: Addiction and Recovery of the Self.* Piscataway: Transaction Publishers.

DiIulio, John D., Jr. 1997. "In America's Cities: The Lord's Work, the Church, and the 'Civil Society' Sector." *Brookings Review* 15:27–31.

Dudley, Carl S., and David A. Roozen. 2001. *Faith Communities Today: A Report on Religion in the United States Today.* Hartford: Hartford Institute for Religion Research. <www.hirr.hartsem.edu>.

Dunne, Joseph. 1995. "Beyond Sovereignty and Deconstruction: The Storied Self." *Philosophy and Social Criticism* 21:137–157.

Eiesland, Nancy L. 2000. *A Particular Place: Urban Ecology and Religious Restructuring in a Southern Exurb.* New Brunswick: Rutgers University Press.

Eiesland, Nancy L., and R. Stephen Warner. 1998. "Ecology: Seeing the Congregation in Context." Pp. 40–77 in *Studying Congregations: A New Handbook,* edited by Nancy T. Ammerman, Jackson W. Carroll, Carl S. Dudley, and William McKinney. Nashville: Abingdon.

Elizar, Daniel J., ed. 1994. *Covenant in the Nineteenth Century" The Decline of an American Political Tradition.* Boulder: Rowman & Littlefield.

Elizar, Daniel J., ed. 2000. *The Covenant Connection.* Boulder: Lexington.

Emerson, Michael O., and Christian Smith. 2000. *Divided by Faith: Evangelical Religion and the Problem of Race in America.* New York: Oxford University Press.

Emerson, Michael O., Christian Smith, and David Sikkink. 1999. "Equal in Christ, but Not in the World: White Conservative Protestants and Explanations of Black–White Inequality." *Social Problems* 46:398–417.

Eng, Eugenia, and John W. Hatch. 1991. "Networking between Agencies and Black Churches: The Lay Health Advisor Model." *Prevention in Human Services* 10:123–146.

Faith & Families of Mississippi. nd–a. "Faith & Families of Mississippi: 'What Is It?'" Jackson: Faith & Families.

———. nd–b. "From a Life of Dependency to a Life of Self Sufficiency." Jackson: Faith & Families.

Fellmeth, Aaron Xavier. 1996. "Social Capital in the United States and Taiwan: Trust or Rule of Law?" *Development Policy Review* 14:151–171.

Finke, Roger, and Rodney Stark. 1992. *The Churching of America, 1776–1990: Winners and Losers in Our Religious Economy.* New Brunswick: Rutgers University Press.

Frank, Thomas. 2000. *One Market Under God: Extreme Capitalism, Market Populism, and the End of Economic Democracy.* New York: Doubleday.

Fritz, Sara. 1999. "'Charitable Choice' Unites Church, State." *St. Petersburg Times*, June 18.

Fukuyama, Francis. 1995. *Trust: The Social Virtues and the Creation of Prosperity.* New York: Free Press.

Gamm, Gerald. 2001. "After the Urban Exodus: Jews, Protestants, and the Erosion of Catholic Exceptionalism, 1950–2000." Pp. 39–55 in *Can Charitable Choice Work?* edited by Andrew Walsh. Hartford: Leonard E. Greenberg Center for the Study of Religion in Public Life.

Gans, Herbert J. 1995. *The War against the Poor.* New York: Basic Books.

Gilens, Martin. 1999. *Why Americans Hate Welfare: Race, Media, and the Politics of Antipoverty Policy.* Chicago: University of Chicago Press.

Glennon, Fred. 2000. "Blessed Be the Ties That Bind? The Challenge of Charitable Choice to Moral Obligation." *Journal of Church and State* 42:825–843.

Gordon, Linda. 1994. *Pitied but Not Entitled: Single Mothers and the History of Welfare, 1890–1935.* New York: Free Press.

Greeley, Andrew. 1997. "The Other Civic America: Religion and Social Capital." *American Prospect* 32:68–73.

Griener, Gretchen M. 2000. "Charitable Choice and Welfare Reform: Collaboration between State and Local Governments and Faith–Based Organizations." *Welfare Information Network*, Volume 4, Issue 12. <www.welfareinfo.org/issuenotecharitablechoice.htm>.

Hall, Peter Dobkin. 2001. "Historical Perspectives on Religion, Government, and Social Welfare in America." Pp. 78–120 in *Can Charitable Choice Work?* edited by Andrew Walsh. Hartford: Leonard E. Greenberg Center for the Study of Religion in Public Life.

Handler, Joel F., and Yeheskel Hasenfeld. 1991. *The Moral Construction of Poverty: Welfare Reform in America.* Newbury Park: Sage.

Handler, Joel F., and Lucie White, eds. 1999. *Hard Labor: Women and Work in the Post–Welfare Era.* New York: ME Sharpe.

Harris, Fredrick C. 2001. "Black Churches and Civic Traditions: Outreach, Activism, and the Politics of Public Funding of Faith–Based Ministries." Pp. 140–156 in *Can Charitable Choice Work?* edited by Andrew Walsh. Hartford: Leonard E. Greenberg Center for the Study of Religion in Public Life.

Harris, Margaret. 1995. "Quiet Care: Welfare Work and Religious Congregations." *Journal of Social Policy* 24:53–71.

Harris, Margaret. 1996. "'An Inner Group of Willing People': Volunteering in a Religious Context." *Social Policy and Administration* 30:54–68.

Harrison, Erik. 1995a. "Religious Groups in Mississippi Take Poor Folks under Their Wings." *Houston Chronicle,* September 17.

———. 1995b. "Welfare Reform: Mississippi Experiment Puts Faith in Religious Groups." *Los Angeles Times,* August 29.

Hart, Stephen. 1996. *What Does the Lord Require? How American Christians Think about Economic Justice.* New Brunswick: Rutgers University Press.

Harvey, David. 2001. *Spaces of Hope.* Berkeley: University of California Press.

Hehir, J. Bryan. 2000. "Religious Ideas and Social Policy: Subsidiarity and Catholic Style of Ministry." Pp. 97–120 in *Who Will Provide? The Changing Role of Religion in American Social Welfare,* edited by Mary Jo Bane, Brent Coffin, and Ronald Thiemann. Boulder: Westview Press.

Heineman, Kenneth J. 1999. *A Catholic New Deal: Religion and Reform in Depression Pittsburgh.* University Park: Pennsylvania State University Press.

Hitchens, Christopher. 1997. *The Missionary Position: Mother Teresa in Theory and Practice.* New York: Verso.

Hobbes, Thomas. [1651] 1994. *Leviathan.* London: Everyman.

Hogstel, Mildred O., and C. Gail Davis. 1996. "Eldercare and Support in the Church." *Journal of Religious Gerontology* 9:43–56.

Hopewell, James F. 1987. *Congregation: Stories and Structures.* Philadelphia: Fortress Press.

Humphrey, Richard A. 1980. "Religion in Appalachia: Implications for Social Work Practice." *Journal of Humanics* 8:4–18.

Indianapolis Star. 1996. "A Role for Churches." *Indianapolis Star,* January 21.

Jewish News. 1999. "Other Voices in the Valley." *Arizona Republic,* May 24.

Katz, Michael B. 1989. *The Undeserving Poor: From the War on Poverty to the War on Welfare.* New York: Pantheon Books.

———. 1995. *Improving Poor People: The Welfare State, the "Underclass," and Urban Schools as History.* Princeton: Princeton University Press.

———. 1996. *In the Shadow of the Poorhouse: A Social History of Welfare in America,* 10th anniv. ed., rev. New York: Basic Books.

Kids Count Data Book. 1998. *State Profiles of Child Well-Being*. Baltimore: The Annie E. Casey Foundation.

Kniss, Fred. 1996. "Ideas and Symbols as Resources in Intrareligious Conflict: The Case of American Mennonites." *Sociology of Religion* 57:7–23.

———. 1997. *Disquiet in the Land: Cultural Conflict in Mennonite Communities*. New Brunswick: Rutgers University Press.

Kniss, Fred, and David Todd Campbell. 1997. "The Effect of Religious Orientation on International Relief and Development Organizations." *Journal for the Scientific Study of Religion* 36:93–103.

Lamont, Michèle. 1992. *Money, Morals, and Manners: The Culture of the French and the American Upper–Middle Class*. Chicago: University of Chicago Press.

———. 2000. *The Dignity of Working Men: Morality and the Boundaries of Race, Class, and Immigration*. New York: Russell Sage.

Lamonte, Edward Shannon. 1995. *Politics and Welfare in Birmingham, 1900–1975*. Tuscaloosa: The University of Alabama Press.

Lincoln, C. Eric, and Lawrence H. Mamiya. 1990. *The Black Church in the African American Experience*. Durham: Duke University Press.

Lindner, Eileen W., ed. 2000. *Yearbook of American and Canadian Churches 2000: Religious Pluralism in the New Millennium* 68th ed. Nashville: Abingdon.

Lockhart, William H. 2001. "Getting Saved from Poverty: Religion in Poverty–to–Work Programs." Ph.D. diss. University of Virginia.

Loconte, Joe. 1995. "Mississippi's New Bully Pulpit." *Wall Street Journal*, October 6.

Lupton, Deborah. 1999. *Risk*. New York: Routledge.

Mansbridge, Jane J. 1980. *Beyond Adversary Democracy*. New York: Basic Books.

Marsh, Charles. 1997. *God's Long Summer: Stories of Faith and Civil Rights*. Princeton: Princeton University Press.

Martin, Emily. 1994. *Flexible Bodies*. Boston: Beacon Press.

McKinney, William. 1998. "Resources." Pp. 132–166 in *Studying Congregations: A New Handbook*, edited by Nancy T. Ammerman, Jackson W. Carroll, Carl S. Dudley, and William McKinney. Nashville: Abingdon.

McRoberts, Omar M. 1999. "Understanding the 'New' Black Pentecostal Activism: Lessons from Ecumenical Urban Ministries in Boston." *Sociology of Religion* 60:47–70.

Mead, Frank S. 1995. *Handbook of Denominations in the United States*, 10th ed., revised by Samuel S. Hill. Nashville: Abingdon.

Mead, Lawrence M., ed. 1997. *The New Paternalism: Supervisory Approaches to Poverty*. Washington, D.C.: Brookings Institute.

Messer, John. 1998. "Agency, Communion, and the Formation of Social Capital." *Nonprofit and Voluntary Sector Quarterly* 27:5–12.

Mills, C. Wright. 1940. "Situated Actions and Vocabularies of Motive." *American Sociological Review* 5:904–913.

Mink, Gwendolyn. 1998. *Welfare's End*. Ithaca: Cornell University Press.

Mishler, Elliot G. 1986. *Research Interviewing: Context and Narrative*. Cambridge: Harvard University Press.

Mississippi Population Data Sheet. 1993. Social Science Research Center, Mississippi State University.

Monsma, Stephen V. 1996. *When Sacred and Secular Mix: Religious Nonprofit Organizations and Public Money*. Boulder: Rowman & Littlefield.

Morris, Aldon D. 1984. *The Origins of the Civil Rights Movement: Black Communities Organizing for Change*. New York: Free Press.

Morrison, John D. 1991. "The Black Church as a Support System for Black Elderly." *Journal of Gerontological Social Work* 17:105–120.

Nathan, Richard P. 1996. "The Devolution Revolution: An Overview." Pp. 5–13 in the *Rockefeller Institute Bulletin*. Albany: Nelson A. Rockefeller Institute of Government.

Nord, Mark, Kyle Jemison, and Gary Bickel. 1999. *Measuring Food Security in the United States: Prevalence of Food Insecurity and Hunger, by State, 1996–1998*. Economic Research Service, USDA.

O'Conner, Alice. 2001. *Poverty Knowledge: Social Science, Social Policy, and the Poor in Twentieth-Century U.S. History*. Princeton: Princeton University Press.

Olasky, Marvin. 1992. *The Tragedy of American Compassion*. Washington, D.C.: Regnery Publishing.

Olson, Lynn M., Janet Reis, Larry Murphy, and Jennifer H. Gehm. 1988. "The Religious Community as a Partner in Health Care." *Journal of Community Health* 13:249–257.

Orr, John, with Carolyn Mounts and Peter Spoto. 2001. *Religion and Welfare Reform in Southern California: Is Charitable Choice Succeeding?* Los Angeles: Center for Religion and Civic Culture.

Park, Jerry Z., and Christian Smith. 2000. "'To Whom Much Has Been Given . . .': Religious Capital and Community Voluntarism among Churchgoing Protestants." *Journal for the Scientific Study of Religion* 39:272–286.

Patillo–McCoy, Mary. 1998. "Church Culture as a Strategy of Action in the Black Community." *American Sociological Review* 63:767–784.

———. 1999. *Black Picket Fences: Privilege and Peril among the Black Middle Class*. Chicago: University of Chicago Press.

Payne, Charles M. 1995. *I've Got the Light of Freedom: The Organizing Tradition and the Mississippi Freedom Struggle*. Berkeley: University of California Press.

Perkins, Douglas D., Barbara B. Brown, and Ralph B. Taylor. 1996. "The Ecology of Empowerment: Predicting Participation in Community Organizations." *Journal of Social Issues* 52:85–110.

Pinkerton, James P. 1999. "Can Faith–Based Groups Resist Uncle Sam?" *Buffalo News*, June 6.

Piven, Frances Fox, and Richard A. Cloward. 1993. *Regulating the Poor: The Functions of Public Welfare*, updated ed. New York: Vintage Books.

Popielarz, Pamela A. 1999. "Organizational Constraints on Personal Network Formation." *Research in the Sociology of Organizations* 16:263–281.

Portes, Alejandro. 1998. "Social Capital: Its Origins and Applications in Modern Sociology." *Annual Review of Sociology* 24:1–24.

Portes, Alejandro, and Patricia Landolt. 1996. "The Downside of Social Capital." *American Prospect* 26:18–21, 94.

Putnam, Robert D. 2000. *Bowling Alone: The Collapse and Revival of American Community.* New York: Simon & Schuster.

Quadagno, Jill. 1994. *The Color of Welfare: How Racism Undermined the War on Poverty.* New York: Oxford University Press.

Raasch, Chuck. 1999. "Religious Alliance Raises Concerns about Gore Idea." *USA Today*, May 26.

Rawlings, Charles W., and Janet W. Schrock. 1996. "The Role of the Religious Community in Shaping Community Partnerships for Health Care." *Journal of Long–Term Home Health Care* 15:57–59.

Reed, Adolf. 2001. *Class Notes: Posing as Politics and Other Thoughts on the American Scene.* New York: New Press.

Regis, Helen A. 1999. "Second Lines, Minstrelsy, and the Contested Landscapes of New Orleans Afro-Creole Festivals." *Cultural Anthropology* 14:472–504.

Regnerus, Mark D., and Christian Smith. 1998. "Selective Deprivatization among American Religious Traditions: The Reversal of the Great Reversal." *Social Forces* 76:1347–1372.

Regnerus, Mark D., Christian Smith, and David Sikkink. 1998. "Who Gives to the Poor? The Influence of Religious Tradition and Political Location on the Personal Generosity of Americans toward the Poor." *Journal for the Scientific Study of Religion* 37:481–493.

Robinson, Dean E. 2001. *Black Nationalism in American Politics and Thought.* New York: Cambridge University Press.

Rogers, Melissa. 1999. "The Wrong Way to Do Right: Church and State Can Work Together without Being Tied by Funding Strings." *Washington Post*, June 23.

Roof, Wade Clark. 1993. "Religion and Narrative." *Review of Religious Research* 34:297–310.

Rowley, Thomas D. 2000. "Food Assistance Needs of the South's Vulnerable Populations." Southern Rural Development Center, Mississippi State University.

Sack, Kevin. 1999. "Gore Backs Federal Money for Church Social Service Programs." *New York Times*, May 25.

Salamon, Lester M. 1995. *Partners in Public Service: Government–Nonprofit Relations in the Modern Welfare State.* Baltimore: Johns Hopkins University Press.

Savas, E. S. 2000. *Privatization and Public–Private Partnerships.* New York: Chatham House.

Schram, Sanford F. 1995. *Words of Welfare: The Poverty of Social Science and the Social Science of Poverty.* Minneapolis: University of Minnesota Press.

———. 1997. "The Cycle of Representation: The House Republicans and the Contract with America." Pp. 63–75 in *Tales of the State: Narrative in Contemporary U.S. Politics and Public Policy,* edited by Sanford F. Schram and Philip T. Neisser. Boulder: Rowman & Littlefield.

———. 1999. "Introduction—Welfare Reform: A Race to the Bottom?" Pp. 1–12 in *Welfare Reform: A Race to the Bottom?* edited by Sanford F. Schram and Samuel H. Beer. Washington, D.C.: Woodrow Wilson Center Press.

———. 2000. *After Welfare: The Culture of Postindustrial Social Policy.* New York: NYU Press.

Schram, Sanford F., and Samuel H. Beer, eds. 1999. *Welfare Reform: A Race to the Bottom?* Washington, D.C.: Woodrow Wilson Center Press.

Schram, Sanford F., and Philip T. Neisser, eds. 1997. *Tales of the State: Narrative in Contemporary U.S. Politics and Public Policy.* Boulder: Rowman & Littlefield.

Schreiter, Robert J. 1998. "Theology in the Congregation: Discovering and Doing." Pp. 23–39 in *Studying Congregations: A New Handbook,* edited by Nancy T. Ammerman, Jackson W. Carroll, Carl S. Dudley, and William McKinney. Nashville: Abingdon.

Schudson, Michael. 1998. *The Good Citizen: A History of American Civic Life.* New York: Free Press.

Schulman, Michael D., and Cynthia Anderson. 1999. "The Dark Side of the Force: A Case Study of Restructuring Social Capital." *Rural Sociology* 64:351–372.

Schwartz, Barry. 1975. *Queuing and Waiting: Studies in the Social Organization of Access and Delay.* Chicago: University of Chicago Press.

Schwartz, Joel. 2000. *Fighting Poverty with Virtue: Moral Reform and America's Urban Poor, 1825–2000.* Bloomington: Indiana University Press.

Seccombe, Karen. 1999. *"So You Think I Drive a Cadillac?" Welfare Recipients' Perspectives on the System and Its Reform.* Boston: Allyn & Bacon.

Seligman, Adam B. 1997. *The Problem of Trust.* Princeton: Princeton University Press.

Sherman, Amy L. 1995. "Michigan Lessons of Looking to God for Welfare Reform." *Detroit News,* October 29.

———. 2000. *The Growing Impact of Charitable Choice: A Catalogue of New Collaborations between Government and Faith-based Organizations in Nine States.* Washington, D.C.: Center for Public Justice.

Shipps, Jan. 2001. "Religion and Regional Culture in Modern America." Pp. 23–38 in *Can Charitable Choice Work?* edited by Andrew Walsh. Hartford: Leonard E. Greenberg Center for the Study of Religion in Public Life.

Sider, Ronald J., and Heidi Rolland Unruh. 1999. "No Aid to Religion? Charitable Choice and the First Amendment." *Brookings Review* (Spring): 46–49.

———. 2001. "Evangelism and Church–State Partnerships." *Journal of Church and State* 43:267–295.

Skocpol, Theda. 1992. *Protecting Soldiers and Mothers: The Political Origins of Social Policy in the United States.* Cambridge: Harvard University Press.

———. 2000. "Religion, Civil Society, and Social Provision in the U.S." Pp. 21–50 in *Who Will Provide? The Changing Role of Religion in American Social Welfare,* edited by Mary Jo Bane, Brent Coffin, and Ronald Thiemann. Boulder: Westview Press.

Smith, Christian. 2000. *Christian America? What Evangelicals Really Want.* Berkeley: University of California Press.

Smith, Steven Rathgeb, and Michael Lipsky. 1993. *Nonprofits for Hire: The Welfare State in the Age of Contracting.* Cambridge: Harvard University Press.

Spillman, Lyn. 1997. *Nation and Commemoration: Creating National Identities in the United States and Australia.* New York: Cambridge University Press.

Stark, Rodney, and Roger Finke. 2000. *Acts of Faith: Explaining the Human Side of Religion.* Berkeley: University of California Press.

Statistical Abstract of the United States. 1995–1997. Washington, D.C.: U.S. Census Bureau. <www.census.gov/statab/www>

Taylor–Goody Peter, ed. 2000. *Risk, Trust, and Welfare.* New York: St. Martin's Press.

Thiemann, Ronald, Samuel Herring, and Betsy Perabo. 2000. "Risks and Responsibilities of Faith–Based Organizations." Pp. 51–70 in *Who Will Provide? The Changing Role of Religion in American Social Welfare,* edited by Mary Jo Bane, Brent Coffin, and Ronald Thiemann. Boulder: Westview Press.

Tolbert, Charles M., Thomas A. Lyson, and Michael D. Irwin. 1998. "Local Capitalism, Civic Engagement, and Socioeconomic Well–Being." *Social Forces* 77:401–427.

Trattner, Walter I. 1999. *From Poor Law to Welfare State: A History of Social Welfare in America.* New York: Free Press.

Uslaner, Eric M. 1999. "Trust but Verify: Social Capital and Moral Behavior." *Social Science Information* 38:29–55.

Walsh, Andrew, ed. 2001. *Can Charitable Choice Work? Covering Religion's Impact on Urban Affairs and Social Services.* Hartford: Leonard E. Greenberg Center for the Study of Religion in Public Life.

Weber, Max. [1904–5] 1958. *The Protestant Ethic and the Spirit of Capitalism.* London: Allen & Unwin.

White, Lucie. 2000. "'That's What I Growed Up Hearing': Race, Redemption, and American Democracy." Pp. 238–265 in *Who Will Provide? The Changing Role of Religion in American Social Welfare,* edited by Mary Jo Bane, Brent Coffin, and Ronald Thiemann. Boulder: Westview Press.

Williams, Rhys H. 1994. "Covenant, Contract, and Communities: Religion and Political Culture in America." *Current World Leaders* 37:31–50.

———. 1999. "Visions of the Good Society and the Religious Roots of American Political Culture." *Sociology of Religion* 60:1–34.

Williams, Roger, and David C. Ruesink. 1998. "The Changing Rural Family . . . and Community: Implications for Congregational Ministry." *Family Ministry* 12:6–21.

Wilson, John, and Thomas Janoski. 1995. "The Contribution of Religion to Volunteer Work." *Sociology of Religion* 56:137–152.

Wilson, John, and Mark Musick. 1997. "Who Cares? Toward an Integrated Theory of Volunteer Work." *American Sociological Review* 62:694–713.

Wineburg, Robert J. 1993. "Social Policy, Community Service Development, and Religious Organizations." *Nonprofit Management and Leadership* 3:283–299.

———. 2001. *A Limited Partnership: The Politics of Religion, Welfare, and Social Service.* New York: Columbia University Press.

Winship, Christopher, and Jenny Berrien. 1999. "Boston Cops and Black Churches." *Public Interest* 136:52–68.

Winston, Diane. 1999. *Red–Hot and Righteous: The Urban Religion of the Salvation Army.* Cambridge: Harvard University Press.

Wolfe, Alan. 1993. "Whatever Happened to Compassion?" *Critical Review* 7:497–503.

Wood, Richard L. 1999. "Religious Culture and Political Action." *Sociological Theory* 17:307–332.

Wuthnow, Robert. 1991. *Acts of Compassion: Caring for Others and Helping Ourselves.* Princeton: Princeton University Press.

———. 1994a. *Sharing the Journey: Support Groups and America's New Quest for Community.* New York: Free Press.

———. 1994b. *God and Mammon in America.* New York: Free Press.

———. 1997. "The Cultural Turn: Stories, Logic, and the Quest for Identity in American Religion." Pp. 245–265 in *Contemporary American Religion: An Ethnographic Reader*, edited by Penny Edgell Becker and Nancy L. Eiesland. Walnut Creek: Alta Mira Press.

———. 1999. "Mobilizing Civic Engagement: The Changing Impact of Religious Involvement." Pp. 331–363 in *Civic Engagement in American Democracy*, edited by Theda Skocpol and Morris P. Fiorina. Washington, D.C.: Brookings Institution Press.

Yamane, David. 2000. "Narrative and Religious Experience." *Sociology of Religion* 61:171–189.

Yardley, Jim. 1996. "Focus on Overhauling Welfare: Mississippi Enlists Church Community." *Atlanta Journal and Constitution*, April 30.

Zand, Dale E. 1996. *The Leadership Triad: Knowledge, Trust, and Power.* New York: Oxford University Press.

Zelizer, Vivianna A. 1997. *The Social Meaning of Money: Pin Money, Paychecks, Poor Relief, and Other Currencies.* Princeton: Princeton University Press.

Index

About the Authors

JOHN P. BARTKOWSKI is Associate Professor of Sociology at Mississippi State University. He is the author of *Remaking the Godly Marriage: Gender Negotiation in Evangelical Families*. His published articles have appeared in various scholarly journals. HELEN A. REGIS is Assistant Professor of Anthropology, Louisiana State University. Her work on New Orleans jazz funerals and second lines has appeared in *American Ethnologist* and *Cultural Anthropology*. She is the author of *Fulbe Voices: Marriage, Islam, and Medicine in Northern Cameroon*.